Strategic Decision-Making

Strategic Decision-Making

Chris Gore

Head of Undergraduate Programmes,
Coventry Business School

Kate Murray

Assistant Dean,
Derbyshire Business School

Bill Richardson

Subject Leader
in Management Strategy and Business Decision-Making,
Sheffield Business School

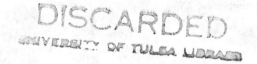

CASSELL

Cassell
Villiers House
41/47 Strand
London WC2N 5JE

387 Park Avenue South
New York, NY 10016–8810, USA

First published 1992

British Library Cataloguing-in-Publication Data
A catalogue record for this book is available from the
British Library.

ISBN 0–304–32559–7
0–304–31965–1 pbk

Typeset by Fakenham Photosetting Limited,
Fakenham, Norfolk
Printed and bound in Great Britain by Dotesios,
Trowbridge, Wilts.

Contents

Preface

This book addresses the issue that is of central concern to the management of the modern business organization, namely effective decision-making at the strategic level. It is written in the belief that the quality of decision-making is not merely dependent on the whim, judgement or experience of individuals but is likely to be enhanced by examination of both decision processes and decision methods. The emphasis is on developing an awareness of how to improve decision-making rather than on describing decision-making phenomena. Not only is strategic decision-making an interesting subject in its own right but the adoption of the concepts and ideas embedded in the subject area will also lead to an improvement in the quality of strategic decision-making and so to an increase in the wealth-producing capacity of business organizations.

A normative approach is used throughout the book along with a rational decision process model, which forms the basis of its structure. The central thrust is one of showing the crucial role of rationality in strategic decision-making. Very few practitioners or theorists propose the opposite – an increase in irrationality! However, studies which highlight the absence of rationality in real business decision-making are sometimes used as a means of justifying suboptimal behaviour. Such studies, while interesting, do not help practitioners to solve real problems and improve decision-making. In contrast, the adoption of a rational framework enables the reader to develop an efficient approach to decision-making and to be aware of both the limitations that work against rationality and the methods that can be used in these constrained circumstances.

At the beginning of the book the reader's understanding of decision-making processes and their rational underpinnings is developed. Later, factors which limit rationality are introduced and methods for overcoming these shortcomings are suggested. An advantage of this approach to decision-making is that it provides a framework to accommodate seemingly diverse models and enables the reader to reconcile the approaches taken and so gain a holistic view of the area under discussion. The framework can be used to assess new theories, approaches and practical experiences as and when they arise. Thus the recipe approach adopted by some textbooks is avoided. A menu of disparate alternative decision-methods and modes of analysis with little commonality is not offered. The framework adopted unifies diverse approaches; it shows how they can be related to each other and enables the reader subsequently to assess new theories and prescriptive advice.

This approach has enabled the inclusion not only of material that has become accepted as the basis for the subject area, but also of some subject matter that is clearly relevant but not as yet normally included in books on strategy. Unusually, the book presents a study of the culture of organizations, an examination of O. E. Williamson's ideas on efficient forms of organizational structure, some of the important contributions made by Porter to competitive analysis, the identification of differences in strategic decision-making between small and large firms and guidance for the reader on the method for undertaking business or case analysis. To ensure that the reader has the opportunity to apply the ideas presented, original case material is included at the end of each chapter.

All case studies are based on real-life experiences but some organizations have asked to remain anonymous. The case material is not intended to illustrate either effective or ineffective handling of business situations but is intended to form a basis for student discussion.

Every effort has been made to trace the holders of copyright material and seek their permission to reproduce the tables and diagrams concerned. The authors and publishers apologize to any who have inadvertently been overlooked.

The book is intended for final-year degree courses and advanced management courses dealing with business policy and strategic management. In relating these issues to decision theory it has the advantage of providing a link between intermediate studies in decision-making and advanced studies on strategy. From a student's point of view elements of the book could be used, with supplementary reading, at both intermediate and advanced stages. To aid tutors and lecturers a comprehensive lecturer's guide has been prepared. It provides review material, discusses questions, and gives case study guidance and sample assignment questions for each chapter. The lecturer's guide is available from the publishers, free of charge, to lecturers who adopt *Strategic Decision-Making* for their course.

The authors wish to thank the many colleagues who have contributed to their understanding of the subject, and in particular Alan Murphy and Maurice Brown.

1 Decision Processes

For the modern business organization ensuring that decision-making is as effective as possible is extremely important. Effective decision-making enables companies to achieve their objectives in an efficient manner and provides a means of establishing working systems of operation and control. However, decision-making involves more than the choice of some preferred alternative. It also involves what can be described as a process[1] that leads up to the choice situation and continues after the choice has been made. If the process can be improved and appropriate methods can be used during the process then decision-making itself will improve. The starting point in understanding decision-making is the development of this process view of decision-making. If decision processes are to be efficient, however, they must be placed within a rational context; this chapter, therefore, also explains the concept of rationality and its limitations and modifications.

The objectives of this chapter are to:

- define a decision;
- identify different levels of decision-making;
- explain rationality in decision-making;
- provide a general decision process model;
- describe some strategic decision process models;
- summarize the literature on decision processes;
- highlight the importance of the methodological approach used to model a decision;
- relate theory to practice so that decision-making can be improved.

What is a decision?

Mintzberg[2] defined a decision as 'a specific commitment to action', so it includes all purposeful behaviour that concludes with a commitment to do something rather than merely to talk about it. Whether or not this definition includes a decision to do nothing is unclear, although it is unlikely because Mintzberg talks of a commitment of resources. Other writers[3] argue that a decision to do nothing needs to be included, as long as it is part of a rational process leading to a conscious choice between alternatives. A decision is made even if the alternative is to do nothing. As will be seen in Chapter 6, it may be vital to consider the zero alternative as a part of the decision. However, as Janis and Mann[4] point out, a no-choice option is frequently selected to avoid conflict or to maintain the status quo and so reduce uncertainty. In such cases there is a decision to do nothing rather than something – but the decision is less than rational, for a full consideration of alternatives has not been made.

Harrison's[5] definition of a decision as 'simply a moment in an ongoing process of evaluating alternatives for meeting an objective' describes a decision as the moment of choice. It presupposes that a decision follows a number of distinct stages or that there is a decision-making cycle. It also assumes that behaviour is purposeful in that objectives are set and attempts are made to meet them, and so it sets the 'decision' within a wider decision process, whereas a broader concept of a decision may encompass the whole of the process of decision-making itself.

Levels of decision-making

It is useful to divide up the generic activity of decision-making into classes of decisions which have common features. In this way appropriate decision processes and methods can be adopted for the different classes.

One such classification is provided by Simon,[6] who has suggested that all decisions can be divided into two groups (see Figure 1.1). First, there are programmed decisions. These can be readily mapped on to a diagram or a computer program and are 'repetitive and routine, to the extent that a definite procedure has been worked out for handling them' (p. 6). Secondly, there are decisions that are non-programmed. These are so complex that the system they follow cannot be predetermined, as each decision is unique so that 'there is no cut and dried method for handling the problem' (p. 6), and its complexity and novelty require a customized solution. Drucker[7] has suggested names for these categories of decisions: 'generic' and 'unique'. Generic decisions are routine, deal with predictable cause and effect relationships, use defined information channels and have definite decision criteria. There is frequently reliance on rules and set procedures to handle such decisions. Unique decisions are novel and require judgement and creativity, since they are complex and are characterized by incomplete information and uncertainty.

Another classification, by Ansoff,[8] is into strategic decisions, administrative decisions and operating decisions. The importance of these attempts at classification is demonstrated by Ansoff, because he shows their implication for management. The first category is a subset of Simon's non-programmed and Drucker's unique decisions, and is concerned with objectives and long-range plans, which are usually the province of top management (see Figure 1.1).

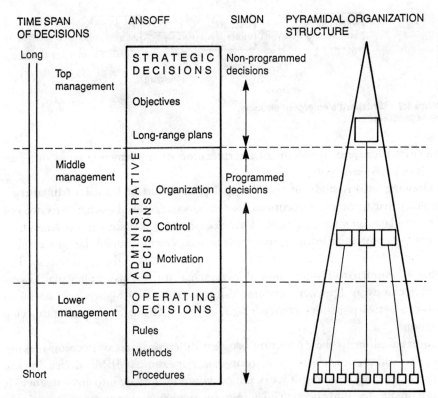

Figure 1.1 Levels of decision-making.

Ansoff divides Simon's programmed and Drucker's generic decisions into administrative decisions, the area of middle management, and operating decisions, the area of lower management. The latter are concerned with routine decisions and can be explained by rules, methods and procedures, whereas administrative decisions are more complex and concerned with control, motivation and organizational systems. This subdivision of programmed decisions is a more realistic approach that identifies useful classifications for management methods. Chapter 4 will illustrate that one of the roles performed by organizational structure is to separate out these decisions to appropriate levels of management. Lower-level decisions are those that may be programmed by firms such as automatic re-ordering decisions linked to stock levels. Such decisions may be delegated but control can be maintained by the use of decision rules.

The disadvantages of this very sequential approach to the categorization of management decisions are highlighted by Mintzberg.[9] He suggests, on the basis of empirical evidence, that a strict classification of decisions misses important aspects of how complex decisions are made. Many strategic decisions emerge as a result of numerous small low-level decisions, which he calls an emergent strategy (see Figure 1.2). Additionally, intended strategic decisions can lead to unrealized

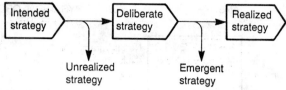

Figure 1.2 Mintzberg's emergent strategy.
Source: Mintzberg,[9] p. 162.

strategies because of problems of interpretation or implementation at different levels of decision-making.

Drawing on his study of the National Film Board of Canada, Mintzberg[10] suggests that in practice intentions are not always realized – objectives are not met, in Harrison's terminology. What does emerge is a strategy as a result of individuals or groups learning from past mistakes or developing new ideas independently. If successful, these are taken up in other parts of the organization. The process is similar to Quinn's logical incrementalism.[11] This implies that lower-level decisions, in Drucker's or Simon's terms, can affect higher-level decisions and can actually be the source of these types of major organization-wide decisions.

In practical terms the distinction between different levels of decision-making will also lead to some classification problems. For example, IBM's decision in the UK to review its smoking at work policy does not fit easily into any category. It was a unique decision affecting all employees and having long-term implications, but it could not really be called a strategic decision. However, it was not programmable, for there were no precedents, and it took years to come to fruition. The decision to implement a partial ban in the UK is now being used by IBM in other parts of the world, such as the USA and France, and so it can now be classified as an administrative decision.

Rational decision-making

Whatever the type of decision, it is important to consider the extent to which it may be described as rational.

The term 'a rational decision' as it relates to a business organization has its roots in neo-classical economics, and refers to a decision based on a logical process of adopting means to achieve a particular end or objective. Objectives may include the firm's desire to maximize its profits, or an individual's desire to maximize his or her utility. According to Parsons[12] an act is rational if: (a) it is orientated to a clearly formulated unambiguous goal or set of values which are logically consistent; and (b) the means chosen to achieve the goal use the best available information. The term 'rational' does not denote approval or disapproval of the objective; rather it refers to the method of achieving the objective.

Rationality in economics is an assumed mode of behaviour by the economic actors involved and, together with a number of other assumptions, allows the construction of closed models which have predictive ability within their limited confines. For example, these ideas can be applied to the theory of the firm to provide an economic profit-maximizing model. To learn about rationality let us examine this model and consider the assumptions made. It requires:

1 An economic objective that can be quantified and that maximizes the utility of the decision-maker.
2 Transitive and consistent preferences of decision-makers for their objectives.
3 Unlimited information processing abilities by those involved and an ability to see their own self-interest and act accordingly.
4 Well defined mutually exclusive alternatives.
5 Perfect estimates of outcomes and calculations of the expected value of each alternative, which may include an estimate of the probability of each outcome.
6 Selection of the alternative that maximizes 'expected utility'.
7 Unlimited information and so no time or cost constraints.

Using these assumptions microeconomics then constructs models that form the basis of market analysis. These assumptions are gross over-simplifications of the real world and thus economic analysis proceeds to construct more complex and realistic models by relaxing them. This approach of starting with simple but unrealistic models and moving towards more complex and correspondingly more realistic models provides a useful approach to the construction of decision models.

As the assumptions of rationality described above provide a basis for this book's approach to rationality in decision-making it is worth while to examine them in greater detail. The assumptions fall into two groups. Assumptions 1, 2 and 3 refer to conditions about the individual decision-maker and the remainder are features of the decision environment. If all of these conditions were met the decision-maker could take fully rational decisions. A clear view of a simple objective could be found. All the alternatives to achieve it would be considered and the best possible alternative chosen. In the real world, however, such full rationality cannot be achieved. Taking each assumption in turn it is possible to see their shortcomings and to suggest ways of overcoming them.

Assumption 1 presumes an economic, quantifiable, maximizing objective. In organizations there are frequently multiple objectives, which may be qualitative as well as quantitative. However, it should always be possible to state some of a business organization's objectives in quantitative terms, as will be seen in Chapter 2.

Assumption 2 of the rational model is that of stability of preferences over time. This assumption anticipates that the evaluation of outcomes will remain stable across time. However, people are constantly learning and adapting their behaviour in the light of their experiences. An implied assumption is that of a fixed time horizon at the moment of choice, but the decision-maker has to live with the consequences of the decision in whatever state of the world actually materializes. This is not attractive to many people and partially accounts for avoidance of decision-making or for a desire to reduce the time span involved. This also explains the popularity of decision rules in financial investments, such as the payback method of investment evaluation, which emphasizes the speed of capital return, and the relative unpopularity of the net present value technique, which evaluates the total investment taking the full period of the investment into account.[13]

Assumption 3 assumes unlimited information processing. It does not, therefore, allow for people's limited cognitive ability, which according to Simon[14] creates 'bounded rationality'. Thus limited knowledge and limited brain power mean that a full evaluation of all possibilities is never carried out, so optimal solutions to complex problems are not found. Furthermore, they may not be necessary; for example, in 'teaching' a computer to play chess, the approach of accepting only satisfactory moves was followed with considerable success.

Also, people do not relentlessly pursue self-interest, and aspirations are modified in the light of experience. Self-interest is not seen only in economic terms but also in social, political and psychological terms. Behaviour can only be seen as 'rational' in the context in which it occurs and there is not a logically derived 'rational' set of behaviours to suit all situations. Philosophically this stance has been taken to its logical conclusion by Oakshott, who points out that at one time bloomers were argued to be the rational style for cycling![15] However, it is difficult to decide just how far Simon wishes to go in his analysis of 'bounded rationality'. The logical philosophical conclusion of the argument does not fit happily with his other work, which is always logical and rationally argued, and his interest in artificial intelligence, which implies a mechanistic mapping of human behaviour after due allowance for the satisficing tendencies of people. It would seem that mechanisms adapted to cope with limited cognitive ability are frequently satisfactory and a satisficing approach might be a way of achieving the most rational outcome in a particular case.

Assumption 4, of the existence of well-defined mutually exclusive alternatives, is affected by information availability and frequently all alternatives are not well defined. As the world is uncertain it is impossible to know if all alternatives have been ascertained. It is often too expensive to explore all possibilities, and sequential consideration of alternatives together with satisfying behaviour means that once an alternative is found which seems satisfactory then often the search will cease. In a study at Leicester Polytechnic of 280 decisions taken by organizations it was found that in 38 per cent of cases no alternative to the solution accepted was investigated. Other alternatives were screened out by the time the choice stage had been reached. This approach is understandable, because it is frequently very expensive to develop a number of custom-made alternative solutions, but it is not advocated. If only one alternative solution can be fully investigated decision-makers must clearly specify objectives and ensure that alternative potential solutions have been evaluated as fully as possible before being abandoned. It needs to be recognized that decision choices are frequently effectively made before the choice stage in a decision is reached.

Assumption 5 requires quantification of information, which is not always possible. Estimates of the expected value of the alternatives considered can be made, but because of the information problems these must often be more in the nature of guesstimates and sometimes alternatives must be compared on qualitative criteria. For example, the quality of a product is measurable over various dimensions but it also depends on people's perceptions of it. Much work in management accounting, marketing and personnel is directed at quantifying seemingly qualitative concepts.

Assumption 6 assumes that decision-makers are fully aware of the benefits arising from a decision and choose the alternative or outcome which provides the maximum benefit. The problem of specifying and quantifying objectives, of the stability of preferences and of the costs of information are all relevant here.

Assumption 7 expects that time and information are never limited and that information is inexpensive to acquire. In many real-life situations the opposite conditions prevail. Much information is gathered in a dynamic and complex world in which it is impossible to know everything, so there is always an element of risk. Knight[16] distinguished between risk and uncertainty. A risky situation is one in which possible outcomes are known and their associated probabilities are also known, but which will occur is not known. Uncertainty exists if possible outcomes are known but not their probabilities. Ignorance occurs if possible outcomes are not known. Using this classification, because many business situations begin with all possible outcomes not being known, businesses are operating in a situation of ignorance! However, information can be gathered to turn a situation of ignorance into one of uncertainty and then to one of risk. More recently, Moore[17] has described risk as 'a scenario in which possible losses are present' (p. 2) and suggests that risk in a business situation has two aspects: the probability of loss occurring and the possible loss level relative to the starting asset base. So the amount of information to be gathered depends on the size of the possible loss if a mistake is made and on the costs of information collection.

Mechanisms for coping with risk or uncertainty due to lack of information include, according to Simon[18] and Cyert and March,[19] establishing an aspiration level that is felt to be a satisfactory outcome. Once this level is reached or a method of achieving it is discovered, no further search is made. The aspiration level concept allows people to reduce information search and evaluation of alternatives, and requires fewer estimates of the probabilities of the states of the environment. It does, of course, lead to suboptimal decision-making. According to Hogarth,[20] limited human information processing capacity arises from selective perception of information, the nature of processing, processing capacity and memory limitations.

Another problem is that perception of information is selective to the extent that only one-seventieth of what is present in the visual field can be perceived at one time. Anticipation plays a large part in what is actually seen, so that sometimes 'people only see what they want to see'. Processing is sequential, for people cannot simultaneously integrate a great deal of information. The order in which information is received will determine the sequence and may bias judgement. However, constant small adjustments as the result of new information lead to satisfactory results in a stable environment; only if it is unstable or given to sudden periods of instability will bad decisions result. People's processing capacity works on a heuristic rather than an optimal basis. Simple decision rules remove the need to consider all information and speed up the process, but can lead to inconsistent choices and to the exclusion of vital information. Memory capacity is limited and memory seems to work by a process of associations that reconstruct past events, unlike a computer, which accesses information in its original form. Reconstruction is useful, for it enables people to organize data into 'patterns', investing them with meaning, and so enables them to remember far more than would have been possible if the data were random.

The existence of these violations of the assumptions required for full rationality necessarily means that we cannot expect decisions or decision processes to be fully rational. What has to be achieved, therefore, is an understanding of the constraints that these violations present, so that the decision process can be made rational within the bounds of these constraints. Thus, if time is at a premium all possible alternatives may not be considered, but as many as the time allows will be, so that the decision will not be arbitrarily made.

In a world where there cannot be full rationality, models of how to make a decision can be of help. These models can be thought of in terms of a spectrum, from the very general to the more specific. The remainder of the book takes us through an examination of these models, starting with the general models of decision processes.

Strategic decision processes

A decision process is concerned with the whole range of activities involved in making a decision, not merely the point of decision. It encompasses everything from the initial stimulus of a need for a decision through to the feedback from surveying events as a result of the decision taken. If the process more clearly approximates the rational model then decisions will be better than if a haphazard approach is adopted, and where applied within firms will lead to an improvement in the process of decision-making and so to a better fulfilment of specified objectives.

Mumford and Pettigrew[21] point out that decisions, especially strategic decisions, are concerned with the allocation of resources in terms of both finance and manpower. These important decisions affect organizations' political structures, and the status and position of those involved. A judicious application of rational principles, including knowledge of practical situations and likely behavioural influences, therefore, will lead to improved decision-making and better business performance.

Before discussing the decision-making process in detail it is worth outlining the advantages of analysing a firm's decision process and trying to create 'good' processes. Scrutiny of a decision process model in the context of actual decision-making approaches enables decision-makers to concentrate on the individual functions within a whole decision. This can lead to greater effectiveness within a decision process of, for example, the search for useful information or the selection of a strategic development. Furthermore, viewing the total process enables decision-makers to consider the interrelationships between the different functions, and enables the dynamism of the total process to be understood so that the decision-maker can direct and control the process. Above all, however, the prescription of a quest for good decision processes is based on the belief that paying attention to the way decisions are made will improve the quality of decision-making and management within the firm.

There is little agreement among writers on decision-making processes about the number of decision-making stages or about what each stage involves, but this is not surprising given the heterogeneity of decision situations, particularly for small firms. Table 1.1 summarizes a number of writers' approaches by marking the stages that they mention. No writer mentions all the stages explicitly, although they may be included implicitly. It can be seen that as the literature has developed over time the number of stages included has increased, so that recent writers mention more stages than, say, Simon,[6] who suggested in 1960 that the decision-making process consisted of three major elements: finding occasions for making a decision (classified in Table 1.1 as 'need for a decision'); finding possible courses of action ('develop alternatives'); and choosing among the courses of action ('choice'). Mintzberg[2] in 1976 defined a decision process 'as a set of actions and dynamic factors that begins with the identification of a stimulus for action and ends with a specific commitment to action' (p. 246). He then identified several different processes as a result of the observation of 25 strategic decisions, which had in common three stages: identification, development and selection. The first corresponds to 'need for a decision' and 'problem definition', the second to 'information gathering' and 'diagnosis', the third to 'evaluate alternatives' and 'choice'. Gilligan et al.[22] also identified six stages, but theirs were concentrated towards the end of the cycle, while Mintzberg's were at the beginning. The two most recent contributions do not agree either.[23, 24]

If the stages of Table 1.1 are all incorporated into one model it suggests that a decision process follows the path outlined in Figure 1.3. It can be seen that no stage is really redundant, yet writers do not include all stages explicitly. Setting objectives is only included by Gilligan et al., Harrison, Gordon and Pressman,

Table 1.1 Stages of the decision process mentioned by different writers

Writer	Set objectives	Need for a decision (problem recognition)	Problem definition	Information gathering (search)	Develop alternatives (diagnosis)	Evaluate alternatives	Choice	Implement	Monitor (follow-up)
Simon[6]		●			●		●		
Janis[25]		●					●	●	●
Schrenk[26]		●			●		●		
Witte[27]				●	●	●	●		
Mintzberg et al.[2]		●	●	●	●	●	●		●
Gordon and Pressman[28]	●		●		●		●		●
Gilligan et al.[22]	●			●			●	●	●
Harrison[5]	●			●			●	●	●
Bridge[23]	●		●		●		●		
Hill[24]		●			●		●	●	

and Bridge. However, this stage is vital in business decision-making as solutions can only be seen as successful or not in the light of both the problem or opportunity and the overall objectives of the firm. The importance of objectives in decision-making is taken up in Chapter 2. Very few writers (only Mintzberg, Gordon and Pressman, and Bridge) include a problem definition stage, although recognizing a problem or a need for a decision, which almost all writers include, is not the same as clearly specifying what is required. This stage can in fact determine the results looked for and so needs careful attention. Lyles[29] highlighted this in her study of organizations' problem formulation activities and found that 75 per cent of the sample initially defined the problem incorrectly and had to redefine it. The search stage is similarly scantily treated, only Gilligan et al., Mintzberg and Harrison recognizing it, but it is one that absorbs most time for firms and can never be taken for granted. Finally, the implementation and monitoring stages are ignored by the majority of writers. Again these stages in practice are vital, for no matter how excellent a solution or decision is, if it is not translated into action and no attempt is made to ensure that implementation is in accordance with plans then the whole effort spent on the previous stages will be wasted.

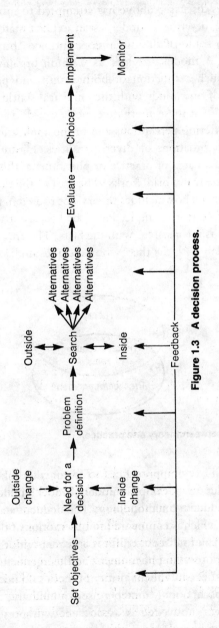

Figure 1.3 A decision process.

A critique of the models

Each of the writers discussed above has attempted to model a decision process. Cooke and Slack[30] describe a model 'as an explicit statement of our image of reality' (p. 22), so some of the differences outlined above arise from different images of reality. A model provides us with an organization of reality. It is, therefore, very much a function of both reality and perception. It links the theoretical world of our minds with the empirical world of our senses. It is no surprise, therefore, that these alternative models of decision-making exist. They are the result of differing perceptions and of the application of these perceptions to diverse decision situations or diverse realities. Figure 1.4 shows an area of theory overlapping an area of practice or phenomena: this area contains theories that explain how the real world works. The area of the theory box that does not overlap the phenomena box includes theory not rooted in reality either because it does not intend to be (for example, logic) or because it is 'bad' theory in Popper's[31] sense that it is inconsistent with the facts. The area of the phenomena box that does not overlap with the theory box includes undiscovered or unexplained phenomena.

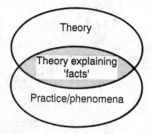

Figure 1.4 The link between theory and practice.

There are basically two approaches to forging the links between theory and phenomena in order to develop a model. Model builders can use deductive methodology or inductive methodology. The deductive approach involves formulating a theory, which is compared to observations of the phenomena that the theory seeks to explain to discover if it is consistent with the facts. The inductive approach involves observing phenomena and then generating theories to explain these observations. Broadly the majority of theories on decision processes follow the deductive approach; only Mintzberg uses an inductive approach.

Usually deductive knowledge is associated with prescriptive or normative advice and inductive knowledge with descriptive advice. A knowledge–source matrix based on Caw's work[32] shows this (Table 1.2). Following Caw's analysis one would expect the different methodological approaches to have been used partly because different uses for the knowledge have been perceived by those generating it. Thus, for example, Mintzberg took an inductive approach as he wished to explain observed phenomena, but like many descriptivists or positivists before him he went on to suggest what should be done to improve strategic decision-making by looking at the detail of his findings. Other writers took a deductive approach as they wished to offer advice, but they had considerable experience of business decision-making, which must have affected their theorizing or model building.

Table 1.2   A source–knowledge matrix

Source	Knowledge	
	'What should be': normative/prescriptive	'What is': descriptive
Deductive	●	
Inductive		●

This brings us to the artificiality in the deductive–inductive split, for in practice no model can be wholly one or the other. Figure 1.5 shows that theory cannot be generated in total isolation from the real world, because awareness of the phenomena it is to explain will influence the model builder's perceptions. Similarly, the selection of an area of interest will be affected by implicit theories affecting selection of 'facts'. Additionally, rules of measurement and of correspondence between phenomena and the names or numbers associated with them are general to both inductionists and deductionists, although they vary over time and between 'scientific periods'.

A particular problem in trying to model a decision process is the huge range of experiences that are covered: although most of the writers mentioned confine themselves to the business area, they frequently include other types of organization. Furthermore, they attempt to cover all types of decision, dealing with different time spans and ranging over different continents. It may therefore be of more use to develop a less general model of decision-making. Features of these general models can be incorporated and refined for use in specific decision areas.

Strategic decision-making models

An important subset of decision models that is a central concern of this book is that associated with strategic decision-making. A review of a number of the models available demonstrates both the importance of understanding the methodological stance taken and the need to relate theory to practice. The earlier models tended to be normative and prescriptive. They assumed a clear distinction between different levels of decision-making and a degree of rationality seldom found in practice. The later models were descriptive and indicated that in the 'real

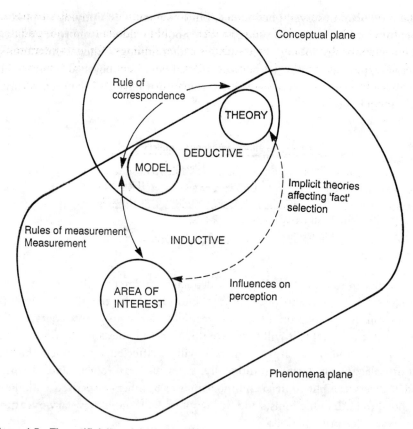

Figure 1.5   The artificiality of the inductive–deductive methodological split.

world' the levels of decision-making are more closely related and rationality cannot be assumed; allowances have to be made for behavioural effects.

The following discussion shows that the Hofer and Schendel model and the Higgins model both develop a rational sequential approach to strategic decision-making which is of necessity 'top-down'. Mintzberg, on the other hand, suggests that because of limited rationality the process is not sequential but involves considerable back-tracking or repetition of stages. Furthermore, there is not a firm distinction between the levels of decision-making because a number of operating or administrative decisions can eventually amount to a perceivable strategy. What emerges in such situations may not, of course, be desirable or what was really wanted. So for a bottom-up approach to be successful in achieving overall objectives, it is essential that an overall strategic direction is given from the top. The strategic management process must guide lower-level decisions to ensure they are in line with strategic objectives.

Hofer and Schendel[33] claim that strategy is an unstructured problem-solving process, which they then describe as a rational sequential process (see Figure 1.6).

Their normative model sees goal formulation as outside the strategy formulation process. In this way the model is more general – of wider applicability and use than if it specified an objective and worked through to specific applications. This model is based on the ideas of limited rationality, so it encompasses uncertainty, complexity of decision and bounded rationality, and provides a model for rational decision-making that takes account of these features. The model begins with identification of the issue. This is not necessarily simple or obvious because of the problem of partial ignorance, so Hofer and Schendel advise the inclusion of contingency planning in the strategy formulation process. Once the decision issue has been identified alternatives are generated, including social and political analyses as well as economic and market forecasts. These must then be evaluated. They suggest that it is difficult to look at problems or projects in isolation, because of the synergistic effects among projects. Additionally, information, especially that concerned with the future, is unlikely to be reliable, so contingency planning at both a business level and an overall corporate level is advocated. The process of evaluation clarifies the multi-dimensional issues. A choice then has to be made, and for this to be done in the most rational way, given the constraints on rationality, the choice situation will involve the use of criteria, or a choice 'model'. These form part of what are called strategic tools and can be found in Chapters 6 and 9. After choice the process ends because Hofer and Schendel exclude implementation planning from the strategy formulation process.

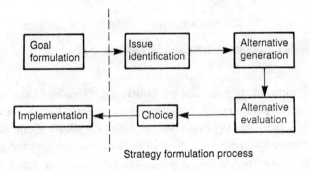

Strategy formulation process

Figure 1.6   Hofer and Schendel's strategic decision-making process.

Even in modelling the more specific decision of strategy opinion is not undivided. To Higgins[34] the main issue in the strategic decision-making process is the identification of information system needs, which will overcome the problems of assimilation that fully rational models would have. In many ways his approach is effectively a practical implementation of Ansoff's ideas (see Figure 1.7). Objectives are compared with required performance (which comes from outside the model) and any performance gap is looked at in the light of forecasts, which are themselves a result of an audit of the company's present position (which may involve, for example, an analysis of strengths and weaknesses) compared with the results of an environmental analysis of the important factors likely to influence the company. From these comparisons of different information inputs an overall corporate plan results, followed by individual business plans and finally operational budgets. Thus Higgins sees the process as one imposed from the top of an organization, using data that can mostly be easily quantified.

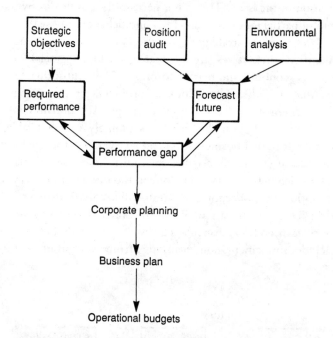

Figure 1.7   Higgins's strategic decision-making process.

Yet another approach is provided by Mintzberg.[2] Unlike Hofer and Schendel or Higgins he adopts a positive approach to theory formation. Mintzberg provides a rather richer model that not only recognizes limitations to full rationality but also incorporates into the model practices that are adopted to overcome these limitations (see Figure 1.8). Using data based on five years of empirical observations, using 50 teams of four or five students, who worked in organizations for three to six months observing 25 strategic decisions, Mintzberg claims that actual decision processes fall into three stages: identification, development and selection. Identification consists of two parts: the recognition of a problem and the diagnosis of that problem. Recognition of a problem is affected by the availability of an answer, or occurs if 'actuals' deviate from 'standard'. The number of stimuli needed before a problem is recognized depends on whether the situation is perceived as being a crisis, a problem or an opportunity. The 25 decisions reported upon fell into the following categories: five opportunities, six opportunities/problems and fourteen problems/crises. The diagnostic part of the

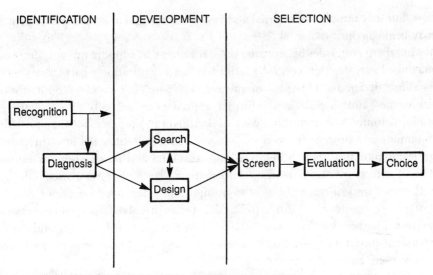

Figure 1.8   Mintzberg's strategic decision-making process.

identification stage involves attempts to clarify issues, open information channels and establish task forces.

The second phase of the process has two distinct parts, that associated with search and that associated with design. Search for solutions begins with the organization's 'memory'; that is, its information systems and the experience of established members of the organization. Search is frequently passive in that, for example, there are alternatives offered for sale by service organizations actively looking for organizations with problems. Finally there is a 'trap' search, which involves letting others know that you require an answer to a problem. The design of solutions is a complex and iterative process. The problem is broken into smaller parts which are handled in a sequential manner, with decisions to move on to the next 'stage' effectively meaning that certain possibilities are ruled out as the decision progresses. Solutions may be custom-made or modified ready-made answers. The former approach is only used if the latter is not available, because it involves complex cycles of design and search activities which Mintzberg calls 'nested cycles'.

The final stage is that of selection. It is usually seen as the last step but as development involves breaking a decision into a series of sub-decisions, each of which requires a selection step, so selection can be part of development. Selection involves screening to eliminate unfeasible solutions and so this stage is often part of the search phase. Next comes evaluation, which was found to be insignificant in this study, with judgement being the most important technique, followed by bargaining between interested parties. Thirdly, selection involves choice, but Mintzberg warns that the ignorance of those with authority to choose and the bias of the sponsor should be remembered. Finally, authorization ends the process, but it is not always internal and is not always given, so the whole process may begin again.

Mintzberg concludes by stressing three routines that support strategic decision-making. First, decision control routines are an organization's particular way of handling decisions. This idea of meta-decision-making involves both routine approaches and flexible and informal approaches. Secondly, in Mintzberg's study, communication routines were of dominant importance, for they provided the inputs and outputs for decision-making. These routines fell into three categories: exploration, which involved both scanning and passive review; investigation, which involved focusing information search, but was often informal and verbal; and dissemination, whose importance depended on the number of individuals involved. Thirdly, political routines involved bargaining between interested parties, persuasion of those necessary to get a project going and the co-option of unwilling participants on to the team, to ensure or encourage their involvement and commitment.

Finally, Mintzberg stresses the importance of dynamics in the decision process. He found no examples of undisturbed progression of a decision through the process stages he identified, because of interferences, feedback loops and dead ends. The process was sometimes speeded up, sometimes delayed and sometimes recycled.

Each of the models presented, in its own way, takes account of some of the aspects of limitations to full rationality, and analyses the decision into a series of stages and steps that are important. As models become 'richer' rather than 'general', so methods of overcoming constraints can be incorporated. In this way Mintzberg's model is particularly interesting. His idea of rational activity and the incorporation of many management features into the process is valuable. Work by Johnson,[35] drawing on Pondy,[36] suggests that real-life strategic decisions are incremental in nature and can be explained by unifying the rational model with an intuitive model. At the same time, of course, it must be recognized that such a model loses its more general applicability. The point to remember is that a model is to be used. One of universal use cannot be expected. It is a question of choosing the most appropriate for the issue at hand.

Practical considerations

What practical reasons are there for studying decision processes? An analysis of the way decisions are taken within an organization can help to give an overall 'picture' of the process normally followed for each organization that develops its own distinctive way of doing things because of the influence of its culture. A model similar to that in Case study 1 can be developed to outline the stages followed. It is then possible to compare the model produced with an idealized model, such as that of Figure 1.3, to see whether stages have been missed out or disproportionate amounts of time and resources have been devoted to one stage. It can also be seen whether the process modelled is unnecessarily erratic. Once a complex decision is broken into stages it is easier to suggest specific improvements at particular points or stages. For example, perhaps the problem was not correctly specified at the problem definition stage, as Lyles[29] found was often true, or perhaps there was a lack of monitoring of results. The Glamorous Nightdresses case study seems to imply that disproportionate amounts of time and resources are devoted to authorization after the choice stage. The evidence that many firms do not use quantitative criteria suggests that the development of such criteria would be a benefit.

The interrelationships between the stages can be viewed, so that management can review the functioning of the whole decision-making process. It may be that there is a great deal of 'back-tracking' or recycling of events, so that stages are repeated. This can often be useful but it can be time-consuming and, if mechanisms can be developed to ensure repetition is undertaken only when essential, resources can be saved. The area of generation of alternatives is particularly suitable for this treatment as evidence suggests that frequently only one solution is considered. If this solution then becomes unsatisfactory the process must be repeated. A system which ensures that specified reasons for the rejection of an alternative, before it is compared with criteria, are listed then the same ground does not have to be covered again. For example, a major tractor company decided at a strategic level to contract out certain stages of production. The implementation of this resulted in the closure of a paint shop and the use of a paint finishing contractor. If this decision had not been investigated fully the service provided by the contractor might not have been of the required quality. Discovering an unsatisfactory service after the decision to close the in-house facility would necessitate very expensive back-tracking of the decision. The tendency at a strategic level to ignore the operational consequences will inevitably have strategic consequences by causing back-tracking.

The dynamism of the process must not be forgotten and frequently the systematic remodelling of a decision enables management better to coordinate and control the groups involved in making a decision.

Conclusion

This chapter has adopted the Harrison definition of a decision as 'a moment in an ongoing process of evaluating alternatives for meeting an objective'. It has suggested that, although different levels of decision-making are identified by various writers, in practice it is often difficult to distinguish between the levels. Some administrative decisions are unique but not of strategic significance and a number of operating decisions can in effect amount to a strategic change of direction. It has been argued that rational decision-making provides a useful model to improve business decision-making. An analysis of a number of writers on decision processes has led to the development of a model of a decision process that involves more stages than any individual writer advocates. A discussion of normative and positive models leads to the suggestion that both approaches are relevant to modelling business decision-making. This is amplified by the description of two examples from each methodological stance. Finally the practical usefulness of modelling a decision process is discussed and demonstrated in a case study.

Case study 1
Glamorous Nightdresses plc

This case is based on a multinational textile and clothing manufacturer. It first illustrates the problem of not clearly distinguishing between levels of decision-making and the tendency to refer decisions upwards. Secondly, it shows that certain stages of a decision process can be needlessly time- and resource-consuming.

A production problem arose at a factory making children's and ladies' wear. A new style of nightdress was proving difficult to embroider and an above average number of seconds was being produced. The factory manager was alerted to the problem by two control reports from the accounts department, which indicated that two styles of nightdress were producing higher than average (3 per cent) seconds. The seconds recovery supervisor gave the reason for the rejects as low-quality decorative stitching on hems and sleeves. The normal procedure in such a situation was for the supervisor to identify the machinists at fault and tell them to improve their standard of work or give extra training if required. However, in this instance the number of machinists at fault was so large that it was felt that the problem had another cause. At a weekly production meeting between the factory manager, chief designer, cutting room manager and purchasing controller/work study officer, which was chaired by the divisional chief executive (CE), it was agreed to search for the cause. The designer, the work study officer and machinists, in conjunction with the factory manager, agreed that the sewing machines in use (with the exception of one machine) could not produce the quality of finish required. The one machine could not cope with projected production volumes. Three alternative solutions were formulated:

1 Buy a new sewing machine with top spreader facilities costing £2401. ▷

2 Hire a suitable machine costing £1300 per annum.

3 Accept the drop in quality.

The factory manager recommended alternative 1 and the divisional CE agreed. However, all capital expenditure had to be authorized by the front-line-reporting body's (FRB) chief executive officer (CEO). In addition, an authorized capital expenditure voucher (CEV) had to be signed by the divisional CEO, the sub-group CEO, the FRB finance director and the FRB CEO.

The CEV contains a financial analysis of the costs and benefits of the proposed capital expenditure together with a short narrative by the proposer, which shows the chain of command linked to the organizational chart for the company (Figure C1.1). The proposal showed an undiscounted payback of under two years and was authorized by all relevant people.

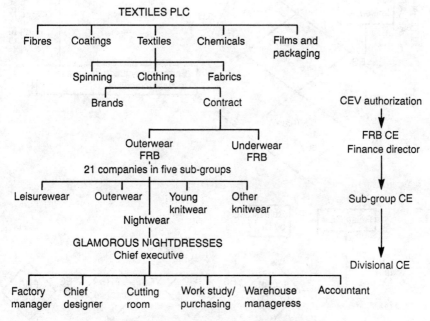

Figure C1.1 The chain of command of Glamorous Nightdresses.

The model of the process in Figure C1.2 shows the stages followed and highlights the stages where resources have been devoted. Using Hofer and Schendel's analysis we can see the disproportionate time directed to choice. Given the amount of money involved (£2401) it would seem that the authorization process was needlessly lengthy and involved too much of the time of several highly paid executives. However, the desire to ensure that a coherent strategy is implemented often leads large firms to have extensive ▷

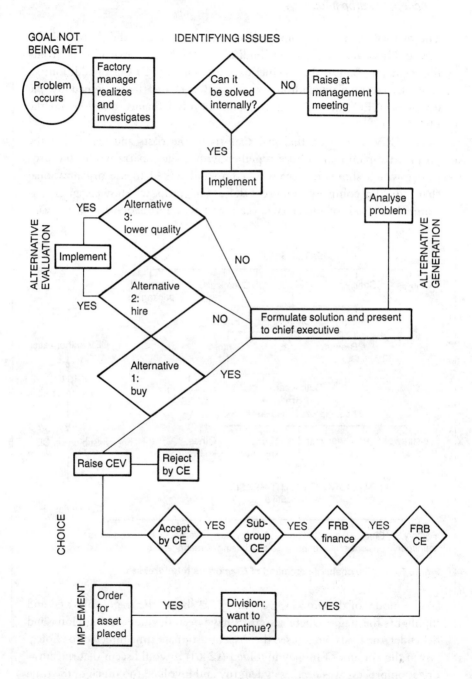

Figure C1.2   A model of the decision process at Glamorous Nightdresses.

authorization procedures. Given that a policy of lower quality or rental could have been implemented without going through such procedures the model helps to highlight areas where the decision-making process needs review.

References

1 E. F. Harrison, *The Managerial Decision-Making Process*. Houghton Mifflin, Boston, 1987; 6–8.
2 H. Mintzberg, D. Rasinghani and A. Thearet, 'The structure of unstructured decision processes', *Administrative Science Quarterly*, 1976; **21**: 246–75.
3 F. G. Castles, D. J. Murray and D. C. Potter, *Decisions, Organisations and Society*. Penguin, Harmondsworth, 1971.
4 I. H. Janis and L. I. Mann, *Decision Making: a Psychological Analysis of Conflict, Choice and Commitment*. Free Press, New York, 1977.
5 E. F. Harrison, *The Managerial Decision-Making Process*. Houghton Mifflin, Boston, 1987; 25.
6 H. A. Simon, *The New Science of Management Decision*. Harper & Row, New York, 1960; 6.
7 P. Drucker, *The Effective Executive*. Harper & Row, New York, 1967; 122–5.
8 H. I. Ansoff, *Business Strategy*. Penguin, Harmondsworth, 1969.
9 H. Mintzberg, 'Crafting strategy', *Harvard Business Review*, July/August 1987; 66–75.
10 H. Mintzberg, 'Strategy formulation in an adhocracy', *Administrative Science Quarterly*, 1985; **30**: 160–97.
11 J. B. Quinn, *Strategies for Change: Logical Incrementalism*. Irwin, Homewood, IL, 1980.
12 T. Parsons (ed.), *Max Weber's Theory of Social and Economic Organization*. Free Press, New York, 1947; 16.
13 See R. W. Mills, 'Capital budgeting: the state of the art', *Long Range Planning*, 1988; **21**: 76–82, for a summary of the use of decision criteria in investment decisioning in the UK.
14 H. A. Simon, 'Rational decision making in business organizations', *American Economic Review*. 1979; **69**: 493–513.
15 M. Oakshott, *Rationalism in Politics*. Methuen, London, 1967.
16 See B. F. Baird, *Introduction to Decision Analysis*. Duxbury, 1980, for a fuller discussion.
17 P. Moore, *The Business of Risk*. Cambridge University Press, Cambridge, 1983; 2.
18 H. A. Simon, 'A behavioural model of rational choice', *Quarterly Journal of Economics*. 1955; **69**: 99–118.
19 R. Cyert and P. March, *A Behavioural Theory of the Firm*. Prentice-Hall International, New York, 1964.
20 R. Hogarth, *Judgement and Choice*. Wiley International, New York, 1987.
21 E. Mumford and A. Pettigrew, *Implementing Strategic Decisions*. Longman, Harlow, 1975.
22 C. Gilligan, B. Neale and D. F. Murray, *Business Decision Making*. Philip Allan, Oxford, 1983.
23 J. Bridge, *Managerial Decisions with the Microcomputer*. Philip Allan, Oxford, 1989.
24 S. Hill, *Managerial Economics: The Analysis of Business Decisions*. Macmillan, Basingstoke, 1989.

25 I. Janis, 'Stages in the decision making progress', in *Theories of Cognitive Consistency*, R. Abdson (ed.), Rand McNally, Chicago, 1968; 577–88.

26 L. P. Schrenk, 'Aiding the decision maker – a decision making process model', *Ergonomics*, 1969; July: 543–57.

27 E. Witte, 'Field research on complex decision making processes', *International Studies of Management and Organisation*, 1972; Summer: 156–82.

28 G. Gordon and I. Pressman, *Quantitative Decision Making*. Prentice-Hall, Englewood Cliffs, NJ, 1978.

29 M. A. Lyles, 'Formulating strategic problems', *Strategic Management Journal*, 1981; **12**: 61–75.

30 S. Cooke and N. Slack, *Making Management Decisions*. Prentice-Hall International, Englewood Cliffs, NJ, 1984.

31 K. Popper, *The Logic of Scientific Discovery*. Hutchinson, London, 1968.

32 P. Caw, *The Philosophy of Science*. Van Nostrand, Princeton, NJ, 1965.

33 C. W. Hofer and D. Schendel, *Strategy Formulation: Analytical Concepts*. West Publishing, St Paul, MN, 1978.

34 J. C. Higgins, 'Management information systems for corporate planning', in *Corporate Strategy and Planning*, B. Taylor and J. R. Sparkes (eds), Heinemann, London, 1982; 299–310.

35 G. Johnson, *Strategic Change and the Management Process*. Blackwell, Oxford, 1987.

36 L. R. Pondy, 'Union of rationality and intuition in management action', in *The Executive Mind*, S. Srivastva (ed.), Jossey-Bass, San Francisco, 1983; 103–39.

2 Corporate Objectives

This chapter looks at corporate objectives. As was seen in Chapter 1 they are the beginning of the decision cycle and also the end towards which it is working. A successful decision is largely assessed on the basis of whether or not outcomes meet the objectives set. The normative decision process models and the rational model suggests that objectives are clear and unambiguous and the process towards their achievement is logical and sequential. The positive models and the example in the case study suggest that the process is less clear-cut and that objectives are vaguer because they are not stated in clear operational terms or because they are multiple and partially conflict.

The focus of this chapter is on achieving objectives. It is argued that economic models of objectives make assumptions about the motivation of individuals concerned with decision-making within the firm. Thus the problems of generating a hierarchical set of objectives from a mission statement are analysed and related to the concept of stakeholders. The importance of individual motivation and reward systems that affect the objectives set is stressed. On the other hand, behavioural models concentrate on the ability of individuals to influence the decision-making process. So organizational political power, structural considerations and communications networks are emphasized, as they affect the ability to translate desired objectives into real decisions and actions. What is suggested here is that a synthesis of the two approaches is required. It is argued that this can be achieved in practical terms by the use of a form of management by objectives and/or strong leadership. The case study shows one firm's approach to creating a corporate philosophy to guide its activities.

The objectives of this chapter are to:

- develop a model for analysing the economic and behavioural approaches to objective-setting;
- identify the factors affecting achievable objectives;
- examine what is meant by a mission statement;
- provide a method for creating a hierarchy of objectives;
- summarize relevant theories on individual motivation and reward systems;
- relate stakeholder analysis to mission achievement;
- outline the need to understand power in organizations;

- highlight the importance of management by objectives and leadership in achieving objectives;
- warn that ethical acceptability should be considered.

Implementing objectives

Before anyone can implement a decision and take action he or she needs to be motivated, that is, have the desire for action, and to be able to influence or control the decision-making process, that is, have the ability to act (see Figure 2.1).

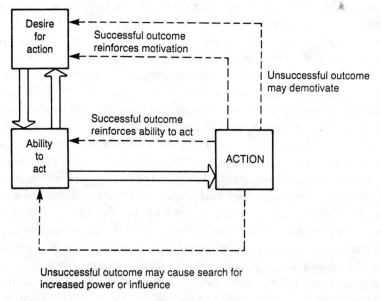

Figure 2.1 Action requires desire and the ability to act.

Reinforcement is an important part of decision-making. Positive feedback increases the tendency for behaviour to be repeated. One aspect of positive feedback is success. If action is successful then motivation is reinforced and so is the influence on or control of the decision-making process by the successful actor. If action is unsuccessful actors may be demotivated, or they may strive to achieve more control of the decision-making process and so work to increase their ability to act. There is also a feedback link between the desire for action and the ability to act, because the highly motivated will search for more power or control and those in powerful positions may realize there is more they can do and so expand their horizons.

The many theories about corporate objectives[1-6] have tended to concentrate on only one element of this model, either the desire for action or the ability to act (see Table 2.1 for a summary). The theories based on economic analysis concentrate on the motivational aspects and tend to assume either that the owners of the firm are in control, as in the case of the neo-classical economic models, and want profit maximization, or that there has been a divorce of ownership from control so that the managers of the firm are in control and can pursue their own objectives at the expense of the owners or shareholders. The extent of this separation of ownership from control has been hotly debated and, although some argue that it has not gone as far as Berle and Means[7] suggested, the 1980s phenomena of employee share ownership schemes and directors' salaries linked to return on capital employed can be traced to a belief in this separation. An attempt to create a coincidence of desires between managers and owners, by rewarding managers using the same criteria that owners use (growth of earnings either paid as dividends or re-invested to lead to capital gains on shares), does in fact imply a recognition that control is in the hands of managers and that takeover threats are insufficient to restrain their behaviour. However, Green[8] argues that the incentive effect of management buy-outs is not just pecuniary and that, by removing constraints, it enables managers to perform their tasks better. Theories have suggested a variety of managerial motivations, such as sales maximization, salary and status maximization and maximization of the growth of the firm. Chapter 1 pointed out the shortcomings of such optimizing models.

Theories based on organizational or behavioural studies, on the other hand, concentrate on the ability to influence or control the decision-making process, or the ability to act to ensure that goals can be reached. These models are all satisficing models because of 'bounded rationality' and informational limitations. Thus people seek only a satisfactory outcome. If the gap between achievement and the objective is too large then the target will be lowered. Using this idea, Cyert and March's[4] model concentrates on both the decision processes found in practice and the coalition forming aspects of groups within real organizations. Subsequent studies have split these two so that, for example, Cohen and Olsen[5] concentrate on decision processes in organizations and Pfeffer[6] concentrates on coalitions and power in organizations. All agree that there is no one goal or objective but that a multiplicity of goals exist. Cohen and Olsen suggest that people often rationalize after the event about what goal they were trying to achieve; others suggest more rational group behaviour but that different groups pursue different goals. This is because of their organizational roles or the environment they work in. They have different external experiences, which lead them to have differing expectations and beliefs as to how to achieve their desired ends. The stakeholder approach is closely aligned to these behavioural models.

If action requires both an ability to act and a desire for action, it would seem that a model incorporating both these aspects is needed. Management by objectives is one way of achieving a synthesis of these ideas because it uses the management hierarchy, where control is often clearly established, and it attempts to align individual objectives with departmental objectives and with overall

Table 2.1   A summary of theories of corporate objectives

Writer	Objective	Ability to act	Desire for action
Neo-classical economists	Profit maximization	Control of organization in hands of entrepreneur	Self-interest of entrepreneur, monetary reward
Baumol[1]	Sales revenue maximization	Divorce of ownership and control means managers can pursue own goals within reason	Increasing sales revenue subject to a profit constraint
Williamson[2]	Managerial utility maximization	Shareholders have very limited impact on decision-making while managers have considerable discretion	Marginal production costs and marginal revenue equate to provide as big a fund as possible to meet managerial preferred expenditure; this is for more staff and generous managerial emoluments, which enhance salary, status and prestige
Marris and Woods[3]	Growth of the firm	Managers are in control but restrained by the need to have a satisfactory valuation ratio (market value to book value of assets) to prevent takeovers	Shareholders want growth of dividends and capital gains and managers want growth of the firm as their salaries are linked to the size of the company they manage
Cyert and March[4]	Each department has its own objective; for example, sales have the goal of value, volume or a market share percentage and production have a goal of smooth and level production, whereas only top management have the goal of profit	Constraints are considerable; information is limited, as is ability to process it, criteria are simple and decisions made sequentially; coalitions of interested groups change over time and vary with different decisions	Multiple and possibly conflicting goals; satisficing behaviour by members of the organization; goals often stated as aspirations and not tested for internal consistency
Cohen and Olsen[5]	No clear objectives; frequently they are after-the-event rationalizations	Constrained by overloaded systems and by random participation in decision-making forums	Participants are not 'motivated' to act; rather they respond to perceived problems or act out of habit
Pfeffer[6]	Each coalition will have its own objectives and seek to gain sufficient power to ensure they are achieved	Depends on control of resources, position in the organizational structure and the interdependence of groups	Each group or sub-group may have a different objective because these derive from differing individual beliefs and differing beliefs about how best to achieve a desired goal

strategic objectives. Strong leadership can also bring together these two strands and ensure that organizational objectives are achieved.

Before a detailed explanation is given of how management by objectives and leadership can ensure that both the desire for action and the ability to act can work together to produce effective achievable objectives, a number of factors which affect each of the areas will be examined.

Figure 2.2 shows the influences on the two aspects of action that are necessary before a decision can be implemented. The desire for action is affected by individual motivation, which arises from personal values and beliefs. These are modified by the experiences individuals have within an organization, and of particular importance is the mission statement and the hierarchy of objectives devolving from it. Reinforcement of these is achieved by reward systems and management systems such as quality teams. An overall influence in this sphere that can be crucial is that of corporate culture; this is taken up in detail in Chapter 3.

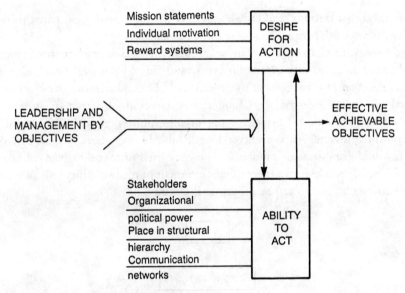

Figure 2.2   Factors affecting objectives.

The ability to act is affected by the power structure in an organization, the position of the decision-maker in the organizational hierarchy and communication networks, which are taken up in detail in Chapter 4. Also of importance can be the configuration of stakeholders. Again corporate culture can be important in affecting individuals' and groups' perceptions of their ability to act. In Figure 2.2 leadership and management by objectives are shown as being capable of influencing both the desire for action and the ability to act. It is because of this that it is suggested that they can play a synthesizing role in bringing together motivational concerns identified by the economic models and behavioural issues identified by the satisficing models, and so ensure that effective achievable objectives are set.

What is a mission?

In 1968 Argenti[9] argued that the fundamental objective, or what is now called the mission, of a business must be an expression of its 'permanent unalterable *raison d'être*', and that it should be to make a profit measured as a return on shareholders' funds. Since then there has been a great deal written about both the theory and practice of objective setting. Practitioners such as Drucker[10] tended to concentrate on the need for unambiguous, measurable and specifically assigned responsibilities associated with objectives. Thus the quantification of objectives together with monitoring of their achievement was essential. More academic writers[11] articulated economic theory arguments of maximizing profits and so implied that all business organizations could or should have the same goal. Compare this with the firm as a wealth breeder (discussed in Chapter 7).

In a more practical sense it can be argued that ways need to be found to translate the mission into clear objectives, and that by far the most influential technique is that of management by objectives.[12] Thus a hierarchy of objectives is needed, as was suggested by Granger.[13] An overall objective or mission is required to give a sense of where the organization is going. This might be relevant for at least ten years and could be devolved into a series of sub-objectives which would give strategic guidance. These are then further devolved into operational objectives which can meet the requirement of measurability and allocation of responsibility, and so can be monitored (Figure 2.3).

Figure 2.3   A hierarchy of objectives.

A practical approach to this process is well explained by Redwood[14] and was used by him when he was General Manager of Corporate Planning at Fisons Limited. His approach results in an ends–means chain like that described by Simon.[15] Each level in the hierarchy of objectives is an end viewed from the perspective of the level below it and is a means viewed from the perspective of the level above it. Cooke and Slack[16] give several examples of ends–means chains and show how there can be several 'routes' or chains to the same objective. In this approach the mission is an end for each strategic objective while each strategic objective is an end for several operational objectives. Hence strategic objectives are the means by which the mission is achieved.

In practice the missions of business organizations vary considerably and tend not to refer simply to profit, as Argenti, Friedman and the neo-classical economic model suggest they should. A survey by Murray[17] found that the most popular stated objective could be categorized as 'market share or sales maximization', closely followed by 'high quality of product/service'. A more recent survey by Gore and Murray[18] showed that customer satisfaction was the dominant mission. Evidence based on asking managers what goals are being pursued usually concludes that financial goals dominate.[19] It should be noted that the time scales and methodological approaches used are different, and this may partly account for the differing results. It could be that one type of survey is measuring stated objectives – what managers say they are doing – while the other, based on asking junior management what their perceptions were, is measuring working objectives. These can be measured by ascertaining what resources and time are devoted to which activities and which measurement systems are employed. It is possible to argue that the market/customer goals act as proxies for profit maximization or are the means to that end.

Some examples of mission statements include:

Constantly seeking ways of improving the total service to customers.

High street retailer

To grow profitably on a world-wide scale through aggressive marketing of high quality branded foods.

Confectionery manufacturer

Profits, growth in a free market economy, quality of products and service to customers, respect for the dignity and worth of individuals, provision of equal opportunities and the desire to be good world citizens.

Multinational industrial company

Mission statements vary considerably because different purposes are envisaged for them. For some firms they are an unvarying statement of the core values – for example, 'The supreme purpose of the whole organization is to secure the fairest possible sharing by all the members of all the advantages of ownership, gain, knowledge and power' – and from them are derived strategic objectives which relate to more practical implementable issues. With such general missions frequently expressing the beliefs of founders of the organization, it is possible for strategic objectives to vary considerably over time, as long as they are consistent with the central belief or mission. For an interesting variation of this approach see Case study 2. For other firms the mission is something that does vary over time and that can be used to signal a change in strategy. Redwood[14] shows how

Fison's mission changed from, in 1967, 'To achieve continuous growth in EPS both in the short term and in the long term', to, in 1976, 'To achieve profitable growth in real terms by increasing EPS and raising return on capital employed'. The move was prompted by an environmental change, that of very high rates of inflation. Another purpose of the mission is to bind together different stakeholders' groups and an example of that is the quote above relating to a multinational industrial company.

Whatever purpose a mission serves it needs to attempt to provide a vision or overall view of the essence of the organization and to express what is distinctive about it. Argenti's[9] suggestion that a mission is an organization's 'permanent unalterable *raison d'être*' provides a good working definition. Michel[20] includes badly worded mission statements as a reason for failures in strategic planning because 'they need to state implicitly or explicitly what is not, as well as what is, intended' (p. 11.12). The greatest flaw is the implicit message in a mission that the organization is better than the competition, as it is statistically impossible for all competitors to be superior. As a result of these difficulties Drennan[21] argues that a few key goals are needed, not 'elegant but anodyne' mission statements; thus communication to the workforce can be simplified and commitment increased.

Motivation of individuals

The theories about objectives demonstrate the effect of personal values and beliefs on organizational objectives. If a manager personifies the organization she or he will reflect completely its mission and strategic objectives and values. However, as there is no such thing as the organization in terms of a specific being, it is dangerous to assume that organizational objectives and values exist in their own right; rather they are reflected in the behaviour of individuals and groups, and together these affect the culture of the firm, which is examined in Chapter 3.

Individual actions are affected by value systems although these are not quantifiable except on a continuum of 'strongly agree' to 'strongly disagree'. There have been many classifications of values: for example, Allport *et al.*'s[22] scale of aesthetic, theoretical, economic, political, social and religious; or Maslow's[23] hierarchy of lower-order needs (physiological, safety, social) and higher-order needs (self-esteem and self-actualization). Individuals are motivated to behaviour in a way that ensures those needs are met. So, for example, for most people in an advanced industrial society the lower-order needs are met and so the satisfactory completion of complex tasks provides a strong motivational force as it satisfies higher-order needs. Alderfer[24] has suggested a simpler hierarchy of needs, which includes existence, relatedness and growth. This view is based on empirical research, and the satisfaction of lower needs is *not* a prerequisite for the emergence of higher needs.

An appreciation of this basis of motivation is important if objectives are to be used as an effective form of control.[25] This requires an appropriate reward system linked to the fulfilment of objectives.

Reward systems[26]

There is a wide variety of human needs or values operating at work. In order to motivate personnel it is necessary to diagnose what needs or values are most important to the organization and then to devise reward systems to ensure these are encouraged, The closer the fit between organizational objectives, personnel needs and values and the reward system, the higher productivity will be because decisions will fit together in a pattern that leads to the achievement of the mission. If higher level needs are to be satisfied then reward systems will have to be complex and varied.

Reward systems work on the premise that individuals repeat behaviour that is rewarded and avoid behaviour that is punished, and reinforcement of behaviour is more effective. Intrinsic rewards, those built into the work itself, which create a challenge or give a sense of accomplishment or a chance for creativity, are more successful than extrinsic rewards.[27] This is because extrinsic rewards require constant adjustment to ensure that pay, bonuses and benefits are comparable with others on offer and to ensure they are most effectively timed. They need to be perceived as 'fair', so performance must be easily measured, the system well understood and equitably applied. Unless there is a high level of trust between management and employees, there will be a tendency to 'play the system'. Taylor,[28] in his pioneering work on 'scientific management', blamed poor management and lax control systems for low productivity. The dangers of devising a 'foolproof' system can be seen by the existence of threats to 'work to rule', which is a severe sanction employees can impose during industrial relations disputes.

The connection between rewards and behaviour is not always direct and simple, so motivating personnel to behave in a way consistent with organizational aims is not a simple task. Group pressures are very important and can override organizational pressures,[29] so it is essential that teams are encouraged to consider how they contribute to overall objectives and are not allowed to develop their own and possibly conflicting goals in the manner described by Cyert and March[4] and experienced by many people in work situations.

Stakeholders

The concept of stakeholders can be traced back to Barnard[30] in management literature but it has always been recognized by political theorists, especially those like Machiavelli, who concentrated on the practicalities of power. Current interest in the topic arose from accountants wishing to define the users of external financial reports. This originated in *The Corporate Report*,[31] which identified seven groups with rights to information concerning the operation of a business: investors, creditors, employees, advisers, customers and suppliers, government and society.

A stakeholder is an individual who belongs to a recognizably separate group of people or institutions who have a special interest in an organization. Figure 2.4, based on Haines,[32] shows the stakeholders normally found in a business organization and their likely interests.

Figure 2.4   Stakeholders and their interests.

Stakeholders will vary over time both in terms of importance and in terms of their interests. At the beginning of the Thatcher era of government in the UK, employees and their trade unions would have been considered more important than in the late 1980s. However, demographic changes putting pressure on labour markets may lead to an increase in the importance of this sector in the 1990s. An interventionist government with a strong industrial policy would probably result in a separate segment being created for 'government', which would not necessarily replace the 'society' segment. Evidence about which stakeholders are recognized is not extensively available, but a survey in the USA in 1984[33] showed the following results when executives ranked stakeholders on a scale from 1 (least important) to 7 (most important):

Customers	6.40
Employees	6.01
Owners	5.30
General public	4.52
Shareholders	4.51
Political figures	3.79
Government officials	2.90

Using stakeholder information for solving the practical problem of establishing corporate objectives is more difficult. It requires that the needs of various stakeholders are established, that their claims are reconciled should they conflict and that a tangible, measurable hierarchy of objectives is created from them.

Establishing the needs of stakeholders or their interests is not usually difficult. However, sometimes an individual has a dual role in an organization, for example employee and shareholder, and which view prevails in the case of any conflicting interests can only be decided by that individual. Reconciling the conflicting claims of stakeholders is generally the task of management. It is necessary to establish key stakeholders who, according to Pearce,[34] can be divided into inside claimants and outside claimants. The former include management, directors, shareholders and employees, and the latter include all others. This special role of management is why Figure 2.4 includes 'strategic management' in the centre as well as 'company', whereas Haines's original does not. Management, having previously assessed the various needs of the stakeholders, must make further assessments of the relative power of the stakeholders so that claims can be prioritized. Pfeffer[6] gives considerable advice on the assessment of power in organizations, which can be useful in this situation. However, the process need not involve conflict at all, for every stakeholder can benefit from the successful operation of the organization. An example of the way one company has reconciled conflicting stakeholder needs and reconciled it to an overall mission of 'our purpose is to create wealth' is shown in Figure 2.5.

Figure 2.5 shows an ideal way of reconciling stakeholder claims. It is not always possible to meet all claims from everyone involved but it is usually possible for satisfactory working conditions to be established. These can be unsettled by major changes, such as competitive shifts or takeover threats.

Although it is possible to show that all stakeholders can and do contribute to the overall success of the organization, it is necessary to recognize that frequently certain stakeholders are more powerful at certain times than others because they have a greater ability to affect the decision-making process. For example, creditors have relatively little say in the running of a business until a crisis situation occurs and cash flow and financing problems arise. They can then become a dominant or key stakeholder. Similarly, many shareholders take very little interest in their company until either profits fall dramatically or a takeover bid is announced.

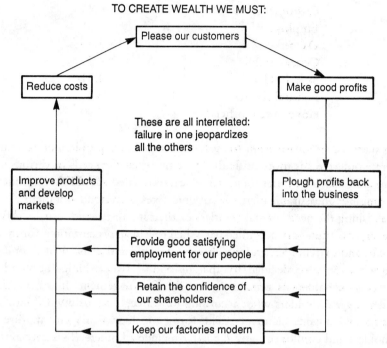

TO CREATE WEALTH WE MUST:

Figure 2.5   How stakeholders contribute to a mission.
Source: *The Corporate Report*[31].

Organizational political power

The ability of certain participants in an organization to affect decision-making frequently depends on their power. Pfeffer[6] claims that in any organization there must be certain conditions before political behaviour is found. These include the existence of different sub-units that are interdependent and staffed by people with different goals and different beliefs about how to achieve their goals. The resulting conflict leads to political behaviour if resources are scarce, the decision is perceived as important and power is not firmly centralized.

'Power resides implicitly in the other's dependence.' It is 'directly proportional to A's motivational investment in goals mediated by B, and inversely proportional to the availability of those goals outside of the AB relationship'.[35] Power can be assessed by looking at control over resources.[36] Particularly important here is the existence of slack and the upward adjustment of aspirations to absorb it, making growth a popular objective because it helps avoid the necessity of making difficult choices.[37] Also of importance is the ability to cope with uncertainty; for example, for maintenance engineers in an automated factory the possession of this attribute increases their influence and power. Similarly the irreplaceability of individuals or groups with special skills or knowledge, such as systems analysts or the boss's personal assistant, will enhance their power.

Control over one stage of the decision process concentrates power into a group or individual's hands; for example, they may be 'gate-keepers' of information or able to set constraints. This effect is more marked if the group concerned shares a strong consensus. Individuals possess certain characteristics which make them more powerful, for example if they are good negotiators,[38] articulate,[39] understand the distribution of power and the decision processes, and believe in their case.[40]

Pfeffer[6] claims that power is important because it has 'consequences in organizations for resource allocations, administrative succession, structures and strategic choices' (p. 231). All of these are affected because the ability of individuals to act and so reach effective achievable objectives is dependent on the power they possess or can acquire. Survey work by Hegarty and Hoffman[41] based on the experiences of 407 European 'top managers' suggests that 'power and influence in strategic decision-making is a complex process' (p. 84). The key participant is the managing director exercising formal authority. However, power bases also exist in the departments most closely involved in the decision. These fall broadly into Miles and Snow's three categories of product-market, technological and administrative.[42] For example, product-market decisions are predominantly influenced by marketing departments because of their formal authority and their information base resulting from environmental scanning. Also of considerable but less dominant influence on product-market decisions are the managing director and product management team. Many of these aspects are taken up in Chapter 4, which deals with both formal and informal structures and so with communication networks.

Thus far this chapter has focused on an analysis of the factors influencing the desire to act on the one hand and the ability to act on the other hand. However, a comprehensive analysis would be more sensibly constructed if a synthesis of the two approaches could be achieved. Two approaches to achieving such a synthesis have been proposed: management by objectives and leadership. Each of these is considered in the following sections of this chapter.

Management by objectives

Earlier it was argued that both the ability to act and the desire for action are necessary if effective, achievable objectives are to be pursued through the decision-making process. Management by objectives (MBO) is one way of achieving this synthesis because it attempts to align individual objectives and departmental objectives with the overall objectives or mission. It uses the formal management hierarchy and if cleverly applied can also use overlapping team membership, as described in Case study 3, to assist in the cascading of objectives throughout the organization so that the vision of the strategists is translated into reality.

Peter Drucker introduced the concept in 1954.[43] It is a rational management technique which involves the identification of long-term quantifiable objectives that can be implemented by discussions, down through the organization, in which individuals set their own targets and contribute to the overall objectives and mission of the organization. There is a strong element of belief in self-control and personal motivation.

Seyna[44] has surveyed the history of MBO, which has both its advocates and detractors. By going back to Drucker's original work it is possible to see what was originally intended and then to assess whether or not this has been implemented. In order for all to contribute to the purpose of the organization all must know its mission. Seyna claims that this is frequently forgotten, but recently organizations such as Esso have held special conferences for staff to publicize their overall strategic objectives and missions. Objectives are essential, for they give a common dimension of vision and can help to encourage team work, as it is possible to establish each team's contribution to the mission. This can only be done if the objectives are clearly understood at all management levels. Objectives are used to help prioritize actions and are the standard against which performance is monitored. Close involvement by everyone is essential as self-control is an important ingredient. Thus imposition from above is not in the spirit of MBO. Neither is setting unachievable objectives, for the idea is that they should be measurable and that regular monitoring of achievements should ascertain the extent to which targets are achieved.

MBO is 'a flexible, rational system that adapts to all situations'.[44] By careful design it is possible to align everyone in the organization behind the strategic objectives so that all have the same desire for action or are motivated to the same end. By using the existing structure and the less formally defined work teams within that structure, it is possible to ensure that everyone has the ability to act or translate objectives into reality. This ideal synthesis is not easily achieved. It requires leadership from the top, excellent communications and a strong personnel policy to ensure that selection, training and reward systems all work together in a coordinated or holistic way. So it moves from being a set of intentions to becoming the basis of corporate strategic thinking, which enables a whole corporate culture to revolve round it.[45]

Leadership

Another way of synthesizing the two aspects of what is required for effective achievable objectives is through leadership. Exerting influence is at the core of leadership. This can be achieved formally as the result of a position in the hierarchy or informally as the result of the personal characteristics or attributes of the leader. Power held in this way can be legitimate if it goes with the position held, or illegitimate if it results from informal offers of rewards or threats of punishment. Etzioni[46] suggests that there are three types of compliance structures. Economic ones are found in all business organizations where people are paid to work. Normative compliance structures rely on personal relations and shared beliefs to influence behaviour. These are used more and more in modern business organizations, especially those with a strong corporate culture. Finally, coercive compliance structures are the type found in prisons and use fear to direct behaviour. These are not often found in businesses but are not unknown.

If leadership is perceived as legitimate it will have more influence than if it is not. Mintzberg[47] ascribes three roles to a leader: the interpersonal functions of liaising, supervising and acting as a figurehead; the informational functions of monitoring, disseminating and speaking for the organization; and the decision-making functions, which call on the previous functions and activities in order to initiate and design changes, handle disturbances, allocate resources and negotiate both between subordinates and with the environment. Leaders can adopt different styles and there is a great deal of literature both categorizing styles and advocating particular approaches as best.

Profiles of actual managers are not generally available but research by Norburn and Schurz[48] summarized the British director:

> [has] had little inter-company experience; likes a 'challenge', but despises creativity; is most likely to have been an accountant, and least likely to have a production, or international experience and considers (falsely) that his company status is growing. He is educated, male, suburban, and maritally stable. He is no longer ambitious but is content with his lot. He does not ascribe his success to patronage, but to hard work and concern for achieving his budget. He is more likely to be authoritarian, and does not consider social adaptability, concern for people, loyalty and lateral thinking, are likely to enhance executive success.

This contrasts starkly with their survey of the literature, which concluded that boards of directors should endorse or set strategy, be adequately informed to evaluate strategy, be independent of the executive and be able to 'hire and fire' the chief executive officer.

A warning note

A clear guiding mission and a well-thought-out set of logically derived strategic objectives can be a strategic asset. They can greatly improve decision-making by making it more rational and by providing a clear set of criteria against which alternatives can be evaluated and performance or outcomes compared. They can act as a motivator for personnel, provide a mechanism to ensure they are accountable for their decisions and enable assessment of their performance. However, there is no guarantee that the mission is the 'correct' one for the organization, or that it is ethically acceptable to the society in which the organization operates. Furthermore, if a very strong mission supported with great enthusiasm at the top prevails, there may be a tendency for bias to permeate the decision-making process. What happens is similar to Janis's 'groupthink'.[49]

The 'correctness' of the mission is very difficult to establish. Most organizations from time to time re-evaluate their mission statements or central objectives. A few never do this because the mission encapsulates core values only and the strategic objectives cover more specific aspirations. The evaluation process is usually set in motion because of obvious failure in some aspect of desired performance. In the Fisons example above, poor earnings per share led to the re-evaluation. A threatened takeover or some other major environmental change may have a similar impact. Although one-off major changes should be responded to, it can be argued that it is better for an organization to anticipate change (Chapter 8 looks at techniques to help in this task). Frequently it is the insidious changes which cause the most difficulty. Some firms responded early to 'green issues' and were in the forefront of creating opinions (for example, The Body Shop), while others did not realize until later that they were good environmentalists (for example, Johnson Polishes) and others ignored green issues until they became a threat (for example, the electricity industry). The problem here is: to what extent and when do organizations accept a trend and respond to it by making fundamental changes? A mission change is a very important decision and the misinterpretation of a trend may lead to unnecessary changes; hence the tendency to 'wait and see' and hope change is not necessary. However, good environmental scanning and flexible organizations are a much better approach.

Ethical acceptability is an issue rarely considered but nevertheless it is very important. For an exception to this see Stieglitz,[50] whose summary of chief executives' views on their roles suggests that some believe moral leadership is important. The corporate report,[31] in a survey of 300 of the *Times* 1000 Companies conducted in 1975, found that 28 per cent of the respondents recognized a responsibility to the community. In the 1980s the philosophy of the new right dominated thinking. This is aptly summed up by Milton Friedman,[11] who regarded political and economic systems as 'markets in which the outcome is determined by the interaction among persons pursuing their own self interest' (p. x), so that the 'free market system distributes the fruits of economic progress among all the people' (p. 247) and consumers should be 'free to choose what chances [they] take with [their] own lives' (p. 227). Relying totally on the economic system to protect the vulnerable is not advocated by Friedman, but government intervention should be severely limited because self-interest can be broadly interpreted so that altruistic acts are not ruled out. An example of this might be Figure 2.5, which shows how stakeholders contribute to a mission, but maximization of shareholder wealth is really the logical outcome of a true free-market approach. A number of major corporate scandals, such as the 'Guinness Affair',[51] have led to questions about just how far self-interest should go or be allowed to go and whether restraints should be self-imposed or imposed by regulatory bodies. There are no ready answers and what is ethically acceptable in one country and one time is not necessarily acceptable elsewhere or at a different time. Pornography is ruled out by many publishers, for example, although it is a profitable area in publishing, whereas this business policy is clearly acceptable to others.

The problem of very strong support for very clear missions only arises if the mission is misconceived. As a behavioural phenomenon it is found sufficiently frequently to be worthy of comment. Janis[49] describes groupthink as occurring in cohesive groups whose members fail to apply independent critical thinking and objective moral judgement, so that the ethical consequences of decisions are ignored, as occurred, for example, in the Guinness case. It also involves the restriction of information that questions the central belief; for example, the Central Electricity Generating Board was accused in a report by the Select Committee on Energy in 1990 of 'applying systematic bias in favour of nuclear power, ignoring the risk entailed, failing to provide adequate contingencies for risk and being insufficiently cautious'.[52] This policy was found after the Board's head, an enthusiastic supporter of nuclear power, had resigned.

Conclusion

This chapter has suggested that both motivation and ability to affect the decision-making process are crucial for setting effective achievable objectives. It has advocated devolving an interrelated hierarchy of objectives from an overall mission statement. A number of factors were identified as influencing the outcome of actual implementable objectives. These include individual motivation and reward systems which, together with the mission statement, affect the desire for action. The ability to translate that desire into effective behaviour is affected by the existence and form of stakeholders, the political power of organizational participants, the structural hierarchy and communication networks. It was argued that all these factors are influenced by leadership and its use of rational management techniques, such as management by objectives. Although taking account of all the above factors would lead to the creation of an implementable hierarchy of objectives, it is essential to check that these are ethically acceptable and fit into the wider context of society so that misconceived missions are not devised.

Case study 2
BBA Group plc

This case illustrates a novel approach to objective setting in that a strong culture, clearly articulated, underpins the objectives set. ▷

Background

BBA is a diversified multinational industrial group serving the automotive, industrial and aviation markets. Sales totalled £1229 million in 1990 of which 52 per cent were associated with the automotive industry, 36 per cent the general industrial market and 12 per cent the aviation industry. Sales by geographical area in 1990 were 32 per cent in Europe, 31 per cent in North America, 22 per cent in the UK, and 15% in other areas. Table C2.1 gives details of operating profit according to market and geographical area. Profits on ordinary activities before taxation rose from £8.7 million in 1984 to £64.1 million in 1988 to £75.1 million in 1990 and dividends per share, in the same period, went from 1.74p to 6.45p to 7.50p.

Table C2.1   Operating profit by market and geographical area, 1990

Market	£m	Area	£m
Automotive	34.6	Europe	22.5
Industrial	46.2		
Aviation	16.1	UK	16.9
Net interest	(21.8)	North America	38.5
	75.1	Rest of world	15.4
			93.3
		Associated companies	3.6
		Net interest	(21.8)
			75.1

BBA's growth has been both organic and through acquisition. Organic growth, according to Dr J. G. White, Group Managing Director, 'justifies [BBA's] preoccupation with running the existing business more efficiently' (1988 Annual Report and Accounts), as demonstrated by operating margins improving from 7.7 per cent in 1987 to 8.3 per cent in 1988. Capital investment of £62 million, which greatly exceeded the rate of depreciation, was primarily aimed at reducing unit costs through improved process efficiency and was funded by internal cash flow. However, by 1990 trading 'proved to be difficult' (1990 Annual Report and Accounts), but BBA endeavoured to structure its business to mitigate these difficulties and then 'operate with diligence'.

Markets

BBA concentrates on products that have reached the mature stage in their life cycle and are beginning to decline. BBA aims to gain market share of these declining markets and increase profitability by raising prices and reducing costs, and encouraging the tail of the product life cycle. So coupled with this sunset industries policy is one of consolidating fragmented ▷

markets. BBA is divided into three distinct segments: automotive, industrial and aviation segments.

The automotive market is served by three divisions: friction materials, automotive components and structural body systems, both as original equipment and in the after market. The friction materials division aims to reflect its present strength in Europe, North America and South-east Asia. The growth in world vehicle numbers, with motorization not yet at saturation point, means the market for automotive components is still growing.

The industrial market is served by three divisions: industrial textiles, producing carpet underlay, speciality tapes and fluid transportation hose; high-performance plastics; and specialist electrical equipment. Expansion in these areas is expected to be both organic and through acquisition.

The aviation market is served by component manufacturing of landing gear and flight controls; and aviation engineering, particularly servicing aircraft and airport services in both the UK and the USA.

Objectives

BBA's primary objective is to enhance shareholders' wealth by consistently improving earnings per share, whilst minimizing risk from over-exposure to any one industrial or geographic area. This is achieved through organic growth and acquisition of under-performing assets so long as they offer above-average profits potential and contribute to the evolution of a balanced and focused portfolio.

Planning is impossible, according to Dr White, because of the number of variables involved and the volatile nature of the business environment. However, it is possible to have an overall sense of direction provided by a clear objective and to heighten a firm's capacity to react to environmental choice.

Management

Management style is characterized by honesty and openness. Table C2.2 shows the organizational structure of BBA. Dr White joined BBA in 1984. A summary of his view of BBA's corporate philosophy can be found at the end of this case study. To overcome communication problems he insists that everyone is clear about who is his or her boss and that everyone answers to only one boss. Dr White believes that people are motivated by bonuses (up to 22.5 per cent of salary at BBA) to achieve targets they set themselves.

Finance

Share price changes are important for the paper financing of acquisitions and for the effect on motivation of employees with share options, so share price movements must be closely monitored. As well as experiencing insta- ▷

Table C2.2   Organizational structure, 1990

	Chairman		
	V. E. Treves		
Group Managing Director Dr J. G. White	*Group Director, Finance* P. E. Clappison	*Non-executive* R. H. Cooper	*Non-executive* L. J. Stammers
	Executive Management		
Chief Executive, Friction Materials G. Cartwright	*Chief Executive, Automotive Components* P. F. Crawford	*Chief Executive, Corporate Affairs* G. E. Howard	*Chief Executive, Pacific BBA Ltd* G. J. Kraehe
President and Chief Executive, Page Avjet Corp. V. DeLuca	*Chief Executive, Engineering* B. G. Hill	*Chief Executive, Engineering Products* I. Williamson	*Chief Executive, Industrial Textiles* M. A. Wright

bility in the financial markets, BBA faces complexity: with a turnover of £1229 million, it operates in 14 different legal, financial and taxation frameworks and has to deal with 14 different exchange rates.

Gearing had reached about 69 per cent by 1990 despite a desire to restrict it to 40 per cent. In 1988 net interest amounted to 32 per cent of operating profit despite the fact that other 'current borrowings are predominantly outside the UK and steps were taken to fix the cost of approximately half of those borrowings before the recent rises in world interest rates' (C. M. Fentam, Chairman, 1988 Annual Report). By 1990 net interest was 22.5 per cent of operating profit.

BBA – A CORPORATE PHILOSOPHY

The inertia of history is a powerful influence on corporate philosophy. BBA in its 103 years of existence has strayed little from:

1 Yorkshire paternalism

2 Weaving of heavy textiles

3 Friction technology via woven or pressed resin media.

The philosophy of BBA for the next few years will be to adapt rather than abandon the inertia.

Management

(a) Grit and gumption are preferable to inertia and intellect.
(b) The Victorian work ethic is not an antique.
(c) One man can only serve one master, to whom he is responsible for a minimum number of succinctly defined tasks.

$\triangleright$

(d) Most companies owned or yet to be acquired possess adequate people waiting to be transformed by dedicated leadership.

(e) The effectiveness of an organization is in inverse proportion to the number of hierarchical layers.

Markets

We shall concentrate in markets where:

(a) The products are in a state of maturity or decline 'sunset industries'.

(b) The scale of our presence in a market segment will allow price leadership.

(c) The capital cost of market entry is high.

(d) Fragmentation of ownership on the supply side facilitates rapid earnings growth by acquisition of contribution flows.

Money

(a) The longer run belongs to Oscar Wilde, who is dead.

(b) The key macro and micro variables of our business are so dynamic that poker becomes more predictable than planning and reactivity more profitable than rumination.

(c) Budgets are personal commitments made by management to their superiors, subordinates, shareholders and their self-respect.

(d) The cheapest producer will win.

(e) The investment of money on average return of less than three points above market should be restricted to Ascot.

(f) Gearing should not exceed 40 per cent. The location from which funds emanate should be matched to the location from which the profit stream permits their service.

(g) We are not currency speculators, even when we win.

(h) Tax is a direct cost to the business and, accordingly, should be eschewed.

(i) Victorian thrift is not an antique.

(j) Nothing comes free; cheap assets are often expensive utilities.

Monday

Our tactic is:

(a) To increase the metabolic rate of BBA through directed endeavour.

(b) To increase profit margins by drastic cost reduction.

(c) To massage and thereby extend the life cycle of the products in which we are engaged.

(d) To become market dominant in our market niches by:
- outproducing the competition;
- transforming general markets where we are nobody to market niches where we are somebody;
- buying competitors.

(e) Use less money in total and keep more money away from the taxman and the usurer.

(f) Avoid the belief that dealing is preferable to working.

▷

(g) Go home tired.

Maybe

(a) The replication of our day-to-day tactic provides long-term growth.
(b) We need to address 'Monday' this week and what our reaction will be to what may be on 'Monday' for the next three years.
(c) Three years is, in the current environment, the limit of man's comprehension of what may be.
(d) Long-term growth necessitates:
   • Resource – notably men and money;
   • Sustained performance rather than superficial genius.

References

1 W. J. Baumol, *Business Behavior Value and Growth*. Macmillan, New York, 1959.
2 O. E. Williamson, *The Economics of Discretionary Behavior*. Prentice-Hall, Englewood Cliffs, NJ, 1964.
3 R. L. Marris and A. Woods, *The Corporate Economy, Growth, Competition and Innovative Power*. Macmillan, London, 1971.
4 R. M. Cyert and J. G. March, *A Behavioural Theory of the Firm*. Prentice-Hall, Englewood Cliffs, NJ, 1963.
5 M. Cohen and J. Olsen, 'Garbage can model of organisational choice', *Administrative Science Quarterly*, 1972; **17**: 1–25.
6 J. Pfeffer, *Power in Organizations*. Pitman, Marshfield, MA, 1981.
7 A. Berle and G. Means, *The Modern Corporation and Private Property*. Harcourt, New York, 1932, revised 1967.
8 S. Green, 'The incentive effects of ownership and control in management buyout', *Long Range Planning*, 1988; **21**: 26–34.
9 J. Argenti, *Corporate Planning*. Allan and Unwin, London, 1968.
10 P. Drucker, *Management Tasks – Responsibility – Practice*. Harper & Row, New York, 1973.
11 M. Friedman, *Free to Choose*. Secker & Warburg, London, 1980.
12 See E. J. Seynow, 'MBO: the fad that changed management', *Long Range Planning*, 1986; **19**: 116–23, for a brief history of management by objectives.
13 C. H. Granger, 'Hierarchy of objectives', *Harvard Business Review*, 1964; May–June: 63.
14 H. Redwood, 'Setting corporate objectives', *Long Range Planning*, 1977; **10**: 2–10.
15 H. Simon, *Administrative Behaviour*. Free Press, New York, 1957.
16 S. Cooke and N. Slack, *Making Management Decisions*. Prentice-Hall International, Englewood Cliffs, NJ, 1984.
17 K. Murray, 'Organisational objectives – an empirical study', *Management Monitor*, 1987; **5**(3): 53–7.
18 C. Gore and K. Murray, 'The Marketing Mission', unpublished survey, 1990.
19 See, for example, A. Francis, 'Company objectives, managerial motivations and the behaviour of large firms', *Cambridge Journal of Economics*, 1980; **4**: 345–61, or R. A. Hill, 'Facts and theory in measuring divisional performance', *Accountancy*, 1982; **93** (1064). *The Corporate Report* (30), in a UK survey of large companies, reported that 58

per cent of them gave their primary objective as profit. However, there was a recognition of their responsibility to other groups, such as employees, customers and the community.

20 P. Michel, 'Failures in strategic planning', in *Handbook of Strategic Planning*, J. Gardner *et al.* (eds). John Wiley, New York, 1986; Chapter 11.

21 D. Drennan, 'How to get your employees committed', *Management Today*, 1989; October: 121–9.

22 G. W. Allport *et al.*, *A Study of Values*. Houghton Mifflin, Boston, 1951.

23 A. H. Maslow, *Motivation and Personality*. New York, Harper & Row, 1954.

24 C. P. Alderfer, 'An empirical test of a new theory of human needs', *Organisational Behaviour and Human Performance*, 1969; **4**: 142–75.

25 E. F. Harrison, *The Managerial Decision-Making Process*. Houghton Mifflin, Boston, 1987.

26 This is only a brief summary of the most important points. For further information see F. Herzberg, *Work and the Nature of Man*. World Publishing, Cleveland, OH, 1966; or E. L. Lawler, *Motivation in the Work Organization*. Brooks Publishing, Monterey, CA, 1973.

27 F. Herzberg, 'One more time: how do you motivate employees?', *Harvard Business Review*, 1968; **46**: 53–62.

28 F. W. Taylor, *The Principles of Scientific Management*. Harper & Row, New York, 1947.

29 E. Mayo, *The Human Problems of an Industrial Civilization*. Macmillan, New York, 1933.

30 C. I. Barnard, *The Functions of the Executive*. Harvard University Press, Cambridge, MA, 1938.

31 *The Corporate Report*, Accounting Standards Steering Committee, London, 1975.

32 W. Haines, 'Corporate planning and management by objectives', *Long Range Planning*, 1977; **10**: 13–20.

33 B. Z. Posner and W. H. Schmidt, 'Values and the American manager', *California Management Review*, 1984, 26: 206.

34 J. Pearce, 'The company mission as a strategic tool'. *Sloan Management Review*, 1982; **23**(4): 15–24.

35 R. M. Emerson, 'Power-dependence relations', *American Sociological Review*, 1962; **27**: 31–41.

36 J. Pfeffer and G. R. Salancik, *The External Control of Organizations: A Resource Dependence Perspective*. Harper & Row, New York, 1978.

37 D. Katz and R. Kahn, *The Social Psychology of Organizations*. John Wiley, New York, 1966.

38 R. Butcher, 'Social process and power', in *Power in Organizations*, Mayer N. Zald (ed.), Vanderbilt Press, Nashville, TN, 1970; 3–48.

39 R. Allan *et al.*, 'Organizational politics', *California Management Review*, 1979; **22**: 77–83.

40 G. R. Salancik, 'Commitment and the control of organizational behaviour and belief', in *New Directions in Organizational Behaviour*, B. M. Stow and G. R. Salancik (eds). St Clair Press, Chicago, 1977; 1–54.

41 W. H. Hegarty and R. C. Hoffman, 'Who influences strategic decisions?', *Long Range Planning*, 1987; **20**: 76–85.

42 R. E. Miles and C. C. Snow, *Organizational Strategy, Structure and Process*. McGraw-Hill, New York, 1978.

43 P. Drucker, *The Practice of Management*. Harper & Row, New York, 1954.

44 E. J. Seyna, 'MBO: the fad that changed management, *Long Range Planning*, 1986; **19**(6): 116–23.

45 J. W. Dudley, *1992: Strategies for the Single Market*. Kogan Page, London, 1989.

46 A. Etzioni, *A Comparative Analysis of Complex Organizations*. Free Press, New York, 1961.

47 H. Mintzberg, *The Nature of Managerial Work*. Harper & Row, New York, 1973.

48 D. Norburn and F. D. Schurz, 'The British board room: time for a revolution', *Long Range Planning*, 1984; **17**(5): 35–44.

49 I. Janis, *Victims of Group Think*. Houghton Mifflin, Boston, 1972.

50 H. Stieglitz, *Chief Executives View Their Jobs*. The Conference Board, Brussels, 1985.

51 See, for example, N. Kochan and H. Pym, *The Guinness Affair*. Christopher Helm, London, 1987.

52 M. Fagan and C. Brown, *Independent*, 28 June 1990; 1.

3 Corporate Cultures

This chapter investigates corporate culture. It takes up some of the issues raised earlier on corporate objectives, for it discusses a concept which lies at the heart of a great deal of organizational activity. Corporate culture affects individuals' behaviour to varying degrees but can provide a strong unifying force, and so if it can be controlled it is potentially a useful management tool. The forms of objectives, the decision processes and the styles of decision-making are frequently substantially influenced by the dominant organizational culture. Thus it is important to try understand what is meant by this somewhat nebulous concept and to ascertain to what extent management can influence and control it. A corporate culture can be a strategic asset and greatly facilitate strategic decision-making or it can be totally inappropriate and lead to the decline and collapse of an organization.

The objectives of this chapter are to:

- explain what is meant by the complex concept of culture;
- relate culture and objectives;
- identify different levels of culture found in organizations;
- analyse the factors affecting corporate culture;
- assess the impact of culture on performance;
- highlight models for changing corporate culture;
- demonstrate how one UK firm has tried to change its culture.

Defining culture

Kilmann et al.[1] define corporate culture as 'a hidden, yet unifying theme that provides meaning, direction and mobilization' (p. ix) to actions within an organization. Deal and Kennedy[2] suggest that having, getting and shaping culture are important matters and that diagnosing and understanding culture are scientifically and operationally possible. By culture they mean:

1 A company's way of doing things.
2 Shared understandings between company personnel.
3 Implicit power balances existing in a company.

They claim that most successful companies have a strong culture. The folk tales and heroes in a company are largely believed and are important in that they affect performance. Culture can be a strategic asset as the 'internalised beliefs motivate people to unusual performance levels'.[2] There is widespread evidence of examples of positive cultures: Honda's culture encourages an emphasis on quality and delivery; Marks & Spencer emphasizes quality and rapid decision-making; IBM concentrates on customer service. However, it can also be a liability if, for example, it leads to intransigency in the face of a need for change. Such an inappropriate culture was British Leyland's centralized production-orientated values, which proved exceedingly difficult to change when more marketing-orientated values were needed to respond to Ford's clever market segmentation policy. Even the appointment of a strong hero (Michael Edwardes) did not lead to very significant or speedy changes. It is possible to overstate the importance of culture. Gould and Campbell[3] suggest as a result of a UK survey that 'corporate ways of doing things and some consensus on underlying values typically exist; but a thorough going commitment to corporate goals or themes is much rarer' (p. 306).

Levels of culture

Just as objectives exist at different levels, creating an interrelated hierarchy, so culture exists at various levels. Culture is a complex concept, and several models have been developed to try to ascertain its important elements. A common feature of these models is that they identify a hierarchy of cultural factors ranging from values and attitudes through to behaviour and procedures. According to Schein,[4] culture exists at three levels. The first is the visible level, which he calls 'artifacts and creations' and which includes technology and audible and visible behaviour patterns. For example, it may be that office doors are open and people walk around chatting a lot. However, it is not possible to infer what this means without reference to the second level, the values level, which can be tested by reference to the physical or social environment found in an organization. To continue the example, doors may be open because it is policy to be accessible and communication may be highly valued, so there is a great deal of chatting. The third level is based on basic assumptions about human nature and relations, human activity, and relationships with the environment. In the example there may be a basic belief that the best ideas require thorough discussion. This level is largely invisible because it is taken for granted.

Kilmann et al.[1] prefer to divide culture into two levels. The surface level includes attitudes or norms such as 'don't rock the boat' or 'treat women as second-class citizens'. A more fundamental culture level exists, which includes hidden assumptions and basic values and beliefs. These often relate to stake-holders within the organization and beliefs about the environment. For example, 'the government will continue to restrict foreign imports', 'the consumer will continue to buy whatever the firm produces', 'employees will always accept current working conditions', 'what worked in the past will work in the future'.

Dyer[5] identifies four levels of organizational culture. The first level, like Schein, he calls artefacts. This level is associated with, for example, rituals, which could include who is or is not allowed to see minutes relating to certain meetings. The second level is called perspective. This involves a 'co-ordinated set of ideas and actions a person uses in dealing with a problematic situation'.[6] As it sets the bounds for acceptable behaviour, the example above may reduce to 'only heads of department are circulated with minutes'. At the third level a value is generated that will generalize from the perspective. In the same example, this may become 'secrecy is a good thing'. The tacit assumption lying behind this perspective is embedded at the fourth level or root of the culture and might, in this example, be 'junior staff cannot be trusted'.

Unlike the hierarchy of objectives, where the flow was one-way from the mission to the individual departmental working objective, cultural levels work both ways. Fundamental levels are the most stable and have arisen as a result of experience and the development of rituals at more superficial levels. Unless and until the fundamental level is challenged and amended, new rituals must conform to the basic assumptions or perspectives already existing (see Figure 3.1).

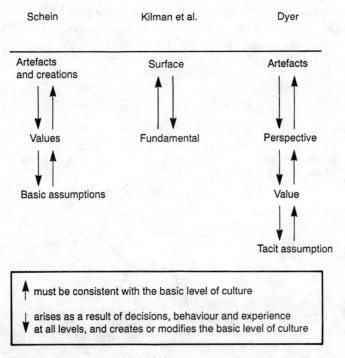

Figure 3.1 Levels of culture.

It is important to remember that most organizations do not have single cultures but are made up of divisions, sections or departments, each with varying cultures. Some may be very different at a fundamental level, such as those described by Cyert and March,[7] where each functional department has a totally different objective and a different working culture, while others will vary slightly only at the surface level. There are a number of reasons for different cultures developing and straying from the corporate culture. Culture is learned, according to Schein,[4] either through positive reward and reinforcement, which leads to successful actions being repeated, or through anxiety and pain reduction when traumas overcome are avoided again. 'Any group has the potential of developing its own culture if it has a stable relationship and a history of joint problem solving' (p. 26). Therefore the extent to which departments are likely to develop cultures that are independent of the corporate culture will be related to the degree of interaction with other elements of the firm and the degree of decentralization that is provided by the organizational structure.

Factors affecting culture

Culture consists of and is affected by a number of factors. Figure 3.2 shows that there are many influences on corporate culture. Employees and stakeholders have norms of behaviour, value systems and beliefs which they bring with them to the organizational setting. These are modified by their experiences within the organization so that norms and values, which are rules of conduct defining acceptable behaviour, show what is important.

Figure 3.2 Factors affecting culture.

These have developed as a result of experience and come from the corporate history. They can be summed up as 'the way we get things done round here'. Also included are beliefs and expectations that show what is believed to be true and so are modified as the result of new experiences and by changes in personnel. Easterby-Smith[8] has suggested that some of the training methods used by firms are aimed at cultural reinforcement and the maintenance of such norms. So, for example, regular sales meetings and training sessions continue to remind everyone of how a particular firm wishes to do business. Gore and Murray[9] have suggested that the influence of culture on the selection process helps to ensure that personnel whose personal characteristics are disposed to the prevailing culture are selected.

Rituals and ceremonies are described by anthropologists as ways of explaining the routine of day-to-day life in an organization. This may involve, for example, the way customers are dealt with, the existence or not of special privileges for certain staff, or the singing of a corporate song by telephone sales people at the beginning of each morning and afternoon to build up enthusiasm and morale. It is not unusual for induction programmes to involve participants in some of these rituals, so that new entrants immediately begin to learn and to adapt to existing acceptable modes of behaviour. In the song example new employees are required to adapt a top twenty hit and rehearse the team so that it can be presented and videotaped. 'In general the stronger the culture of the organisation, the tougher will be the socialisation process for new entrants'.[8]

Communication networks either formally or informally let people know what counts. Frequently the formal system sends one message and the informal another. For example, although formal equal opportunities policies exist in many organizations, sometimes informal messages suggest that women are not suitable for management tasks. The need for a unified approach requires methods of linking layers vertically in the hierarchy and laterally across functions and departments or divisions. Case study 3 is one example of an attempt to do this, in which overlapping team membership enables ideas to cascade down through the systems in the organization. Ineffective formal communication systems can lead to the informal system taking over and creating its own messages. If management ignores the informal system of communications then rumours are likely to develop to satisfy the need for information and an alternative undesirable culture may develop.

Views vary about the importance of leaders in affecting culture. Schein[10] argues that one of the most powerful forces for embedding and reinforcing culture is what leaders pay attention to, and measure and control. Leaders' reactions to critical incidents, their behaviour in crises and their attempts at deliberate teaching and coaching are thus important ingredients in the culture creation process. Systematically paying attention to things they believe count supplements the formal control mechanisms and 'hammers home' what matters in an organization. Thomas J. Lipton[11] asserted that 'every organisation is, in reality, the lengthened shadow of its leader' (p. 125). However, it can be argued that a leader is just one human being in the organization and his or her impact is therefore limited, so it is the top team that matters. Goldsmith and Clutterbuck,[12] using UK data, suggest that leadership which is visible and has a clear mission is one of the ten reasons for a company to have a successful corporate culture. Implicitly, too, leadership provides the driving force for the design, implementation and cultural reinforcement of successful US organisational forms.[13]

Heroes, frequently in the form of leaders with charismatic qualities, contribute to the embedding of culture. Myths develop to explain past behaviour and at social occasions or in meetings such things as the retelling of the vision and perseverance of the founder of the company may occur. References 2, 12 and 13 all repeat stories about the importance of heroes to firms. The founders or their families are frequently of significant influence. For example, John Sainsbury's values of 'orderliness, detail and selfhelp' and his belief in 'low prices and wholesomeness' still pervade the company over 100 years later.[12] Heroes 'personify an organisation's values and as such provide a tangible role model for employees to follow'.[2]

Reinforcement of corporate culture also takes place as a result of reward systems that reward acceptable behaviour and do not reward unacceptable behaviour. Thus a reward system draws employees' attention to what is required and helps to transmit culture through the organization. Richardson and Morris[14] suggest that management can attempt to redesign all aspects of its organization to create an all-pervasive and often unseen force for indoctrination towards the preferred way of doing things.

Finally, culture is affected by societal norms, which will include expressions of beliefs about how business should be run.[15] It will therefore be of particular importance to establish the impact that stakeholders in the organization are likely to have on culture. Earlier it was argued that the fundamental values and beliefs that underlie culture are often based on relationships between the organization and its environment, and between its stakeholders. However, such relationships are very long term. The role of business in society has moved over the past decade from being 'a necessary evil' to becoming 'the engine of social growth'. Such changes in societal attitudes may also act as a spur to explicit attempts to affect culture within firms.[9] Similarly, there have been enormous changes in the relative importance of different stakeholders to the culture of organizations; the importance of employee attitudes and of government influence has waxed and waned over the period. In a study of the motor manufacturing industry Krafick[16] found that organizational norms imported from another country (Japan) can take precedence over national norms. Japanese-owned firms employing local labour in Europe import their preferred cultures, and successfully change traditional nationalistic approaches at work.

The impact of corporate culture on performance

Peters and Waterman[13] tried to ascertain the characteristics or culture of success-ful companies. The sample was drawn from high-technology, consumer goods, general industrial, service, project management and resource-based industries. The companies were selected as being the top performers (in the top half) of their industries using the measures below.

1 Long-term growth over 20 years (1961–80) of assets, equity and the ratio of market value to book value.
2 Return on capital and sales (1961–80) measured by net income over total investment, average return on equity and average return on sales.

From their list of 62 'continually innovating big companies' 19 dropped out and the remaining 43 were interviewed 'in depth' and by the use of secondary sources. The validity of the sample has been questioned by Saunders and Wong[17] because it is not random and there are no control groups. Carroll[18] also points out methodological problems, including the biased nature of the sample and the possibility that an important characteristic has been missed. It is interesting to note that purely financial data are used yet the reasons advanced for success are not directly financial. Peters and Waterman begin by advocating the use of McKinsey's 7-S framework as a means for thinking about and analysing what comprises the organization (see Figure 3.3). They suggest that management should concentrate on the 'soft S's' (style, skills, staff and shared values) and not on the 'hard S's' (strategy, structure and systems), which have traditionally been the 'obsession of Scientific Management' (p. 11). The hard S's are assumed to be satisfactory so the emphasis must be to keep them simple and to try to improve the soft S's summed up by corporate culture. They argue that companies with only financial goals are not as successful as those with a broader set of values. Dynamic structures, although 'untidy', are most effective in modern environ-ments and can be held together by shared values, thus removing the need for strict hierarchical bureaucratic procedures. In essence they are advocating man-agement recognition and utilization of informal organizational structures, giving as an example IBM's experience, which is that new products do not come through the formal system but from 'outside the system Zealots' (p. 115). This tendency seems widespread and is called 'bootlegging' at General Electric and 'scrounging' at 3M.

Peters and Waterman's findings are detailed in eight chapters, each of which concentrates on a particular point.

1 *Bias for action* Successful firms have devised ways to counter the tendency to conformity and inertia by encouraging organizational fluidity, 'management by walking about', solving problems in a series of clearly defined chunks

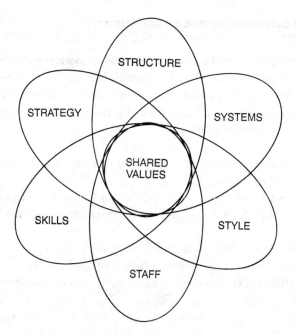

Figure 3.3 The McKinsey 7-S framework.

sequentially, being willing to experiment, setting tight deadlines and simplify-
ing systems.

2 *Close to the customer* Successful companies are customer-orientated and focus
on revenue generation through market segmentation.

3 *Autonomy and entrepreneurship* Excellent companies have grown through innovation and retain their ability to innovate. This was frequently achieved by
decentralizing, by encouraging product 'champions' and by tolerating failures.

4 *Productivity through people* Excellent organizations trust their employees, and
have high expectations of their performance. The attitude of top management
towards trusting people not only manifested itself in quality circles, management by objectives and job enrichment schemes, but pervaded the whole
organization. Great care was taken to select new managers who would fit the
company culture. Above all the excellent companies had a definite philosophy
of which all employees were aware and which affected their behaviour so that
the company (wo)man was created.

5 *Hands-on value-led* Leaders of excellent companies created 'exciting environments through personal attention, persistance and direct intervention' (p. 279).
Every excellent company was clear about what it stood for and took the

process of shaping values seriously. The dominant beliefs of excellent companies usually included:

(a) a belief in being best;

(b) a belief in the importance of doing the job well;

(c) a belief in the importance of people;

(d) a belief in superior quality and service;

(e) a belief in innovation;

(f) a belief in informality to enhance communication;

(g) a belief in the importance of economic growth and profits.

These were constantly reinforced by top management, who espoused these beliefs.

6 *Stick to the knitting* Organizations were most successful if they stuck closely to their central skills.

7 *Simple form, lean staff* Size led to complexity. Complex organizational structures should be avoided.

8 *Simultaneous loose–tight properties* Excellent organizations were 'on the one hand rigidly controlled and yet at the same time [allowed] autonomy, entrepreneurship and innovation from the rank and file' (p. 318). Separate sub-units were united by strong value systems, which provided a stable framework.

Changing corporate culture

A number of similar surveys have been carried out in the UK. Goldsmith and Clutterbuck[12] took the same approach as Peters and Waterman (interviewing top management and using secondary sources), but the companies were mostly in mature industries, whereas the US sample had been concentrated in the high technology area. Areas highlighted by Goldsmith and Clutterbuck were similar but explicitly included leadership and corporate social responsibility. Saunders and Wong's work[17] used a control group, a matched sample of Japanese companies, and concluded that there was no evidence of shared values. Successful companies were planning-orientated, not action-orientated, and had long-term objectives. The latter point is important because some of Peters and Waterman's excellent companies have since failed to meet the test of excellence: hence Peters's recent emphasis on adapting to environmental change.[19]

The problem with the approach used by these best-sellers is that there is an implied assumption that some of the management ideas and techniques outlined can be copied by others, applied as a winning formula or used as what Grinyer and Spender[20] call management recipes. These are unlikely to work at all times and in all environments; they are at best rules of thumb. Looking at decision models for changing corporate cultures shows that the process is likely to be lengthy, expensive and difficult.

If company cultures can and do differ and certain cultures are more successful than others then the notion of trying to change culture must be considered. A decision to change a corporate culture is always a strategic one and will involve many aspects of the organization and all levels in the structural hierarchy. Ironically, culture is easier to change if there is a belief in change embedded in the organizational culture.[21] Johnson[22] has suggested, based on a study of UK menswear retailing, that if there is a homogeneous system of beliefs, change is likely to be successful if the proposed change is small. If beliefs are heterogeneous then larger changes can be successful.

The idea of changing corporate culture, so that it is supportive of particular strategies, is dependent on the belief that culture is an internal organizational variable, susceptible to moulding or shaping by management in particular ways that are consistent with desired strategies.

Smircich[23] has questioned whether corporate culture is manageable because of the existence of multiple subcultures and the absence of suitable technical managerial tools. However, there have been a number of decision frameworks offered to assist in the process of changing culture. Models have been refined as experience of changing corporate cultures is acquired. They began with those offering tips about what seems to be important,[2] but they quickly matured into analysis of organizational cultural norms,[24] and have reached the point of suggesting specific stages in the change process.[25] Case study 3 provides an example of changing corporate culture.

Deal and Kennedy[2] stress the cost of change. They estimate the cost of a culture change to be between 5 and 10 per cent of the budget, so that any change must be estimated to increase profits or reduce costs by at least that amount in order to make attempts at a cultural change worthwhile. It may be that a capital investment programme would be more worthwhile. Having given a warning about cost, Deal and Kennedy then point out that there are no tried and tested management tools but there are a few tips about what can be done. They suggest:

1 Recognize the importance of peer group consensus. For example, if a working team shares a belief in the need for the proposed changes, and has arrived at this view through consensus, then change will be likely to be more successful.
2 Convey and emphasize two-way trust in communications, so that, for example, misunderstandings are not interpreted in the worst light but the real meaning is sought.
3 Ensure that personnel have sufficient training and skills to implement the new change. However keen or highly motivated people are, if they do not have the ability to act they are unlikely to meet the desired objectives.
4 Allow sufficient time for change.
5 Encourage personnel to think of how they can adapt to meet the change ideal.

Commitment or ownership are more likely to develop in those from whom the ideas have come.

Kilmann[24] advocates an analytical approach, which he calls 'a five step process to change corporate cultures'. First, members of the organization must list existing norms that guide behaviour and attitudes. Examples of these in a business wanting change might be 'cheat on your expenses', 'openly criticize company policies' or 'don't reward merit'. Most of these will have been learnt when the employee joined and will be more generally accepted the more cohesive is the group of which the employee is a part. The second step requires that the type of behaviour needed in the future is identified. Overlapping membership of working groups will greatly facilitate a common approach. The third step involves creating new norms so that hidden pressures for dysfunctional behaviour are eliminated. They may include 'becoming cost conscious', 'showing pride in the organization' or 'being enthusiastic'. Kilmann advocates the use of a survey to identify the culture gap in the fourth step. So, for example, if it is considered desirable to share information to help improve decision-making, but the norm is to share only when it benefits one's own work, then the gap is the change in behaviour required to move from one situation to the other, the difference between desired and actual norms. It is usual for the culture gap to widen down through the organizational hierarchy, being narrowest at the top and widest at the bottom. The final step is to close the culture gap. This involves presenting the information gathered and rewarding new behaviours and attitudes.

Allen[25] suggests 'a four phase normative systems change process' (p. 334). The first phase begins with leadership commitment to change, followed by analysis of the situation so that objectives can be set and a programme of events designed. Models outlining levels of culture can be employed at this stage, or more complicated models such as those of Mattsson.[26] The second phase requires that leaders are trained and workshops run to introduce personnel to the new objectives and involve them in the change process to encourage 'ownership'. Ideally, at the end of this phase workshop groups should be in the position of asking what they can do to aid the change process. The third phase pushes forward development of the programme of events at individual level, group level and intergroup level. It enables participants to try out what they have learned and begin to implement change. Leaders must continue to be involved at all stages so that their commitment to change is perceived as continuing. The final phase is one of evaluation and renewal. Given that this model is based on a systems theory approach Allen believes there is always a tendency for an organization to revert to its former state, so there must be regular review of progress.

Case study 3 demonstrates how a firm might actually go about trying to change its culture. It is interesting in that a decision process approach is taken. The team approach is likely to build up commitment to change and the quality team work schedules are an excellent way of focusing attention on to the issues identified by management as being important. In many respects the approach is closely aligned to that suggested by Allen.

Conclusion

This chapter has accepted Deal and Kennedy's definition of corporate culture as a company's way of doing things, shared understandings between company personnel and implicit power balances in a company. It has linked culture to the objective setting process and suggested that, as with objectives, different levels of culture exist. The most important factors affecting culture were considered to be employees and stakeholders, ritual and ceremonies, communication systems, leadership, heroes, reward systems and societal norms and values. The impact of corporate cultures on performance was discussed and it was concluded that in the absence of proper survey techniques it was impossible to recommend the adoption of any of the 'success factors' identified. Environmental changes mean that cultures are likely to have to evolve and adapt, but the costs of change are considerable and success is limited. However, decision models are being developed that are likely to be beneficial by assisting in making the corporate culture change process more rational. It must be remembered that the changes discussed here only refer to internal changes[27] – external changes in terms of technology, products, markets, competitors, and government regulations are taken up in later chapters.

Case study 3
Changing corporate objectives and culture

This case is based on a major high street retailer. It illustrates a rational decision process modified for behavioural problems associated with team working and the implementation of new ideas. It offers a possible model for changing both corporate objectives and corporate culture.

In January 1989 the managing director of a major high street retailer announced a new strategy, aimed at ensuring that the company remained one of the best known and most successful retailers in high street trading. The strategy was really a statement of the company's guiding beliefs in quality, service and truly caring for customers, and a means of ensuring that they were translated into action. Thus it encompassed changes in both corporate objectives and corporate culture. It employed a rational process modified for behavioural influences to do this.

Seven requirements were identified as being necessary: ▷

- welcome for shoppers;
- quality products;
- competitive prices;
- a wide selection of merchandise;
- good information about products;
- guarantees of satisfaction and peace of mind from a pleasant shopping experience.

Only by ensuring that *every* customer was completely satisfied under each of these headings would the company be certain of being the best in an increasingly competitive environment.

These guidelines were to be more than a commendable set of business principles: they were to be a way of life for all employees. Complex procedures were developed to ensure that this expression of hope could be translated into reality. First, staff were made aware of the new objectives through a launch-day conference. This was reported and reinforced by staff newspapers and by videos explaining the concepts. Secondly, all the functional directors announced how they saw their departments contributing; for example, merchandising stressed value for money, more in-store information and a better selection of goods, while warehousing and distribution wished to get closer to store staff (their customers) and to improve computer schedules. Thirdly, quality teams were established. These start at the top with the managing director chairing a meeting of the ten functional directors. Each of these then chairs a meeting of departmental managers who in turn chair meetings of their section heads (see Table C3.1). Thus there is overlapping membership of the teams, and information and decisions can cascade systematically down through the organization, through every function and every level.

Table C3.1 Quality team membership

Management meeting
  Managing director and functional directors

Subordinate quality team I
  Function director and department managers

Subordinate quality team II
  Department manager and section heads

Subordinate quality team III
  Section heads and staff

Each team sets its own objectives, in the light of the overall policy, as it has the specific knowledge needed to develop individual targets which can contribute to the overall achievement of the objective.

▷

The quality teams all follow the approach outlined in Figure C3.1, concentrating on how their own areas of expertise can contribute overall to the section's, department's or function's efforts. Overlapping membership means that different levels in the hierarchy are informed of what is going on and work is not unnecessarily duplicated; nor should it lead to conflicting objectives. The cascading effect down through the organization means there is the widest possible dissemination of information but no great need for bureaucracy. Objectives are aligned throughout the organization and responsibility and accountability are clear at each level.

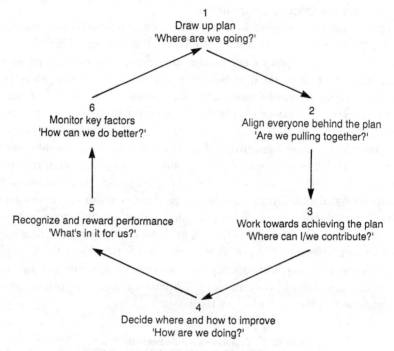

Figure C3.1 Quality team work schedules.

The top quality team gets reports from and sends reports to the ten functional quality teams, who receive reports from and send reports to the subordinate quality teams II, who in turn receive reports from and send reports to the subordinate quality team III. The involvement of as many staff as possible enables the changes made to pervade the organizational culture at all levels. Furthermore, it ensures, because of overlapping membership, that there are no significantly different developments at different levels of the hierarchy that could lead to, for example, middle management interpreting the policy in a very different way from junior management or staff. Functional membership of the top team is a way of ensuring that no function develops policies that may differ or even conflict, ▷

but there may not be enough cross-fertilization. To develop an overall culture there need to be methods of integrating the different parts of a large organization. Either there must be more overlapping membership of quality teams between functions or there should be methods of disseminating the approaches adopted by the different functions. Staff newspapers are unlikely to be sufficient, but cross-functional meetings are likely to be more successful.

The quality team work schedules follow a rational decision process, adapted to cope with behavioural problems associated with team working and the implementation of new ideas, which is presented in a series of simple but relevant questions. 'Where are we going?' corresponds to the objective setting stage and also includes the problems definition stage. 'Are we pulling together?' draws attention to some of the problems teams encounter when they are first established. 'Where can I contribute?' suggests that an answer is needed and corresponds to the alternative generation stage in a decision process. 'How are we doing?' suggests both a review of activities and an attempt to maintain interest in the team's activities. 'What's in it for us?' further reinforces the latter. 'How can we do better?' is the choice stage of the decision, whose outcome is compared to the first stage of the process to see if the objectives set were actually achieved. The choice stage implicitly includes criteria setting and these stages are likely to make use of the overlapping membership of teams throughout the hierarchy, but especially higher up it.

Drucker[28] makes certain requirements of objectives. They should:

1 Be more than good intentions – the launch of the scheme.

2 Degenerate into work – establishing the quality teams.

3 Have specific objectives – quality teams set their own objectives.

4 Have unambiguous measurable results – quality teams develop their own targets and conduct appraisals.

5 Have deadlines – quality teams meet regularly.

6 Assign specific responsibilities – quality teams report upwards and monitor the achievement of targets which are rewarded.

In terms of meeting Drucker's requirements, the quality teams have been well designed. Time will tell how successful they are.

References

1 R. H. Kilmann, M. J. Saxton and R. Serpa, *Gaining Control of the Corporate Culture*. Jossey–Bass, San Francisco, 1985.

2 T. Deal and A. Kennedy, *Corporate Cultures*. Penguin, London, 1982.

3 M. Gould and A. Campbell, *Strategies and Styles*. Basil Blackwell, Oxford, 1987.

4 E. H. Schein, 'How culture forms, develops and changes', in Kilmann *et al*. (1): 17–63.

5 W. Dyer, 'The cycle of cultural evolution in organizations', in Kilmann *et al*. (1): 200–29.

6 H. S. Becher, B. Geer, E. C. Hughes and A. L. Strauss, *Boys in White*. Transaction Books, New Brunswick, NJ, 1961.

7 R. M. Cyert and J. G. March, *A Behavioural Theory of the Firm*. Prentice-Hall, Englewood Cliffs, NJ, 1963.

8 M. Easterby-Smith, 'Evaluating the development of corporate cultures', *Management Education and Development*, 1988; **19**: 85–99.

9 C. Gore and K. Murray, 'Enterprising personnel', *International Journal of Manpower*, 1991; **11**(6): 17–20.

10 E. H. Schein, *Organizational Culture and Leadership*. Jossey-Bass, San Francisco, 1985.

11 G. Gordon, 'The relationship of corporate culture to industry sector', in Kilmann *et al*. (1): 105–25.

12 W. Goldsmith and D. Clutterbuck, *The Winning Streak*. Weidenfeld & Nicolson, London, 1984.

13 T. J. Peters and R. H. Waterman, *In Search of Excellence*. Harper & Row, New York, 1982.

14 B. Richardson and D. Morris, 'Reorganising towards responsiveness', *Management Monitor*, 1987; Summer.

15 S. Davis, 'Culture is not just an internal affair', in Kilmann *et al*. (1): 163–83.

16 J. P. Krafick, 'Triumph of the loan production system', *Sloan Management Review*, 1988; summer; 41–52.

17 J. Saunders and V. Wong. 'In search of excellence in the U.K.' *Journal of Marketing*, 1985; 119–37.

18 D. Carroll, Book review, 'Disappointing search for excellence', *Harvard Business Review*, 1983; November–December.

19 T. Peters, *Thriving on Chaos*. Macmillan, London, 1988.

20 P. Grinyer and J. Spender. *Turnaround: Managerial Recipes for Strategic Success*. Associated Business Press, London, 1978.

21 J. B. Quinn, *Strategies for Change: Logical Incrementalism*, Irwin, Homewood, IL, 1980.

22 G. Johnson, *Strategic Change and the Management Process*. Basil Blackwell, Oxford, 1987.

23 L. Smircich, 'Concepts of culture and organisational analysis', *Administrative Science Quarterly*, 1983; Sept.: 339–58.

24 R. L. Kilmann, *Beyond the Quick Fix*. Jossey-Bass, San Francisco, 1984.

25 R. Allen, 'Four phases for bringing about cultural change', in Kilmann *et al*. (1): 332–54.

26 J. Mattsson, 'Developing an axiological method to measure company values', *European Journal of Marketing*, **22**(6): 21–35.

27 J. Coyne and M. Wright, *Divestment and Strategic Change*, Philip Allan, Oxford, 1986.

28 P. Drucker, *The Effective Executive*. Heinemann, London, 1967.

4 Organization Structure

Previous chapters have drawn attention to the need for rational decision-making and the difficulties, or indeed the impossibility, of achieving a state of full rationality. From an organization point of view one of the major difficulties in achieving rational decision processes is the existence of a variety of goals and the ability of management to pursue them, as discussed in Chapter 2. For an organization as a whole to be effective, however, the decision-making process should be organized along rational lines. Coase[1] in 1937 emphasized that the role of the firm is to enable low costs and flexible coordination of resources, which can only be achieved with the use of rational decision processes. The issue is explained by Barnard,[2] who says that within an organization decision-making must be a 'logical process which must and can characterise organisational action as contrasted with individual action'. The task, therefore, is to ensure that an organization's decisions are as rational as possible and in line with its mission, while participating in that process are non-rational individuals who wish to pursue their own objectives.

One of the ways of achieving this is the careful design of an appropriate organization structure. Such a structure can ensure that decisions are handled at the appropriate levels according to the type of decision (see Figure 1.1). The structure also formalizes the decision process and acts as part of a control mechanism to limit the extent to which individuals can pursue their own objectives. It therefore affects not only the efficient operation of the company but also everyone within it, and plays a vital role in the decision processes.

The objectives of this chapter are to:

- examine the decision-making role of structure;
- analyse the effect of formal and informal aspects, mechanistic and organic organization, and the extent of decentralization;
- identify models of structural form along with their advantages and disadvantages;
- identify the most common form of organization;
- examine reasons for the adoption of a divisional structure;
- examine management policies associated with divisionalization.

The role of organizational structure

The most important role of an organization's structure is that it shows the established pattern of relationships between parts and members of the organization. It is a useful tool because it sorts out decisions into levels of management and identifies the form of the decision process. Thus, it ensures that the different types of decisions are associated with the appropriate level, as shown in Figure 1.1. It sorts out the operational from the strategic decision and ensures that the managing director does not waste his or her time photocopying! In doing this it provides a pattern of formal relationships so that each employee is aware of his or her role and responsibilities, and it enables task coordination and integration. Each employee knows who to report to because the structure establishes an authority system and provides a framework for administrative procedures. So if an employee needs a new piece of equipment he or she will know who must provide authorization.

Thus, structure may be said to define the general shape of the organization. It facilitates and constrains activities, and is characterized by roles, rules and power relationships. According to Mintzberg[3] structure is 'a hierarchy of authority through which flows the formal power to control decisions and actions with common groups to facilitate co-ordination'.

The structure can be seen as a management arrangement to ensure that the desired objectives of the firm are met. It also serves as a control mechanism by limiting the extent to which individuals are free to follow their personal objectives, because it sets their actions within a task-orientated framework. Of course, the idea that the self-seeking, non-rational behaviour of managers could be entirely eliminated is rather idealistic; as Selznick[4] points out, in every organization the goals of the organization are modified by the processes within it. In fact it is more than plausible that in some circumstances organization goals may be subverted by the personal goals of the senior management. Nevertheless, because the structure identifies the pattern of authority it plays an important part in control issues. It is through these structural relationships that the tasks are assigned and formalized. When authority and control are exercised in this way they become accepted as a legitimate use of power and contribute to the willingness of subordinates to comply with the directives of their superiors. So the creation of a structure and hierarchy facilitates the exercise and acceptance of authority and control.

Control systems, however, involve not only the delegation of responsibility but also the monitoring of activities to ensure efficient and effective performance. In simple structures, such as can be found in very small businesses, authority and responsibility can be clearly allocated to specific department managers, who can then be monitored on the basis of performance. In more complex structures where there is substantial integration and coordination, the separation of tasks into a form in which they can be easily monitored is more difficult but no less important; this is an issue which, as will be seen, enters into the discussion of alternative types of structure.

Another aspect of the role that structure may fulfil is that of reducing alienation. It does this by providing justification for authority and facilitates the generation of criteria against which judgements can be made. Junior managers accept the instructions of senior managers because they recognize the authority structure and, in being aware of their own position and role, feel a part of the organization. If a decision is made that is contrary to the interests of the junior it is more acceptable if it appears to have been generated as a result of the application of individual rules. If a junior is not allowed membership of an important committee, less rancour occurs if he or she has been omitted because of not meeting some criterion, such as length of time with the firm, than if the lack of selection was on a personal basis. So the use of structure reduces the extent to which personal judgements and biases appear to influence decision-making. Thus, contentious management decisions can be more acceptable if they are seen to be the outcome of a 'rational system' rather than emanating from a prejudiced manager. Once again this is not a universal advantage. It varies with the circumstances and the type of structure and control. Too tight a control can have the opposite effect of encouraging bureaucratic and ineffective management.

Aspects of structure

Formal and informal

As it forms the basis for decision processes, the organization structure has considerable effect on the operation of the firm. It affects control, the process of decision-making, authority patterns and the extent of alienation. However, the structure can take many forms or patterns and identifying it is not easy. The structure of some systems, such as plants, can easily be detected because it is visible, but in an organization the structure has to be inferred from the actual operations and behaviour of the individuals within it.

To identify the structure, communication flows, authority relationships and roles have to be analysed. The complexity of this task is increased by the fact that there are several other aspects that have to be considered if a good analysis is to be provided. One of the things that makes the issue so complex is that structure can take two forms, formal and informal, both of which affect decision-making.

The formal structure is the intended decision-making process. It represents the design intentions of senior management to ensure that the objectives of the firm are met. It is typically the result of explicit decision-making and is prescriptive in nature, as it identifies a plan of the way that activities should be undertaken and prescribes functions and areas of responsibilities.

This type of structure provides a map of reporting arrangements and details of roles, tasks and groupings within the firm. According to Mintzberg,[5] grouping in the units of formal structure is on the basis of:

1 *Knowledge or skill*: typical of such a structure would be a hospital with departments arranged around specialist areas of medicine.
2 *Work process or function*: this type of grouping is commonly found in manufacturing industry.
3 *Time*: commonly found in manufacturing, where workers may be organized on a shift basis.
4 *Output*: provides the basis for groupings at several levels within the organization. The firm may be split into divisions on the basis of types of output, or workers on the shopfloor may be grouped on the basis of common output.
5 *Client*: a market orientation is another grouping that can occur at several levels where there are distinct groups of clients with distinct requirements; for example, British Gas has different departments for industrial and non-industrial gas users.
6 *Place*: a grouping on the basis of a market characteristic. Such a grouping is common in the sales force of a company, which will frequently have regional offices.

The size of groupings is also related to the limited span of control of individual managers. This means that, because there is a limit to the number of staff that can be controlled, as the firm grows so the hierarchy will expand.

To identify only the formal structure would be an inadequate analysis of the decision process. Decisions are sometimes made by individuals not identified as decision-makers by the formal structure and informal communication channels are often used. Indeed, in some circumstances the formal structure may only identify the nominal decision-maker, and the effective decision-making lies elsewhere. While a director may have to agree to a major investment proposal, if he or she always says yes then the effective decision-making power lies elsewhere. The informal structure may, therefore, suggest that the prescribed relationships in the formal structure do not correspond to reality. It may also identify a structure of relationships, communication networks and methods of decision-making outside the formal process that arises spontaneously out of the activities and interactions of participants. Thus no analysis of structure is complete without an examination of the informal structure.

The importance of informal structures to the operation of the organization has been stressed by writers who take the human relations approach to organizational behaviour, such as Roethlisberger and Dickson.[6] They made their case on the basis of three hypotheses:

1 Every organization creates an informal structure.
2 In every organization the goals and methods of the organization are modified by the processes within it.

3 The process of modification is effected through the informal structure.

This later point is extremely important. A major problem with providing an analysis of the decision-making of a firm purely on the basis of the formal structure is that such a model does not help to explain change. Organizations are not static entities: they are constantly in a state of change and development in response to changes in the external environment and internal resources. By examining the networks and interactions within the informal structure, modifications to the formal structure can be explained. In a study of a hospital, for example, Strauss et al.[7] based their analysis of the dynamic aspects of decision-making on the interaction of identified power groups of workers. Even the decisions involving medical treatment were arrived at through a process of bargaining between professional and non-professional groups. This was not recognized in the formal structure but served to provide the flexibility of responses that was necessary in practice. To explain the decision-making of the firm, therefore, both the formal and informal elements must be analysed; as Mintzberg[3] says, we need to examine both because they 'intertwine'. The extent to which they intertwine is important and firms will differ in the relative importance of the two forms of structure. Sometimes the informal may create problems: it can be counter-productive, causing distrust of the hierarchy, it may increase alienation, facilitate rumours and uncertainty. On the other hand, in some firms it may increase efficiency and harmony among the workforce and encourage initiative, as can be seen from Case study 4.1.

Mechanistic and organic firms

The effect of formal and informal relations within firms has been examined by Burns and Stalker.[8] They suggest that there are firms that are dominated by the formal system: they operate like a machine with fully elaborated operating procedures, where each task is broken down into smaller tasks and where there are established methods for carrying out any particular job. In such a system the decision-making is characterized by the operation of rules and there is very little scope for individual judgement. They used this model to analyse a viscose rayon filament fibre factory employing about 900 workers. Cellulose went through a series of carefully controlled stages of production. The tasks of the workers in the production process were specified in detail and designed to maintain each stage of the process within the standards laid down in the factory 'bible', a term for the rule book. This type of firm is called mechanistic by Burns and Stalker. The role of the informal structure in such a firm is small and, therefore, the management processes are not flexible or adaptive. As a result of this, the organization will only succeed where there are stable market conditions which do not require rapid changes and responses on the part of the firm.

In contrast to this, a second form of organization structure is noted as associated with dynamic firms that respond to changes in market conditions. These are firms where the informal structure plays a very important part in the decision-making processes. Burns and Stalker refer to these firms as organic. In such firms the roles are less clearly defined and are subject to relatively frequent changes in response to changing conditions, there is continual interaction between the staff, particularly in terms of a great deal of group and team working, and there is a strong emphasis put on the importance of individual contributions, in the form of ideas and judgement, to the decision-making process. In contrast to the mechanistic firm, tasks are not broken down into smaller tasks, responsibilities are not clearly defined and there is no factory bible. Instead individuals are encouraged to perform tasks in the light of their knowledge of the tasks and of the firm as a whole. Burns and Stalker based this analysis on an examination of the operation of firms in the electronics industry, where written communication was discouraged and individual jobs were defined and redefined in response to the rapidly changing market requirements, which necessitated continual product changes.

In assessing the value of these two different combinations of the formal and informal decision-making processes it is important to remember that the most appropriate form will be contingent on the problems faced by the firm. Both methods have advantages and disadvantages. In a stable market, with a complicated but repetitive production process, the mechanistic approach may be efficient. It reduces disagreement and minimizes control costs, information costs and learning costs because it uses a system of established and unchanging practices. The inadequacy of such a system, however, to respond to rapid market changes is likely to be exacerbated by the fact that the management style within such a firm is more likely to be authoritarian in nature. Employees are likely to be characterized by a respect for rules and authority. A part of this syndrome is that they require the stability and assurance that such a system provides. Over a period of time those employees who do not have such characteristics will leave. The remaining workforce will be suited to the decision-making structure. To respond to market change is an exceedingly difficult task for such a firm, not only because of the structure but because the personnel are suited to the mechanistic approach to management and are unlikely to be able to adapt.

In firms that have a greater role for the informal type of organization a very different working environment is provided for the workforce. It is unstable and subject to considerable change in terms of tasks and job requirements. With an unclear specification of roles and tasks, and little in the form of job specification, considerable strain can be imposed on the people involved, and conflict in terms of job area and responsibilities can result. A great deal of time may be spent in resolving disagreements between staff, and control is difficult, so that there is a greater need for coordination and expensive coordination meetings have to be held. In fact it has been found that in such an environment all managers some of the time, and many managers all of the time, yearn for more definition and structure. Nevertheless, such a system does increase commitment by the individual because he or she is recognized as being responsible for fulfilling an objective instead of referring to authority.

Centralization and decentralization

There are two other aspects that are relevant to the discussion of structure. These are centralization and decentralization. These terms describe the extent to which decisions are taken at the centre of the organization, and the extent to which effective decision-making power is devolved throughout the organization. For example, operational decisions could be decentralized while strategic decisions are centralized. In a company such as Unilever advertising expenditure would be decided in a product marketing group but strategic direction is provided by Unilever itself. In contrast, in a company such as Lonrho even strategic decisions are far more decentralized.

This dispersion of decision-making power can occur by means of the informal structure as well as the formal structure. It is very important that any assessment of the degree of decentralization should take account of the effect of the informal structure in the process and make careful distinction between nominal and effective decision-making, because it may well be that the effective decision-making is far more dispersed throughout the organization than is indicated by the formal structure.

The centralization of decision-making does present certain advantages for some organizations. It means that diverse information from all parts of the business is funnelled through some common control point. Because of this coordination is relatively easy, with senior management aware of the state of operations of each department. Furthermore, because the senior managers are armed with this information they may be able to ensure that their assessment of strategic options is realistic and appropriate to the capabilities of the company. They may also be able not only to identify potential growth areas but also to ensure that decisions are made to facilitate development.

Centralization under some circumstances can also provide rapid strategic decision-making. When problem identification, the search for alternatives and choice in strategic issues all occur at the centre rather than being undertaken throughout the management structure, the decision-making process can be very rapid. In companies that are very exposed to changes, in exchange rates for example, this can be a tremendous advantage.

Clearly, however, if every decision was taken at the top of the organization there would be overloading of top management, and one predictable effect of this is that strategic decision-making would be crowded out – the company would simply muddle along, making short-term adjustments to problems as they arose. Unless it is a very small company it is obvious that some amount of decentralization must occur. The issue is of the extent of decentralization.

Decentralization of operational decisions undoubtedly has certain advantages.

It is more rapid and thus provides increased flexibility. For example, minor short-term changes in the market can be immediately responded to with stock adjustments. To refer such decisions up a long hierarchy would incur considerable cost. Decentralization is also likely to improve the motivation of staff and increase their commitment to the decision by giving them a feeling of involvement and responsiblity. As workers' cooperation is usually essential in ensuring successful implementation of any decisions this is an important factor.

The more contentious aspect of decentralization is the extent to which strategic decision-making should be devolved. A large conglomerate will be involved in diverse areas of operation, such as BAT's involvement in tobacco and financial services. Since future developments in these areas involve an assessment of the strengths and weaknesses of the operations of the company in those markets, clearly the particular expertise may not be present on the central board. As Sir John Harvey-Jones, former Chairman of ICI, said: 'How the hell can I know whether the guy in India should be changing his product or whether somebody in Argentina should be changing his technology?' (*Guardian*, 5 March 1987).

There may simply be too many issues of too great a complexity for the central board to cope with. In such circumstances there is likely to be some degree of decentralization of strategic decision-making. One of the difficulties involved in this is to determine the degree to which these decisions are decentralized. If there is not a clear definition of which decisions may be taken at which levels the confusion that results causes delays and expense, so that decisions are perhaps needlessly referred through long management hierarchies. On the other hand, if employees have too much discretion in decision-making, management loses control, experiences frustration and has to set up costly control procedures.

Peters and Waterman[9] have argued that the objective is to provide an optimizing balance of these factors. What is required is a combination of central control plus flexibility and innovations from lower levels, so that a company is characterized by 'loose–tight properties'.

Models of structure

The formal structure of an organization can usually be described by drawing an organizational chart to illustrate the hierarchy. If such charts are compared, certain common features tend to emerge and can provide the basis for modelling different types of structure that are commonly found. These models isolate the main features and so enable identification of the advantages and disadvantages of forms of organization structure.

Simple structure

Many small businesses may be described by a very simple structure with a high degree of informal networking. Frequently the owner or partners undertake most of the judgemental decision-making and there is little in the way of delegation of decision-making powers. Such an organization is characterized by strong personal interaction between the owner and employees. This personal interaction reduces staff costs in the form of turnover, control is direct and supervision and information costs are minimized. The problem arises, however, with growth. At some point there are simply too many decisions to be made and a management structure has to be created. The entrepreneur has to take a conscious decision to delegate decisions by creating roles for other decision-makers. This facilitates the development of specialization. As management expands, some staff will be able to concentrate on building up an expertise in, say, dealing with VAT and wages while others deal more directly with customers. This forms the basis of development into functional areas.

Functional structure

The model of a functional structure, as shown in Figure 4.1, describes a company organization that is arranged around areas of specialization and expertise, such as accounting, marketing and personnel. The grouping it provides has certain efficiency advantages. First, economies of specialization are obtained. Secondly, information costs between different operations within the same area are minimized. Thirdly, control costs are low because role specification is easy and a clear hierarchy of control can be established.

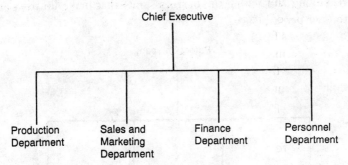

Figure 4.1 Functional structure.

In some circumstances, however, these advantages may be inconsequential or outweighed by the disadvantages of this form of organization. If, for example, the company is operating in diverse market conditions, in home and overseas markets, or with different products, then there may be little to gain from the functional grouping of marketing. The characteristics of each market may be so different that there is little need for them to communicate with each other and there are no advantages of specialization to be gained. The main information flows may be not between the marketeers but between each marketeer and, say, the accountant dealing with his or her product and market. In such a case the functional structure is not suitable. It provides coordination difficulties and high information costs.

Another difficulty associated with diverse or changing markets is that the functional structure is slower to adapt. If certain rules, procedures and conventions are provided as operational guidelines for the functional department as a whole, then changes in those rules which are required for one section to meet a particular market need become a source of difficulty.

While, of course, functional decision-making could be associated with a high degree of decentralization of decision-making power, it could also be associated with centralization. Under such circumstances it may well prolong the decision-making process, over-burden senior managers with routine decisions and lead to the neglect of strategic decision-making.

The holding company structure

In its purest form a holding company is really an investment company that holds a portfolio of shares in several business operations (Figure 4.2). The term also applies to a company that operates as a parent company with its operations divided between business units operating independently, frequently under their own independent names. Such parent companies do not exercise control over the operations or strategic directions of those businesses or provide any form of coordination between the various units. The role of such companies is, therefore, confined to buying and selling the business units that make up the portfolio in response to their performance.

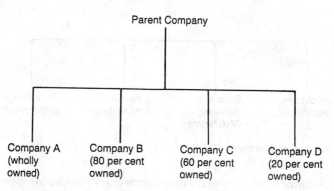

Figure 4.2 **Holding company structure.**

There are some advantages to this form of organization. The threat of sale if there is poor performance by a unit may well act as a spur to the constituent companies to ensure efficient performance. This competitive force means that efficiency can be achieved with a very low cost to the conglomerate because it minimizes the need for central overheads.

Another advantage is that the company comprises a portfolio of business concerns. Thus variability of return is reduced because of the wide spread of assets held. Adverse market conditions in one area of operation can be expected to be offset by operations in other areas. The reaction of BAT to the risk associated with the tobacco market was to offset that risk by entering very different markets, such as finance, where returns would not be affected by changes in consumer taste for tobacco. Overall, the return for the company as a whole is likely to be more stable and that factor in itself should add value to the shares of the holding company so that its value is greater than the mere addition of its component parts. It should be noted that this argument depends on the assumption that shareholders are not themselves holding diversified portfolios. If they are then they would not be prepared to pay a higher price for the reduced risk offered by the holding company.

The holding company offers another advantage that exists because of imperfections in the capital market with regard to the cost of finance. If there are imperfections and rigidities present in the capital market the rate of interest charged for a loan to a business may be inappropriately high, or the loan may not be available. One of the imperfections that may cause this is a lack of information on the company. In contrast, this is not a problem for the holding company, so it will be in a better situation than the capital market for assessing the profitability prospects of an investment proposal. Thus a holding company can, by providing internal finance, facilitate developments and growth which would not otherwise take place and so increase the value of the company.

The main advantages, therefore, to be gained from this form of organization are related to inefficiencies in the capital market. If the capital market is slow to achieve restructuring and does not provide a threat to force firms to be efficient, then the holding company, with its threat of divestment for poorly performing firms, can do the task. If shareholders do not hold diversified portfolios, then the holding company can increase value by holding the portfolios itself. If there is a shortage of capital for investment and growth the holding company organization can facilitate this.

The disadvantages stem from what is lacking from a management point of view. The constant threat of being sold off may lead to short-term decision-making by the management of the business units, with the result that there is less emphasis on long-term decision-making and planning. This is particularly so if the stock market is myopic. The parent company will respond to expectations of stock market valuations and thus will assess its individual business units on short-term performance.

It can also be suggested that in some circumstances competition between the component parts can lead to inefficiencies that could be eliminated with planning and coordination between the units. The lack of internal strategic cohesion may lead to duplication of efforts in the business units, such as duplication of the sales staff, who may even work in competition with each other, duplicating visits to buyers and even reducing prices in competition with another division.

A fourth form of organization provides a mechanism for overcoming some of these weaknesses.

The multidivisional structure

A multidivisional structure (Figure 4.3) describes a firm that is organized into units which are responsible for defined markets, services or products, or for some combination of these. Such a structure has the advantages that emanate from a concentration on business areas in that it minimizes information flows between sections. It also enables the measurement of unit performance, so that the relative profitability of different products and markets can be identified. This, of course, is essential information for strategic decision-making. However, a multidivisional form of organization not only provides this information but also, because each unit is to some extent a separate and definable entity, enables the easy implementation of strategic decisions involving divestment or additions through mergers. A divisional company has decentralization of operational decision-making, which frees senior managers to concentrate on strategic issues. It may also be associated with some degree of decentralization in strategic decisions.

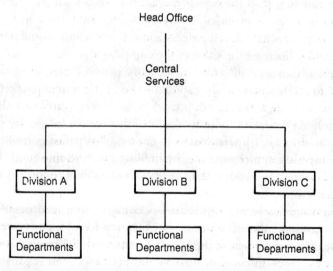

Figure 4.3 Multidivisional structure.

It is just as well to be aware that there are also disadvantages to a multidivisional form of organization. The extent to which decentralization should occur will be a contentious issue, not only in terms of ensuring control and direction for the organization as a whole, but also whether the same degree of decentralization is appropriate in all divisional areas. Too much decentralization may result in the same problem as occurs with a holding company, in that divisions are expensively competing against each other. In addition, if each division is assessed in terms of performance the pricing of inter-trading between the divisions will be an extremely contentious issue and may create considerable conflict.

Another problem that might be associated with too much decentralization is dispute over the allocation of funds for investment. A manager of a profitable division may become uncooperative and his or her staff demotivated if the allocation is reduced in favour of a more profitable area.

There may also be a problem associated with the size of the divisions. As each division is organized along functional lines, if it is too small it will not gain any of the advantages of specialization within the functional areas, whereas if it is too large it will have all the problems of functional organization: as the number of divisions increases so the complexity of resolving the relations between the divisions and coordinating their activity becomes too expensive and may well lead to an undervaluing in the stock market of the combined company, resulting in an asset-stripping takeover. It can be seen, therefore, that there are reasons to suggest that both efficiency gains and efficiency losses can be associated with each type of structural form.

Prevalence of structural form

As it is to be expected that all types of structural form will exist in a developed economy, it is useful to find out how prevalent each form is. Divisional organization as a form of structure was first analysed by Chandler,[10] who used case studies of large American companies and identified the form as emerging in four companies in the 1920s. The diffusion process for this innovation in management was slow, however, and its spread has occurred mainly since the Second World War. Williamson and Bhargava[11] suggest that the 1950s was a time in the USA when many firms were subject to re-organization. In continental Europe, the process of change was slower, and very little change had occurred before the 1970s. As far as the UK economy is concerned there is clear evidence to suggest that firm size has been growing in the post-war economy and by 1980 British industry was more concentrated than elsewhere in Europe or the USA.

Not only has firm size been increasing but the diversity of operation has also been increasing. According to Channon[12] in a study of the top 100 UK manufacturing firms, the percentage of firms that were diversified by 30 per cent of sales or more rose from 25 to 60 per cent between 1950 and 1970, and the percentage that were diversified by more than 5 per cent of sales rose from 66 to 94 per cent. Other work suggests that, in 1958, 16 large enterprises were active in ten or more industrial groups and 38 were active in only one, whereas by 1968, 32 large enterprises were active in ten or more industrial groups and only 19 were active in one.

Given this increase in the size and diversity of firms in the economy it is to be expected that the period will be associated with changes in the form of structure as well. Indeed, Channon[12] found that the use of a divisional structure in the firms in his study increased from 13 to 72 per cent. Steer and Cable[13] suggest that the change-over to the divisional form of organization occurred in the 1960s for UK companies, so that by the 1970s functional organization was very uncommon in large-scale firms. Of the 100 companies studied by Channon only eight were functional and Hill[14] found in 1984 that of the 144 firms he examined 82 per cent were divisional, 16 per cent were holding and only 1.4 per cent were functional. It would seem that the divisional form of organization has become very common among large UK firms.

Reasons for the movement towards a divisional structure

As a result of his case studies in 1962 and his business analysis in 1977 Chandler[10, 15] suggests that changes in organizational structure result from initial changes in strategy, so that strategy precedes structure. A strategic decision to diversify into different market areas is best implemented with the use of a divisional structure. He suggests that in time strategy determines structure and the common denominator of both is the application of the enterprise's resources to market demand, with structure being the means for integrating these resources with demand. Thus, he suggests, strategy is the plan for the allocation of resources to anticipated demand. Case study 4.2 provides an example supporting this view. Further evidence of this strategy–structure link has been provided by Channon[12] and Rumelt.[16]

It can be argued, however, that the structure itself is more than a means of implementing such diversifications, and that it does in fact facilitate and lead to them. The divisional structure provides a separation of strategic and operational decision-making which provides the means for major expansion and contraction decisions to be taken. It may provide the information necessary to take such decisions by separating out the cost centres of the divisions. It overcomes managerial constraints on the rate of growth, such as those suggested by Penrose,[17] as new acquisitions can readily be integrated into the corporate structure by the addition of a new division. The overloading of senior management is reduced and they are able to cope with a greater spread of activities, which will encourage the consideration of diversification.

The effect of the external environment is further considered by Channon,[18] who suggests that while demand is important other factors must also be considered. It should be remembered that the change to divisionalization can be retarded by things like family control and a reluctance of management to move away from the management methods and markets with which they are familiar. To some extent the changes in structure are also the result of natural evolution associated with growth and the information and control problems inherent in the functional form of organization. There is also an element of fashion: in the spread of any innovation there is a point during that spread when adopters merely follow a trend.

Another environmental factor that can cause the company to become divisionalized is the level of competition in the market. Channon suggests that the rise in international competition in the 1950s and the increase in competition that resulted from the restrictive trade practices legislation had the effect of making firms seek the safety of diversification and hence restructuring to divisionalization. Thus, it seems that the strategy of corporate diversification is associated with organizational change towards the adoption of divisional structure, but it is likely that the divisional form of organization in itself may enable diversification strategies and lead to a consideration of such strategies. The decision mechanism used for this transition appears to be more commonly one of incremental changes rather than radical upheaval. Hoskisson and Galbraith[19] found that of 12 reorganizations undertaken by six companies, five involved radical changes and seven incremental changes. According to Chandler[10] the incremental change is explained by an evolutionary process. First there is initial expansion and accumulation of resources. This leads to vertical integration and internal rationalization, which results in a functional structure. As a result of the problems previously mentioned this leads to a pressure for change. The need to exploit new markets and other external factors affect the situation, and cause diversification to take place. Alongside this a market orientation develops. The combination of these forces leads to a change to a divisional structure, as can be seen from Case study 4.2.

The M-form firm

It seems that organizational change for large firms has initially been away from functional arrangements to a structure based upon divisions, which for large companies is now the dominant organizational form. It is more than possible, however, for the divisional structure to coexist with very different forms of managerial systems and behaviour. There may well be wide variation between companies in the type of internal arrangements they adopt. There could be considerable differences in the amount of decentralization of decision-making, the degree of accountability and responsibility, and the reward and motivation systems.

The next issue to be addressed, therefore, is the extent of autonomy to be provided for the divisions. The type of management behaviour and style associated with the divisionalized structure is of crucial importance. In this area Williamson has provided some useful ideas. His approach is to add specified forms of business behaviour to the models of structure, thus providing categories based on structure and behaviour. With the addition of the divorce of ownership from control some interesting implications emerge.

In his early work Williamson[20] provided an analysis of the implications of the divorce of ownership and control in firms organized along functional lines. He suggested that because of imperfection in the goods and capital markets there is inadequate discipline for such firms. This allows scope for senior managers to maximize their utility, subject to the constraint that reported profits should not fall below the minimum level acceptable to shareholders. Williamson suggested that managers' utility is a function of expenditure on excess staff, some degree of managerial slack and some discretionary investment. Such factors lead to a firm that is growth-orientated and profit-satisficing rather than profit-maximizing. It is argued that the functional form of organization facilitates this approach to management. The contribution of each department to profit is not measurable or observable and the allocation of funds to departments is more likely to be based on bargaining power than on an assessment of profitability. In this bargaining process, status is gained by the department manager from the department's size and importance. There is an in-built pressure to increase the size of the department beyond efficient staffing levels, senior managers experience control loss and there is little effective pressure to minimize costs.

Williamson called this type of firm 'U-form', and suggested that it is indicated by the presence of a functional structure and the pursuance of managerial utility, which leads to a growth orientation. As the firm grows, however, the U-form structure itself provides a limit to further growth because of the poor internal control, the existence of conflict in the bargaining processes, and the lack of attention at senior management level to strategic decisions. As the firm grows there is a tendency to move to a form of divisional structure that is combined with certain other behavioural characteristics, which Williamson referred to as the M-form structure.

Such a company is not just organized along divisional lines but also has other management characteristics. In an M-form firm, along with decentralization of decision-making to the divisions, there is financial control. Each division is a profit centre and can be monitored and assessed by the central office on its performance. Furthermore, as the divisions are removed from the central office senior management is able to make impersonal resource allocation decisions on the basis of objective criteria, such as return on investment. This enables relatively rational decision-making, which results in the allocation of funds from the central office to the profitable areas of the business so that expansion takes place in the strong business areas. In this way the firm is operating as an internal capital market with the allocation of resources being decided on the basis of an objective analysis of performance. It can also be suggested that as the head office will have better information on the financial performance than is available in the capital market, this system operates more efficiently and exercises more discipline than the capital market does on the U-form firm.

The Williamson approach therefore fits quite nicely with the ideas of Chapter 2 because each division will have a clear objective of profit-maximization. However, to complete the effectiveness of this approach to decision-making, the issue of motivation also has to be addressed. As was shown in Chapter 2 it is not enough to provide an objective: staff have to be motivated to achieve it. An important part of the Williamson approach, therefore, is that it is accompanied by a reward system for managers that is performance related. Such an approach provides both the desire and the ability to act.

The central office of an M-form firm controls corporate funds and operates a mini capital market which, combined with an appropriate reward system, will ensure that the efficient parts of the corporation grow. Williamson[21] is thus able to formulate what has become known as the M-form hypothesis: 'The organiz-ation and operation of the large enterprise along the lines of the M-form firm favours goal pursuit and least cost behaviour more nearly associated with the neo-classical profit maximization hypothesis than does the U-form organizational alternative' (p. 134).

Implications of the M form of organization

There are several interesting implications of this analysis.

1   In such a firm it would seem that the discretionary behaviour that character-izes the U-form firm has been superseded by least cost behaviour. The firm is orientated towards profit-maximizing rather than profit-satisficing goals and is able to re-allocate funds between divisions on the basis of objective profit-based criteria. The most important implication of this analysis is, therefore, that it is to be expected that M-form firms will out-perform U-form firms.

2   The M-form firm is associated with an internal capital market that has better information on the state of the company than the external capital market. This information enables the central office to intervene quickly in the operations of non-profit-maximizing divisions to ensure profit-maximizing behaviour. In contrast to this constructive behaviour, the external capital market activities are limited to non-trivial displacement costs, such as takeovers. There is considerable evidence to suggest that the external capital market provides imperfect discipline for non-profit-maximizing firms.[22] As a result the M-form firm is seen as being a more efficient form of capital provision than the external market system. This suggests that the greater the incidence of M-form firms in society the greater the efficiency of resource allocation.

3   As an M-form firm is associated with diversified divisions, there are impli-cations for competitive conduct. Edwards[23] and Blair[24] among others suggest that M-form firms may follow anti-competitive practices, such as cross-subsidization between divisions. This could enable such firms to gain a competi-tive advantage over smaller single-market firms and result in the creation of a monopoly position. In particular, transnational firms may engage in transfer pricing across national borders to minimize taxation and thereby maximize

profit. The management system of an M-form firm makes this strategy unlikely, however, because it would violate the necessity of ensuring the accountability and responsibility of each division for its profitability. If each division is held accountable for its profits it will not be prepared to reduce them by subsidizing another division, for example by supplying it with products at too low a price (transfer pricing). If this is the case then there is less argument for a strong anti-trust attitude to be taken by government bodies towards conglomerate mergers. An M-form conglomerate is likely to increase the pressure of competition between the market areas and improve resource allocation.

Other behavioural characteristics

The problem arises in that not all divisional firms adopt M-form management styles. Many large companies use a divisional structure but the central office becomes involved in the policies of the divisions. A supporter of the Williamson approach would argue that this practice is likely to result in prejudicial attitudes being formed by central management, which limits rational decision-making. In addition central management will have less time for taking the global strategic decisions that should be their domain.

In practice, divisionalized firms may fail to establish competition between the divisions for the re-allocation of funds. Instead, profits are left with the source divisions and the full benefits of an internal capital market are not achieved. While the ideas for the M-form firm may be very interesting, they do depend critically on the assumption that the central management will take profit-maximizing decisions. In reality there are many firms where senior officers are concerned with other objectives such as growth or security. In such cases strategic decisions will not be taken on the basis of the relative profitability of the divisions, and practices such as cross-subsidization and the allocation of profits for re-investment on grounds other than relative profitability will take place.

This leads to an even more fundamental criticism of the approach and provides one of the reasons why not all divisionalized companies follow it. The M-form method suggests an almost automatic response by the centre to current profitability of the divisions. It does not take full account of the dynamics of the market and the power a large firm can exert over its market position and thus its long-term profitability. Ideas of strategic management would suggest that more attention should be paid to the future development of markets, and in order to do this company-wide strategies should be followed, which may involve more than a narrow consideration of current profitability of the divisions and take into account top management choice and political considerations within the firm. Views such as this would suggest that it is better to use ideas and models from strategic planning than simply to follow the guidelines of the Williamson approach. So there is disagreement over the 'likely' effect of the organizational form on performance. Empirical research could potentially provide some guidelines but it is beset with problems.

Empirical evidence

Problems with the empirical work

The empirical work within this area is fraught with problems. Classifying firms by their organizational form involves judgement, and a great deal of detailed information on the management practices associated with the structures is needed. As a result it is difficult to conduct work on the basis of large samples. There are also problems with the hypothesis. Although the M-form hypothesis suggests that those firms which are classified as M-form will outperform others this is not to be expected under all environmental conditions. To test the hypothesis it is necessary to compare M-form firms with non-M-form firms that face similar environmental conditions, and matched pairs are hard to find.

In addition, the period of time for which the firm has been an M-form firm is also likely to affect the analysis. If a firm has recently changed to M form then its results are likely to be affected adversely by the process of change. Another problem is that the hypothesis of superior performance refers to a comparison of M-form firms and those U-form firms that should be M form. It does not necessarily apply to a comparison of M-form firms and all other firms. What is needed is a comparison of firms at particular times in their life cycle.

Another problem is that, if the sample isolates those firms which are at a stage of development suitable for M-form organization but have not yet adopted it and compares them with M-form firms, it is possible that the innovators that have adopted the M form are also innovators in aspects of management other than organization, so that superior profits are the result of their being innovators rather than M-form organization alone. Finally, as performance measures use accounting data there is the ever-present problem of inconsistency of treatment of the data between firms. Such factors as these mean that the results of empirical work, while useful, must be treated with some caution.

Empirical work

The tests of a firm's performance usually involve a measurement using some form of accounting data. Two main methods have been used in the empirical studies. One method involves using a regression model of interfirm differences in accounting profits and using the organizational form as an explanatory variable. Such an approach is capable of standardizing for other explanatory variables, such as firm size and growth. Typical of such work is that by Steer and Cable,[13] who include other variables related to managerial and behaviour theories.

A second approach that has been used is residuals analysis. Based on the efficient market hypothesis, this assumes that share prices provide accurate signals for optimal resource allocation and the return on each share forms a linear relationship with the market index measured by the beta factor of portfolio analysis – the systematic risk of the share, i.e. the degree of covariance between the return on the asset and the market as a whole. The approach uses this model to predict what the stock market valuation of the share would have been if the firm had not adopted the M form and then compares this with the actual valuation, thus providing a residual.

Residual analysis uses available data and avoids the problems encountered with the diverse accounting practices of firms. However, it depends heavily on the very questionable assumptions of portfolio analysis and the efficient market hypothesis. It also deals less well with a situation where the movement towards an M form has been made gradually by the firm over a long period of time.

The findings

Some of the studies in the area test only for the effect of the divisional structure on performance. These studies include in their sample divisional firms regardless of the form of management that such firms follow. These include work carried out by Rumelt,[16] Channon[18] and Grinyer et al.[25] Using a sample of 40 per cent of the US Fortune 500 between 1950 and 1970 Rumelt found that product divisional companies had better performance in terms of profitability and growth than functional companies. But when this work was repeated by Channon using UK data in the service industries, it was found that the best rates of return were achieved by the functional companies (although only low levels of significance were achieved); however, divisional firms were found to be superior in terms of growth rates measured by absolute sales. Grinyer et al. also failed to find evidence to support the proposition that companies with a divisional structure tend to outperform others. They examined 48 large UK companies and found that return on investment and net profits were negatively correlated with the degree of divisionalization. Overall, therefore, these studies failed to find consistently strong evidence to support the proposition of superior performance by divisionalized companies per se.

Other studies address the management behaviour issue more explicitly and test for the performance of firms which are associated with M-form characteristics. These include work using US data,[19, 26–29] and work using UK data.[13, 30–33]

Findings that supported the hypothesis that M-form firms outperform U-form firms were reported by some,[13, 26, 27, 30–32] mixed results were obtained by one[28] and negative findings were the result of one study.[29] It would therefore seem that there are a considerable number of results which may be interpreted as supporting the M-form hypothesis in both the USA and the UK. However, these findings are not universally robust, which may suggest that other factors, such as the environment, may well override the effect of the organizational form.

This lack of strong and clear universal findings in support of any particular form of structure raises the question of whether there can be such a thing as an optimal structure.

Contingency theory

In recent years considerable attention has been paid to the ideas of contingency theory. This view suggests that there is no single universal structure that is better than all others under all conditions. An optimal structure for a firm will depend not only on such factors as its size, the diversity of its operation, economies of scale and problems of internal control, but also on its technology and the environment within which it operates.

The importance of the effect of technological considerations has been highlighted in work by Woodward[34] and the Aston Group.[35] Woodward examined the effect of the technological process on management and organization and found that structural characteristics were contingent on the technology used. She came to the conclusion that different structures are required for different technological demands.

While some work[36] provided some support for Woodward's results subsequent work by the Aston Group suggested that, although technology affected the organization of smaller companies, in larger organizations managers are removed from the effects of the specific form of technology used. They suggested that for such organizations size was a better predictor of structure than technology.

Mintzberg[3] suggests that these two views can be reconciled. He points out that the technology can affect the degree to which management methods can be systematized and controlled. Both the market and technology are important. The market can play its role in affecting whether a firm is organic or mechanistic but the type of technical process can as well. Technology, therefore, plays a role in the extent to which management is separated from the effect of the production process. According to Mintzberg sophisticated technologies will require professional staff and decentralization of decision-making. It therefore seems that technology, size and external factors are likely to be important in determining the optimum form of organizational design.

One of the external factors of importance is the social environment. A study of coal-mining methods by Trist and Bamforth[37] was the first to draw attention to the need to change work methods and organization to suit societal needs and norms.

Conclusion

This chapter has highlighted the importance of organization structure in the decision-making process within the firm. In a general sense the purpose of the structure is to organize the decisions within a rational framework. The form that the structure takes and the extent to which the decisions are centralized or formalized varies as a function of the firm's size, technology and environment, but perhaps the last word on the quest for a search for an optimal structure should be left to Mintzberg.[5] He summarizes the thinking by saying that it has moved from believing that there was 'one best way' to 'it all depends, that is the contingency approach, that a structure should reflect age, size, productive system, environment complexity or dynamism'. Thinking has now moved on from this to a 'getting it together or a configuration approach'. This approach maintains that aspects of design should fit together. What is required is a holistic approach to the issues involved in structure, which ensures that the structural form, the control methods, the degree of decentralization, the market situation and the type of environment are all considered and an appropriate structure is one in which constituent elements are consistent. (This theme is continued in Chapter 7.) Mintzberg suggests that the 'conclusion of this approach is that organizations can select their situations in accordance with their structural designs just as much as they can select their designs in accordance with their situation' (p. 277).

Case study 4.1
IBM UK Ltd

This case highlights the interaction of formal and informal structures in a large corporate organization.

IBM UK Limited was established in 1951 with six employees on assignment from other companies in the organization around the world. Today it employs around 17 100 people, nearly all of whom are British. The new company grew rapidly and by 1954 had already built a new manufacturing plant at Greenock in Scotland.

Since that time there has been a dramatic expansion in the market for computers and office equipment, both in the UK and overseas. This has been associated with considerable growth for the company. The company's international subsidiaries, of which the UK company is one of the most important, have grown at a rapid pace.

This growth has required a great deal of capital investment in new plant and equipment over many years. The investment in manufacturing plants at Greenock and Havant, in laboratories at Hursley, in the headquarters of an international teleprocessing network at North Harbour, and at over 40 ▷

other locations around the country, is large and still growing, with major construction projects in Hampshire, Warwickshire and Scotland.

Today, the company develops, makes and sells information processing equipment, and related services and products, but the equipment sold is very different from that of 30 years ago.

A basic aim of the company has been profitability. This has led to considerable attention being paid to the cost basis of the company and a continuing drive for improved productivity. Another dominating objective of the company has been related to its area of market operation. The company regards it as an issue of prime concern to provide products that will improve the customer's information-gathering and processing ability. To do this it committed resources to a heavy programme of research and development.

From the beginning, the company's interest in Britain was more than just in getting the opportunity to sell its products. A manufacturing plant was soon established in Scotland, and later, a development laboratory and another manufacturing plant were established in the south of England.

IBM UK's management organization principles and culture, as well as its product line, are basically the same as those of the parent company. From the very beginning the company recognized that its major resource was the skill, energy and loyalty of its employees. Ever since the company was founded in 1924 it has striven to maintain a high standard of family feeling towards its employees. What this means is that it has attempted to create a community atmosphere among its employees, encouraging social activities linked with the company. Examples include subsidized excursions and sports facilities, which create the opportunity for employees to get to know their fellow workers as well as giving them a chance to communicate with management in a more relaxed atmosphere.

This is associated with the development of a management style orientated to a key phrase, 'respect for the individual'. Because of this approach the company has been concerned to develop a stimulating culture in which employees are encouraged to assess and report on their working situation and environment. One way in which this has been encouraged is by means of the communications systems. The company, as a world leader in information technology, has, as one would expect, many impressive means of communication, the most prominent of which is the National Office Support (NOS) system. This offers employees a means of communication with any other company employee, be it the chief executive or the postroom, via electronic screen mail. There are also diary information, document production facilities and location information and news; and since each person has a personal ID, any can log on anywhere in the world and communicate to any other employee.

Other forms of formal communication include a telephone network spanning the company worldwide, and – still not replaced by the NOS ▷

system completely – letters, memos and print-outs. To overcome any possible problems or disagreements, there are two means of communication specifically set up to deal with them. First is 'Work Out', which is a method for an employee to tell the management if he or she considers a job to be unnecessary, or if it is being duplicated. Second is 'Speak Up', which is a method of voicing a complaint about company work practices. This gives the employees an answer from the top line management and can be used to settle disagreements.

On a group basis, departmental meetings are held regularly. Managers ask all their employees to meet together to voice any problems or even to praise their efforts. This enables both management and employees better to understand their working environment. Twice-yearly 'Kick Off' meetings are held for whole departments, by the management, to show annual targets and to congratulate on previous target fulfilments.

The system works with speed. For example if a customer complaint is received querying the use of some software, and it is of a particularly urgent nature, the customer relations officer can send a note electronically to a user of the software within the company. He or she will then receive an answer within hours via the electronic screen mail. Thus the formal system – of contacting the customer's dealer first, who if unable to answer the query would have to contact the technical support department of the company for the answer – is not used because the informal link is quicker. However, this does not mean that the formal communication network is valueless. On the whole, this type of query would not be urgent, and non-urgent queries are far too numerous to be answered in the informal manner.

So, although a formal hierarchical structure is important at the company there is also the possibility of horizontal communications via formal and informal means, whereby any member of the company is accessible to any other.

Case study 4.2
College Publishers Ltd

This case highlights issues involved with structural change.

College Publishers is a very successful publishing company. It publishes a wide range of textbooks covering GCSE and A level work.

Over a game of golf with a few senior colleagues, the managing director suggested that it might be time to consider doing something new. That night the head of marketing gave some thought to the matter. Expansion was of course possible, by expanding their range of publications, but he ▷

thought that it might also be worth considering entry into other market areas. He had heard, only the previous week, of growing interest in 'companions' for the standard textbooks. These took the form of workbooks. He decided to look into it a bit more closely.

During the next few weeks, he did indeed discover that in many of the subject areas on the firm's publication lists a new trend was emerging. This involved the publication of workbooks and revision guides. Some of these were associated with existing texts but most were free-standing.

A meeting was held to discuss the issue and to choose the way ahead. The head of marketing explained the findings of the survey to the meeting, which then considered the implications. Editorial and sub-editorial were not happy. The change to producing workbook material would require the implementation of a different house style as the format, size and production of such books were very different. This view was extended by the representatives of other functional areas, who pointed to the changes that would be required in working practices. One member of the meeting suggested that the form of material used in the workbooks and the type of presentation were particularly amenable to a greater integration of computers into the process than was the case at present. In other companies producing similar material, for example for the National Extension College, authors were required to submit work in disk form for further processing. He pointed out that this enabled a faster production process, which was essential, for such material as revision aids must include up-to-date questions from examination boards if they were to sell well. This raised a storm of protest.

During the following debate the managing director asked the marketing director whether he had investigated markets with which his department was not familiar, such as the scope for entry into higher academic work, or the provision of computerized educational packages. The reply was that his review of such areas had been limited, as the area of workbooks required attention first. His view was disagreed with and the meeting was adjourned to allow further investigation to take place.

During the next few months the issues raised were carefully considered. It was decided that expansion should take place in two areas, the provision of workbook/study guide material and computer-guided learning aids. It was realized that this was a large change for the company and considerable internal changes were necessary to accommodate the development.

In the event, a new division of the company was formed around the implementation of new methods of production involving extensive use of computers. Because of the 'new' approach taken, the division recruited its own staff, operated on a separate location and was able to separate out its cost and revenue functions from the original company. After considerable initial problems the division proved a success.

References

1 R. H. Coase, 'The nature of the firm', *Economica* (new series), 1937; **4**: 386–405.
2 C. I. Barnard, 'Decisions in organisations', in *Decision Organisations and Society*, F. C. Castles, D. J. Murray and D. C. Potter (eds). Penguin, Harmondsworth, 1971; 31–6.
3 H. Mintzberg, *The Structuring of Organizations*. Prentice-Hall, Englewood Cliffs, NJ, 1979.
4 P. Selznick, *TVA and the Grass Roots*. Harper & Row, New York, 1966.
5 H. Mintzberg, 'The structuring of organizations', in *The Strategy Process*, J. B. Quinn, H. Mintzberg and R. M. James (eds). Prentice-Hall, Englewood Cliffs, NJ, 1988; 276–303.
6 F. J. Roethlisberger and W. J. Dickson, *Management and the Worker*. Harvard University Press, Cambridge, MA, 1939.
7 A. Strauss, L. Schatzman, P. Ehrlich, R. Bucher and M. Slasin, 'The hospital and its negotiated order', in Castles *et al.* (2): 103–23.
8 T. Burns and G. M. Stalker, *The Management of Innovation*. Tavistock, London, 1961.
9 T. J. Peters and R. H. Waterman Jr, *In Search of Excellence*. Harper & Row, New York, 1982.
10 A. D. Chandler Jr, *Strategy and Structure. Chapters in the History of the Industrial Enterprise*. MIT Press, Cambridge, MA, 1962.
11 O. E. Williamson and N. Bhargava, 'Assessing and classifying the internal structure and control apparatus of the modern corporation', in *Market Structure and Corporate Behaviour*, K. G. Cowling (ed.), Gray-Mills, London, 1972.
12 D. F. Channon, *The Strategy and Structure of British Enterprise*. Macmillan, London, 1973.
13 P. Steer and J. Cable, 'Internal organisation and profitability: an empirical analysis of large UK companies', *Journal of Industrial Economics*, 1978; **27**: 13–130.
14 C. W. L. Hill, 'Organisational structure: the development of the firm and business behaviour', in *The Economic Management of the Firm*, J. F. Pickering and T. A. J. Cockerill (eds). Philip Allen, Oxford, 1984; 52–71.
15 A. D. Chandler Jr, *The Visible Hand: The Managerial Revolution in American Business*. Belknap Press, 1977.
16 R. P. Rumelt, 'Diversification strategy and profitability', *Strategic Management Journal*, 1982; **3**: 55–70.
17 E. T. Penrose, *The Theory of the Growth of the Firm*. Basil Blackwell, Oxford, 1959.
18 D. F. Channon, *The Service Industries: Strategy, Structure and Financial Performance*. Macmillan, London, 1978.
19 R. E. Hoskisson and C. S. Galbraith, 'The effects of quantum versus incremental M form reorganization on performance: a time series exploration of intervention dynamics', *Journal of Management*, 1985; **11**: 55–70.
20 O. E. Williamson, *The Economics of Discretionary Behaviour and Managerial Objectives in a Theory of the Firm*. Prentice-Hall, Englewood Cliffs, NJ, 1964.
21 O. E. Williamson, *Corporate Control and Business Behaviour*. Prentice-Hall, Englewood Cliffs, NJ, 1970.
22 See, for example, M. Firth, 'The profitability of takeovers and mergers', *Economic Journal*, 1979; **89**: 316–28, and A. Singh, *Takeovers*. Cambridge University Press, Cambridge, 1971.
23 C. F. Edwards, *Conglomerate Bigness as a Source of Business Power in Business Concentration and Price Policy*. Princeton University Press, Princeton, NJ, 1958.
24 J. M. Blair, *Economic Concentration: Structure, Behaviour and Public Policy*. Harcourt Brace, New York, 1972.

25 P. H. Grinyer, M. Yasai-Ardekani and S. Al-Bazzaz, 'Strategy, structure, the environment and financial performance in 48 UK companies', *Academy of Management Journal*, 1980; **23**: 193–220.

26 H. O. Armour and D. J. Teece, 'Organizational structure and economic performance: a test of the multidivisional hypothesis', *Bell Journal of Economics*, 1978; **9**: 106–12.

27 D. J. Teece, 'Internal organisation and economic performance: an empirical analysis of profitability of principal firms', *Journal of Industrial Economics*, 1981; **30**: 173–200.

28 G. S. Roberts and J. A. Viscione, 'Captive finance subsidiaries and the M form hypothesis', *Bell Journal of Economics*, 1981; **12**: 285–95.

29 B. C. Harris, *Organization: the Effect on Large Corporations*. University of Michigan Press, Ann Arbor, MI, 1983.

30 R. S. Thompson, 'Internal organization and profitability: a note', *Journal of Industrial Economics*, 1981; **30**: 201–11.

31 R. S. Thompson, 'Diffusion of the M-form structure in the UK: rate of imitation, interfirm and interindustry differences', *International Journal of Industrial Organization*, 1983; **1**: 297–315.

32 C. W. L. Hill, 'Internal organization and enterprise performance: some UK evidence', *Managerial and Decision Economics*, 1985; **6**: 210–16.

33 C. W. L. Hill and J. F. Pickering, 'Divisionalization, decentralization and performance of large UK companies', *Journal of Management Studies*, 1986; **23**: 26–50.

34 J. Woodward, *Industrial Organization: Theory and Practice*. Oxford University Press, Oxford, 1965.

35 The work of the Aston Group is reported in D. J. Hickson, D. S. Pugh and D. C. Pheysey, 'Operations technology and organizational structure: an empirical reappraisal', *Administration Science Quarterly*, 1969; **14**: 378–97.

36 W. L. Zwerman, *New Perspectives on Organization Theory*. Greenwood Press, Westport, CT, 1970.

37 E. A. Trist and K. W. I. Bamforth, 'Some social and psychological consequences of the Longwall method of goal-getting', in *Organisation Theory: Selected Readings*, 2nd edn. Penguin, Harmondsworth, 1984.

5 Business Analysis

Decision analysis can be of use in two ways. It can be developed into an analytical framework to enable the business analyst to evaluate an organization and it can be applied by the individual to his or her own decision processes. In order to facilitate these developments this chapter provides guidance for the analysis of cases that represent real businesses, or of businesses themselves. It provides a framework for the analysis before examining in detail the models and ideas used in strategic decision-making. This will enable the reader to fit these models into an overall perspective as the reading progresses, rather than struggling with the individual models with no integrative perspective until the end.

The smaller cases in this book and the Triumph case study in this chapter, which is typical of large strategic case studies used on courses of strategic decision-making, are of course a summary of business situations and provide the basis for business analysis. For this reason the use of case studies is extremely important, as they develop the conceptual skills that are so important to senior management. Such exercises develop an understanding of the interrelationships between the political, social and economic aspects of the environment and the internal operation of the firm.

As with other skills, the ability to analyse a case or business takes time to acquire even if the student is quite aware of the analytical tools and models that can be used in the process. This learning process can be shortened by addressing the issue specifically and paying attention to the development of a methodology that can form the basis for business or case analysis. The specific objectives of this chapter, therefore, are to:

- explain the role of case studies in the learning experience;
- identify a framework that can be used as a basis for case and business analysis;
- highlight good and bad practice in case and business analysis.

Reasons for the use of case studies

A case is a written document covering a certain period of time. Most strategy cases contain some information about the company's history, internal operations and external environment. They may also contain information on the state of physical facilities and technology. Cases usually present actual business situations and enable the examination of successful and unsuccessful companies. Each situation is different and requires unique diagnosis and evaluation as a prelude to action, because ready-made answers do not exist for most managerial problems. By simulation, cases provide experiential learning of decision-making.

It is important to realize why case studies are used and what their objectives are if full advantage is to be gained from them. There is considerable agreement on the reasons for the use of case studies. Schoen and Sprague[1] identified four.

1 Cases require the application of theoretical knowledge and an understanding of management practice. Only in this way can the case be turned from a mere descriptive account into a useful analysis.
2 Cases require the processes of decision-making – the diagnosis of problems, analysis of alternatives and formulation of plans of action – to be practised by the participants. All of these require clear rational thought.
3 Cases provide exposure to a range of decision situations that expand the students' experience.
4 Cases provide practice in problem-solving.

In addition, cases may be used to develop communication skills and to draw attention to the influence of personal values on organizational decisions. Many cases illustrate that problems are rarely confined to neat functional areas such as marketing or finance. While students may be aware of this intellectually it is only when cases are used that this is understood emotionally and so the point is driven home. If these reasons for studying cases are borne in mind when analysing a case the outcome is likely to be more fruitful.

From a strategic decision-making viewpoint, one of the most important reasons for using case material is that it provides the ground work for a methodology for business analysis. Nevertheless, some writers suggest that there are disadvantages to case analysis. They point out that students are usually presented with imperfect information. Some information is redundant, while other pieces of information are missing. However, this is very like reality, in which executives never have perfect information. The challenge is to ascertain if the information is based on reasonably predictable factors rather than on highly contentious or uncertain events. Risk is a ubiquitous phenomenon in the business world and good decision-makers have to evaluate information in such a world and so develop their judgement.

Another contentious issue is that frequently the issues are not stated and the instructor may not provide a nice neat solution or even direct discussions. Indeed there may be no unique answer to the case. The point to remember here is that it is the process of analysis and the application of ideas, i.e. it is the exercise itself, that is important. Note-taking may well be difficult but textbook learning is not the point of case study analysis. That takes place before the analysis. It provides the ideas to be used during the analysis. The process of analysis is more important than the generation of specific accurate answers.

Whatever framework is chosen it should be remembered that the focus should be the development of critical analysis and logical argument. Solutions should resolve identified problems and be capable of successful implementation. This means that they should be realistic in taking account of constraints. Failure to achieve this is a frequent weakness of case analysis by students. Too often conclusions ignore features that will hinder successful implementation, such as manpower problems or a lack of financial resources.

The use of models in business analysis

The organization of a case study on business analysis resembles very closely the rational decision-making process previously introduced. When conducting an analysis it is useful to use a series of steps. First the case should be examined to identify the problem. Then there has to be an investigation of the problem and its causes. This should be followed by a search for alternative lines of action, and a consideration of constraints that would reduce the effectiveness of some possible courses of action. From this it should be possible to recommend a strategy.

In each of these steps the analyst has help from the theories of decision-making and strategic management in the formulation of analysis. The choice of appropriate models for use in the analysis will enable identification of the major issues and act as an organizing device. This is where the use of theory is essential, as it enables analysis of the descriptive material.

For a strategic decision-making case the following chapters discuss several models that can be used to sort out the issues and provide information for the decision analysis. One of these has a widespread use and serves the explanatory purpose of this chapter, namely SWOT analysis. This involves the organization of material into the categories of strengths, weaknesses, opportunities and threats facing the firm in the case study. This form of analysis is important, because business success depends upon successfully capitalizing on strengths while minimizing the effect of weaknesses, in order to take advantage of opportunities and avoid or overcome threats. In order to organize the material into such an overall framework appropriate models from several study areas must be utilized. In this way models of financial analyses, marketing, organizational structure and management style will be used to build up a general picture of the strengths and weaknesses of the firm. This, in turn, provides the information to enable problem diagnosis and a search for alternative lines of action, as well as giving an awareness of the constraints within which the firm operates. It is important, therefore, to examine the SWOT model in more detail.

The SWOT model

The identification of strengths and weaknesses is very much a part of the analysis of internal characteristics of the organization. Strengths are special attributes or distinctive competencies that an organization possesses, which give it an advantage over other organizations, especially competitors. It is not, for example, a strength of Holland & Barrett that the market for health foods is growing rapidly. Rather, its strengths may lie in its product development and marketing expertise, which identify it as 'special'.

Another point to be borne in mind when identifying strengths is that they are only relative, not absolute. For example, a large asset base is not a strength if the main competitors of a company have even larger asset bases. It is the relative size that matters. It must be remembered that the identification of a strength requires a comparison to be made. Usually, this comparison is on the basis of other firms operating in the same market or the firm's past performance.

The analysis of weaknesses is also internal and again can only be conducted in relative terms. Weaknesses are the aspects of organizations that make them less effective than other companies. Once again, care must be taken with the application of this idea. Serving a declining market in shipbuilding is not a weakness of Harland & Wolff; rather, the weakness would lie in a management's failure to respond to that market, not in the market condition itself. So the interpretation of strengths and weaknesses requires considerable care. The concentration of an industry in a declining market may be a part of the reason for a lack of success but one can point to firms that have designed a strategic approach under such conditions, leading to success in terms of profit and growth. For example, British Belt Asbestos operates in declining markets but by adopting a strategy of buying on an international basis to create monopoly power it has achieved success. Thus, the value of the analysis depends on the interpretation of the information. If, for example, a company is concentrated in a particular market there are likely to be detrimental and beneficial effects. Along with the strength of being a more competent producer of goods and services than a diversified competitor, there is the detrimental aspect that it is likely to be exposed to cyclical instability. The analysis of strengths and weaknesses, therefore, must be conducted with considerable care and, according to Argenti,[2] 'it is doubtful if any company will have more than half a dozen strengths and weaknesses of strategic significance' (p. 103).

Opportunities and threats are external to the company. An opportunity is any chance to follow a new or revised strategy that could be of benefit. Opportunities represent potential new initiatives. While they exist for all organizations they are certainly easier to identify for some than for others. For example, when market patents expire the opportunity for other firms to produce previously patented goods is obvious. Most opportunities, however, have to be sought and in some cases even created. For example, the research development investment in IBM is very market-orientated.

Threats are possible events which, if they occur, may seriously hamper an organization's ability to serve one or more of its stakeholder groups or achieve its mission, or even threaten its entire existence. This means that the analyst should examine and identify possible threats from the point of view of all the various stakeholders in the company. The interpretation of a threat may well vary as a function of stakeholder perception. While possible redundancies can be seen as a threat to employees, for shareholders the fall in share price is a threat. The more severe threats are likely to affect all shareholders. Any event that is likely to decrease the value of the company's output will be a threat to all shareholders; for example, entry into its market by a large conglomerate could be a threat to its continued existence, which of course would damage employees and shareholders alike.

Scanning of the environment to identify threats is very important, but it must be accompanied by realistic appraisal of them. In practice, participants in the business may exercise selective perception to downgrade the importance of threats. If competition brings out a refinement to an existing product or new product, an attitude of complacency or wishful thinking may result in the under-estimation of the effect this product will have on the market. Sometimes, as in the case of the development of Whisk liquid detergent, the impact on the market can be considerable. So the analyst must be careful to avoid being affected by the distortions created from the effect of self-interest on perception. The importance of the analysis is that, while there are always threats present in the environment, if a threat is identified soon enough it can be guarded against and sometimes even turned into an opportunity. For example, if a bypass is planned that is likely to reduce the number of customers to a town café, then selling the café for an alternative use and constructing a new building at a bypass intersection may well be an opportunity that has emerged from a threat, as long as the threat is recognized and reacted to before the business runs into financial problems.

It must be appreciated, therefore, that the interpretation of strengths and weaknesses is a very complex process, involving judgement and analysis of the complexities of the organization as a whole, and as this is based on relative measure the analysis is not done in a world of absolutes or optimum choices. To simplify the process the analysis may be initially applied only to the separate business functions. Eventually, and most importantly, such information must be coordinated and the business as a whole will be analysed.

Each reader will eventually develop a technique for acquiring an overall method but those new to the area will find the following method useful:

A method for case analysis

Reading and researching the case

Obviously the first step in case analysis is to read and re-read the case and take full notes. On first reading, the details of the case should be sorted out and the main characters, situations and problems identified. The second reading should provide more details and substantiation or revision of the superficial views of the main issues. This reading can enable identification of data deficiencies and classification of the assumptions that may be necessary to overcome such a weakness.

To help in the construction of the analysis, research should be conducted into the environmental setting of the business or case using as many external sources as possible. Where applicable, these include business periodicals, subject indexes and newspapers. This background provides an appreciation of the situation as experienced by the people in the case. To achieve empathy is an important part of the understanding that is necessary for a thorough analysis. Furthermore, of course, any strategy recommendations that result from the analysis have to be appropriate for the environment of the business. If this were not taken into account there could be a serious error in the analysis, suggesting, for example, a sale of stock when the stock market is at an all-time low, or an increase in gearing when interest rates are rising. In the Triumph case study at the end of this chapter it would, for example, be unwise to proceed to a decision without an analysis of currency movements.

These external sources can also be of use in helping the formation of judgements of relative strengths and weaknesses. It would be very difficult to judge performance, for example, without some standard to judge it against and figures provided for industry averages or the reports and accounts of competing companies can be very useful for this.

So an essential part of business analysis is the consideration of external factors. Sometimes the case will provide information on the firm's major competitors, market conditions, legal restrictions and so on, but in most instances a richer understanding of the environment can be obtained from an examination of outside information relevant to the industry. Chapter 8 discusses some models that can help the analyst to organize and interpret this material.

Data preparation

The next step is to organize the data. The point of examining the data presented in the case is to identify patterns, so that an overall perspective of the issues can be obtained.

To interpret the figures, the first step is to work out summary statistics and ratios. The problem is that there is usually a wide range of ratios that could be worked out from the data provided; Table 5.1 provides a list of some of the possible ratios that could be used. The analyst must be careful to choose the most appropriate and meaningful ratios. In producing them care must be taken to ensure that the correct data for the concept being measured are used. The definitions of concepts that are appropriate may not coincide with those that have been used as the basis for the presentation of the accounts. More detailed information on the use of these in analysis is provided by Weston and Brigham.[3]

After the most useful forms of ratios have been decided upon and worked out, problems frequently arise at the stage of interpreting them. Ideal values for ratios cannot be determined and because of this it is difficult to know what value the ratio should have. This means that there is a great deal of scope in the interpretation of ratios for the influence of value judgement and as a result diverse inferences can be drawn from the same value. Because of this it is useful to use a ratio in terms of comparisons, either by comparing a firm's financial ratios with those of similar firms, or by comparing a firm's present ratio values with its own previous ratio values.

Other summary statistics that might be useful can represent personnel issues, such as the turnover rate. This can provide useful information about the state of labour relations, but it is particularly important to relate this to a careful comparison either with past trends or with similar operations, because turnover levels will be strongly affected by the skill level, hours of work, male/female staff ratio and age distribution of the workforce. There may also be useful statistics that can be worked out from marketing information, sales data or any market research information that is supplied.

Statistical analysis

Income statements and balance sheets provide many of the data needed for the financial analysis. A typical financial analysis would include a study of the operating statements and the identification of trends in sales, profits and various ratios. In addition, there should be a comparison of these to industry averages, which can be obtained from external sources. An important part of the analysis is to identify changes over time in both sub-categories and aggregate values. Any changes should be considered in percentage terms as well as absolute amounts, and preferably also adjusted for inflation. Once the trends in the statistics have been identified, they must be examined in relation to each other in order to gain an overall view of the company. For example, an upward trend in sales revenue may not be as satisfactory as it would otherwise seem if there is a greater increase in costs during the same period.

As most companies have some form of profit objective financial data play a crucial role, but in this process of analysis there may be a danger of an overreliance or over-emphasis on the financial data, because they are perceived as

Table 5.1   Financial ratios

Liquidity ratios

Current ratio

$$\frac{\text{current assets}}{\text{current liabilities}}$$

Quick ratio

$$\frac{\text{current assets} - \text{inventories}}{\text{current liabilities}}$$

Inventory to net working capital

$$\frac{\text{inventory}}{\text{current assets} - \text{current liabilities}}$$

Cash ratio

$$\frac{\text{cash} + \text{cash equivalents}}{\text{current liabilities}}$$

Profitability ratios

Net profit margin

$$\frac{\text{net profit after taxes}}{\text{net sales}}$$

Gross profit margin

$$\frac{\text{sales} - \text{cost of goods sold}}{\text{net sales}}$$

ROI

$$\frac{\text{net profit after taxes}}{\text{stockholders' equity}}$$

EPS

$$\frac{\text{net profit after taxes} - \text{preferred stock dividends}}{\text{average number of common shares}}$$

Activity ratios

Inventory turnover

$$\frac{\text{net sales}}{\text{inventory}}$$

Net working capital turnover

$$\frac{\text{net sales}}{\text{net working capital}}$$

Asset turnover

$$\frac{\text{sales}}{\text{total assets}}$$

Fixed asset turnover

$$\frac{\text{sales}}{\text{fixed assets}}$$

Accounts receivable turnover

$$\frac{\text{annual credit sales}}{\text{accounts receivable}}$$

Leverage ratios

Debt to asset ratio

$$\frac{\text{total debt}}{\text{total assets}}$$

Debt to equity

$$\frac{\text{total debt}}{\text{stockholders' equity}}$$

Long-term debt to capital structure

$$\frac{\text{long-term debt}}{\text{stockholders' equity}}$$

Table 5.1   Financial ratios (*continued*)

Current liabilities to equity	$\dfrac{\text{current liabilities}}{\text{stockholders' equity}}$

Other ratios

Price/earnings	$\dfrac{\text{market price per share}}{\text{earnings per share}}$
Dividend payout ratio	$\dfrac{\text{annual dividend per share}}{\text{annual earnings per share}}$
Dividend yield	$\dfrac{\text{annual dividend per share}}{\text{current market price per share}}$

For an in-depth discussion of ratios see J. F. Weston and E. F. Brigham, *Managerial Finance*, 2nd UK edn. Cassell, London, 1988.

'hard' data. However, ratios should only be regarded as warning signals. Too much importance should not be placed on a single ratio that is out of line. It may quite easily be the result of some temporary factor. For this reason it is particularly unwise to base decisions on ratios that have been derived from interim data. Such data, for periods of less than one year, may well be expected to be influenced by temporary abnormalities. They may also be out of line simply because there were mistakes in collection, and so not reflect the underlying issues at all. An even more important reason not to over-emphasize financial ratios is that they necessarily reflect what has passed rather than what is currently happening, and they may well not indicate future performance. They will have resulted from the 'real' issues within the firm and its environment. In a sense they only describe an effect; in themselves they say little about cause, and the importance of identifying cause must be remembered. It must also be remembered that extrapolation is based on the assumption that none of the determining factors have changed or are likely to change. Finally, although comparison with industry ratios can be useful, there are also problems involved in this. Firms in the industry use diverse methods of deriving their accounts and this can conceal important differences. All these factors illustrate that data that seem 'hard' or 'reliable' may have been subject to manipulation or error, and can be open to considerable misinterpretation.

A general understanding of the case

The quantitative data provide a start for the analysis. The calculations involved are the easiest part: the interpretation requires more care. Even that, however, only provides a limited view of the business. This information has to be fitted into the 'real' side of the business concern. Examination of the marketing, behavioural and managerial aspects of the firm is probably even more difficult than data analysis. Because fewer formulas or other precise tools are available, it is much more an issue of judgement.

The key point is to try to develop a feel for the case, and it is at this point that the ideas and models of strategic management should be used. Models must be chosen to help to explain the issues and to sort out the important determining factors.

It was seen in Chapter 2 that identification of the firm's mission is of vital importance to the whole of the decision process. It provides the driving force and the direction for the firm and pervades its culture. Furthermore, it was shown that it cannot just be assumed that the objective of the firm is to maximize profit. However, the identification of objectives is not always easy. They are frequently not stated explicitly, and even if they are the stated objectives may only be nominal because they have been given a particular form to serve a public relations purpose or to reassure some of the stakeholders. A mission statement incorporating, for example, employee welfare as an objective may well be a platitude to the employees rather than an effective operational aspect of the mission. So the case has to be examined very carefully to determine the true working objectives, which in practice affect the operation of the company. This can sometimes be done by examining behavioural aspects, such as the attitude displayed by the senior management, targets set for departments and the reward system. Even with careful reading, however, it is sometimes difficult to discern clear objectives; the very fact that none exist may be very relevant to the analysis. In these cases it is usually safe to assume that the firm is concerned to improve its position, particularly with regard to profit. Here, ideas of stakeholder analysis, along with the other models of objectives introduced in Chapter 2, can be useful. The analyst should try to sort out what the corporate, business and functional objectives are, where the main problems are and, most importantly, whether the layers of objectives are consistent with each other and to what extent the personal objectives of individuals within the organization can exert an influence. It must also be remembered that the mission itself should not necessarily be accepted in an uncritical way. Sometimes the specification of the mission can lead to an inadequate consideration of opportunities; for example, some time ago Bassett, a sweet manufacturing company, defined its mission as being concerned with the sugar confectionery industry, thereby excluding possibilities which would have been included if the mission had been concerned with the impulse snack market.

The next issue to address is that of the organization or management structure, as covered in Chapter 4. The type of structure can be identified, along with its degree of formality and centralization. When the structural issues have been identified decisions can be made as to whether the structure is an appropriate one to maximize the objectives and whether it is suited to the internal and external environments. As shown in Chapter 4, structure should be appropriate to the environmental conditions, so factors that affect the market should be examined, including its state of change or stability, the firm's market share and the state of competition. In this analysis issues such as duplication of work and information or control loss can be addressed and a view can be formulated about the management style, control mechanisms and the culture of the organization.

The quality of the top management is an important issue that should be assessed in terms of their characteristics, such as knowledge base, commitment to the company, responsibility, interaction with lower management and methods of decision-making. So the next stage is to address functional issues. The point here is to identify the policies that are being pursued in each of the functional areas to see how they relate to each other and to the overall position of the firm. Personnel policies should be reviewed in relation to theory, the environment, the structure and many other practices. As Gore and Murray[4] argue, a holistic approach should be adopted. Policies should be seen in terms of their effectiveness in contributing to the achievement of objective management tasks and to the generation of an appropriate culture.

Finally, financial policies should be examined, with particular attention being paid to the financial risk, measured by the level of gearing, and the risk of failure, measured by insolvency and liquidity. Overall measures of financial performance need to be assessed, bearing in mind the normal relations with risk and return that have been established within the capital market for that industrial sector.

When these assessments of the various aspects of business operation are complete, it is time to list them in terms of SWOT analysis. During this analysis care should be taken to ensure that symptoms are distinguished from problems. Treating symptoms provides only temporary relief. Frequently the information gained from financial analysis indicates symptoms rather than the problem itself. Cash flow trouble really indicates that the basic problem may well lie in an area such as sales.

After this stage of analysis it is time to take advantage of any available group interaction. Discuss the analysis with the members in the group. This will help to reduce the influence of individual perception and bias on the analysis. If it is an effective group a consensus will eventually be reached. However, one of the dangers of this is the development of such tight group norms that the phenomenon of 'groupthink' emerges, with the concomitant danger that inappropriate views are reinforced by other members of the group. To avoid this, adequate preparation is very important so that clear alternative views are already held within the group. Another way of reducing this effect is for the group to allocate the role of devil's advocate to one of its members, or to split into smaller competing groups.

Once there is a consensus on the major problems and the strengths and weaknesses of the organization, it is time to think of possible solutions. At this point group interaction is invaluable to generate diverse ideas, but care must be taken to examine the implications of the suggestions from all points of view. This ensures that the positive and negative points of each solution and implementation issues are considered fully. For example, if a solution requires that the firm raises a large amount of capital, consider whether realistically it is in a position to do this.

After consideration of the alternative solutions, the next step is to select a solution. There may well not be a clear-cut answer. Diverse solutions may be associated with ranges of implications, some of which are beneficial and some of which are detrimental. The construction of a decision tree can enable the methodical examination of alternatives in terms of the different facets they present under different states of nature. When an opportunity was perceived by Fort Stirling to use a new technology to turn recycled paper into a high-quality product it had to be assessed in terms of its many facets, such as its possible contribution to profits, whether it fitted the corporate image and corporate portfolio, and the different possible reactions of rival paper manufacturers. This type of reasoning is a major part of the analysis and as such must be included.

The selection of a solution is not the end of the analysis. The complete development and provision of plans for implementation and control must also be addressed. A good plan should first review the firm's current and future positions, particularly its financial positions. It should pinpoint particular strengths and minimize weaknesses, and then address the implementation issues and policies to be adopted.

Presentation of the analysis

A good presentation is of course very important. The standard is very largely determined by the thoroughness and appropriateness of the preparatory analysis and group work. If this is well done there will be no temptation to present a simple story rather than an analysis. The work can be presented in clearly defined sections according to the format chosen.

As far as presentation is concerned there is no single best way. One way is to follow the plan of a strategic audit, another is the McKinsey 7-S framework, composed of the seven organizational variables of structure, strategy, staff, management style, systems and procedures, skills and shared values, as discussed in Chapter 3. Another alternative is to follow decision process steps or, if an argument can be presented justifying its choice, to use a particular model, such as the Boston Consultancy Group or Porter's analysis.

The investigation will have identified the central problems and constraints and provided a thorough justification for the views put forward. The material will include a consideration of the possible strategies considered and present a well argued case for the one chosen. This, of course, requires a careful discussion of the implementation policies that are required for its success. Even though it is clear that the success of the presentation depends on the preparation work and analysis, style is also relevant. The provision of exhibits to emphasize the main points is useful and if the presentation is aural a group rehearsal is advisable.

Case study 5
Triumph Motorcycles

This case illustrates the problems of business analysis. The analysis of the situation undertaken by a major management consultant was generally accepted and the findings were used to illustrate the experience curve effect. Hindsight shows us that the implied strategy of the Japanese competitors was not articulated and probably did not exist. An explanation could have been that the Japanese firms learnt by trial and error but had a long-term commitment to the industry. Such a simple strategy can now be discerned in other areas of Japanese investment. The models of strategic analysis and strategic options identified by academics and consultants should always be viewed with scepticism. A holistic view and an ability to assess these models critically are essential.

Background

BSA/Triumph, the largest British motorcycle manufacturer, was modestly profitable during the 1960s. In the early 1970s it was making losses of sufficient magnitude to threaten its survival, while Japanese manufacturers were making satisfactory profits.

Triumph Motorcycles (Meriden) Limited (TMM) was formed as a co-operative on 6 March 1975 following an 18-month picket of the factory gate by the workforce, who were attempting to preserve their jobs. TMM was established with a loan from the Department of Industry of £4.2 million, which was paid directly to Norton Villiers Triumph (NVT) for the assets of the business (between July 1973 and March 1975 NVT lost £5.7 million). A grant of £500 000 was provided to TMM by the government in May 1977 for working capital. Trading results are shown in Table C5.1. The cooperative only once made a profit before interest, in 1979. The balance sheets show a continued deterioration until 1980, when the government loans and grants were written off and the amounts due to the Export Credit Guarantee Department (ECGD) were waived. There was a continual decline in the numbers employed by Triumph and in the level of output (see Table C5.2).

In its short history TMM faced several crises. First, there was a stock build-up in 1977 because of a dispute about ex-works prices with Norton Villiers Triumph, who marketed the Meriden output. Secondly, there was another stock build-up in 1979 in the USA because of adverse currency moves, which made motorcycles imported from the UK relatively expensive. This second stock build-up was financed by a facility from the ECGD that was never repaid. The government loans were written off in 1981 and the company was left without any source of working capital as the ECGD withdrew its facility.

▷

Table C5.1   Triumph Motorcycles (Meriden) Limited

	1977 (78 weeks) (£000)	1978 (£000)	1979 (£000)	1980 (£000)	1981 (£000)
Consolidated profit and loss account to 30 September					
Sales	10 337	10 370	11 274	7 855	5 681
Cost of sales	(11 024)	(10 888)	(10 531)	(9 993)	(6 260)
(Loss)/profit	(687)	(518)	743	(2 138)	(579)
Interest	(669)	(786)	(1 195)	(1 019)	(118)
Loss before tax	(1 357)	(1 304)	(451)	(3 157)	(697)
Consolidated balance sheet at 30 September					
Fixed assets	2 396	2 269	2 094	1 877	1 703
Current assets	6 039	6 189	8 510	3 834	2 837
Less current liabilities	5 117	7 018	9 855	7 770	2 075
	921	(830)	(1 345)	(3 937)	762
	3 318	1 439	749	(2 059)	2 464
Share capital	£3	£3	£3	£3	£3
Capital reserve	1 250	1 250	1 250	1 250	1 250
Accumulated deficit	(2 661)	(4 010)	(4 490)	(7 702)	365
	(1 411)	(2 760)	(3 240)	(6 452)	1 615
HM Government loan	4 729	4 200	3 990	3 570	–
Moritorium balances	–	–	–	822	849
	3 318	1 439	749	(2 059)	2 464

The audited accounts were qualified because insufficient working capital was available for the business to be considered on a going concern basis. The 1980 accounts were qualified because of the absennce of proper stockkk records.

Government grants: £750 000 in the period to 31 March 1976
£500 000 May 1977

HM Government loan: £4.2 million pre-June 1976

1980 accounts show write-off of:
Waived 6 October 1981,   £6 409 828 Department of Industry
Waived 30 September 1981, £3 003 557 ECGD

£9 413 385 (included interest)

Source: Published accounts and TMM.

The market

The UK motorcycle market has moved from being one dominated by UK producers to being one dominated by imports. Table C5.3 shows motorcycle production, imports and exports. It shows production and exports steadily falling and imports rising until by 1981 home production accounted for about 1 per cent of the total UK market. Since the mid-1970s UK police forces had been using BMW motorcycles. Over 90 per cent of new ▷

Table C5.2   Numbers employed by TMM and output

	1977–8	1978–9	1979–80	1980–1	1981–2
Numbers employed	720	500	150	170	188
Output*	10687	10416	5881	4133	1333
Output per person	15	21	39	24	7

* Based on sales, which, because of stocks, does not give a very accurate picture of productivity.
Source: TMM.

registrations in 1981 were of Japanese models with Honda taking 41 per cent (see Table C5.4). Distribution by the Japanese was through wholly owned subsidiaries to multi-franchise retail chains. In the UK in 1981 Honda had 900 distributors and Triumph had 150, 40–50 of which were active. The UK market expanded over the period but UK manufacturers were not competitive.

Table C5.3   Motorcycle production, imports and exports in the UK

Year	Production	Exports	Imports
1976	19000	14800	228300
1977	14400	10900	184000
1978	23900	19900	224000
1979	16600	16000	205000
1980	11600	9100	267100
1981	3100	3600	271000

Source: Retail Business, no. 295, September 1982.

Table C5.4   UK market shares in 1981

Company	Percentage of total market	Percentage of superbike segment
Honda	41.3	18.5
Kawasaki	10.6	17.7
Suzuki	18.2	20.5
Yamaha	22.4	16.8
Triumph	0.8	6.4
Harley-Davidson	0.2	0.7
BMW	1.5	11.4
Moto Guzzi	0.8	4.0
Others	4.2	4.0

Source: Motor Cycle Association.

Motorcycle users varied from primary users who could not afford any other transport to secondary users who were youngish (25–34), with a high propensity to car ownership and large disposable incomes. The latter category of user tended to go for the superbike market segment. Associated with motorcycling was the image of leather-jacketed trouble makers, partly arising from a 1953 film in which Marlon Brando starred riding a 650 cc Triumph. This image was taken up in a 1960s cult film, *Easy Rider*, in which the star rode a Harley-Davidson motorcycle. Honda, moving away from these images, started a very successful advertising campaign in the early 1960s based on the slogan, 'You meet the nicest people on a Honda'. The original work for the campaign was based on an idea by an undergraduate student from the University of California, Los Angeles.

In 1959 the UK motorcycle industry had 49 per cent of the US motorcycle market. By 1973 this had fallen to 9 per cent and it was below 1 per cent in 1980. In 1959 Honda established an American subsidiary – American Honda Motor Company – at a time when only 4 per cent of Japanese motorcycle production was being exported. Further US market share data are contained in Tables C5.5 and C5.6. This shows the Japanese manufacturers moving from having no share of the market in the USA in 1959 to dominating it with over 90 per cent in 1980. By 1980 British firms' market shares were negligible. The American firms had 5 per cent of their own market.

The US market is important because of its size (see Table C5.7). This is particularly so in the superbike on-the-road segment, which was Triumph's market segment. These machines have an engine capacity of above 450 cc. In the superbike segment Japanese volume in the USA went from 27 000 units in 1969 to 218 000 units in 1973. In this market segment in 1969 four of the eight models from the 450–749 cc range in the USA were British but by 1973 only two of the ten available models were British. Market share had moved from 49 to 9 per cent. The US manufacturer, Harley-Davidson, had 25 per cent of this segment in 1981. By 1981 the Japanese had 70 per cent of this market in the UK and the USA. The market size in 1981 is shown in Table C5.7.

Table C5.8 shows TMM's sales by geographical area between 1977 and 1981 and further illustrates the importance of the US market, which generally accounted for 50 per cent of TMM's business. However, TMM's share of this market segment declined consistently from 1976 (see Table C5.9).

Production

In 1975 the Boston Consultancy Group (BCG) reported to the House of Commons on the state of the British motorcycle industry. BCG pointed out that 'the sales of Honda, the largest competitor, were of the order of two million units in 1974/5. Sales of the British industry in the correspond- ▷

Table C5.5   Market shares of the US motorcycle market

	1966	1980
Market size		
Estimated retail units	1 382 000	1 065 000*
(after stock adjustments)		
New registrations	n.a.	838 000
Percentages:		
American firms		
Harley–Davidson	4.0	4.9
British firms		
BSA		
Triumph	11.0	0.3
Norton		
German firms		
BMW	–	0.5
Japanese firms		
Honda	63.0	38.8
Yamaha	11.0	23.4
Kawasaki	–	15.7
Suzuki	11.0	15.2
Others	–	1.2

* Excludes mopeds, estimated to be 180 000.
Source: Motor Cycle Association.

Table C5.6   US market shares for superbikes (850 c.c. upwards)

	1980	1981	1982	1983	1984	1985	1986
Harley–Davidson	30.8	29.6	28.8	23.0	26.9	27.8	33.3
Honda	25.6	33.9	35.9	44.3	38.1	38.8	33.1
Kawasaki	16.3	15.1	12.5	9.4	11.7	10.7	12.7
Yamaha	13.3	9.6	10.1	13.1	13.8	13.8	12.6
Suzuki	12.0	9.9	10.5	8.1	7.1	5.6	6.9
BMW	1.6	1.5	1.9	1.8	2.3	3.3	3.4

Source: Harley-Davidson Annual Report, 1986.

Table C5.7   Superbike market size in 1981

	501 to 750 c.c.	501 to 1050 c.c.
UK	13 515	21 652
USA	240 490	366 964
Australia	3 926	8 840

Source: Motor Cycle Association.

▷

Table C5.8 Triumph sales by geographical area 1977–1981

	1977	1978	1979	1980	1981
UK	3 028	2 951	1 714	1 176	379
USA	5 299	5 020	2 060	2 202	374
Europe	694	922	725	360	245
Australia	914	784	180	258	232
Rest of world	752	739	1 175	137	103
Total	10 687	10 416	5 881	4 133	1 333

Table C5.9 TMM's share of the superbike market (per cent)

	UK market		US market
	501 to 750 c.c.	501 to 1050 c.c.	> 450 c.c.
1976	na	na	7.6
1977	na	na	3.6
1978	19.5	13.1	3.8
1979	18.4	10.1	2.8
1980	14.7	8.5	1.3
1981	10.2	6.4	1.0

ing period were approximately twenty thousand units.' They suggested that Honda's experience curve had an 87 per cent slope, which meant that costs fell by 13 per cent each time cumulative production doubled. BCG suggested that Honda had an implied strategy of increasing output so that costs per unit fell, enabling it to lower prices and increase sales so that a virtuous circle developed. As Honda grew it could afford to spend more on research and development and became in the space of a few years the technological and production leader in motorcycle manufacture throughout the world.

Sochiro Honda was a flamboyant engineer who designed the original four-stroke engine in the 1950s on which Honda had built its home reputation. He had teamed up in 1949 with Takeo Fujisawa, whose expertise was in marketing and finance. Sochiro Honda was interested in racing and decided to try to win the Isle of Man race as it was the most prestigious in the world. In 1958 his machines won the manufacturer's prize and in 1961 Honda won all five first positions. In 1958 he designed the supercub, a 50 cc motorcycle that was unlike any other available and that got away from the undesirable image associated with motorcycles. Honda then turned from concentrating on a strong home market to the world market.

UK reaction to the Japanese threat

As imports of Japanese motorcycles increased the UK companies adopted a strategy of segment retreat. They decided that they could not and did not wish to compete with the small motorcycles that were first imported and so ▷

concentrated on the larger bikes. The market consisted of five segments: those below 100 cc engine capacity, 125 to 349 cc, 350 to 449 cc, 450 to 749 cc and those over 750 cc, the superbike market segment. By the late 1960s most UK manufacturers were concentrating on the superbike segment. The market segmentation was partially affected by legal restrictions and by insurance problems for motorcycle users and owners.

The BCG suggested that the loss of market share by British manufacturers was a result of 'a concern for short term profitability'. For any model in which the industry was confronted with Japanese competition the British found it difficult to make profits and responded by withdrawing. However, in the 1970s the Japanese entered the superbike market segment, and continuing the previous strategy would have meant ceasing manufacture altogether. The superbike market segment was the fastest-growing segment and was dominated by UK producers until the late 1960s (Table C5.10).

Table C5.10   Growth of the superbike market segment

Country	1968–74 (% p.a. increase)	UK producers' market share	
		1968 (%)	1974 (%)
Europe	19	2	1
USA			
450 to 749 c.c.	16		
Over 750 c.c	47	49	9
UK	16	34	13
Europe	19	2	1

The BCG suggested that any commercially viable long-term strategy for the British motorcycle industry should recognize the nature of the relationship between market position and profitability. They went as far as to say that 'it is in fact the loss of share [of the market] by the British industry which has caused the low profitability'. Profit pressure did not result from lower prices on unit sales but from a cost position that was fundamentally uncompetitive.

The key factors identified by BCG were technology and scale. The rate of technological learning tended to be related over time to accumulated production experience. Furthermore, manufacturers with the highest annual model volumes could benefit from methods embodying up-to-date technology and gain scale advantages associated with, for example, machine tool development.

The BCG identified three stages of the prrocess of manufacturing and selling motorcycles at which costs and value added could be identified. They suggested that they were of equal importance. The first was concerned with selling and distribution. They estimated that approximately 2 ▷

per cent of sales was spent on advertising by all manufacturers, which in 1972 amounted to $8 million by Honda and $1.3 million by all the British manufacturers. Not mentioned by the BCG but quoted by R. T. Pascale in 'Perspectives on strategy'[5] was Honda's decision in 1964 to re-organize its relationship with its dealers so that it sold directly to the retailer on a cash on delivery basis, just as it had done in Japan in 1958. Triumph, which sold through a subsidiary in the USA, never had that advantage, although once financing was withdrawn by the ECGD, sales to anywhere else in the world had to be on that basis.

Production at the factory was the second source of value added and costs, and BCG concluded that real costs rose in British industry but fell in Japan, with net fixed investment amounting to £1300 per employee in Britain but £5000 in Japan in 1975. The third area identified was bought-in components and materials, with the Japanese having a considerable advantage because of the scale of their purchases and their strong negotiating position.

Overall, despite higher labour costs in Japan, the value added per employee in Honda was £18 000, in Yamaha and Suzuki between £8400 and £12 600 but in Britain only £4200. These enormous advantages resulted from the size of the market share held, which the British strategy of seg-ment retreat had denied.

The Japanese strategy

The BCG claimed that the Japanese had a marketing philosophy that emphasized market share and sales volume. Richard Pascale interviewed the two executives who set up the original Honda subsidiary in 1958. Mr Kawashima claimed, 'In truth, we had no strategy other than the idea of seeing if we could sell something in the United States.' The Japanese Minis-try of Finance only allowed them to invest $250 000 of which $110 000 could be in cash. Stock was divided into an equal number of each of the four products made. 'We were entirely in the dark the first year. We were not aware the motorcycle business in the United States occurs during a seasonal April-to-August window – and our timing coincided with the closing of the 1959 season.'

By the spring of 1960 a few models had been sold but they were returned, leaking oil and with the clutches failing. They were flown back to Japan to find the problem, which was diagnosed as overuse because the Americans drove bikes further and faster than the Japanese. A redesign of a number of components was necessary. There was no alternative but to try to sell the small 50 cc bikes – the supercubs – which were felt not to be suitable for the US market although they were very successful on the home market in Japan. These bikes were used by the directors themselves for running errands and had attracted considerable interest.

Retailers who were not motorcycle dealers were interested in selling ▷

supercubs and reluctantly Honda dealt with them. Advertising was still directed at all customers and there was a desire not to alienate the 'black leather jacket' customer. In 1963 the 'You meet the nicest people on a Honda' advertising campaign was adopted after a split between the president and treasurer and the director of sales. Success was phenomenal and was used to insist on a cash on delivery basis for sales to outlets. 'In one fell swoop Honda shifted the power relationship from the dealer to the manufacturer.'[5]

The US strategy

In 1980 Harley-Davidson (IID), the only indigenous manufacturer of motorcycles in the USA which concentrated on the superbike market segment, faced the same problem as the British manufacturers, the seemingly unbeatable competition from the Japanese. HD's share of the superbike market segment (>850 cc) fell from around one-third in 1977 to one-quarter in 1980. In 1981, using 'junk bonds', management bought out the company from the owners AMF for $65 million. Their publicly stated strategy was to develop and launch 'an entirely new advanced design of motorcycle', aimed at appealing to a new type of biker: 'ageing but affluent, not dirty and downwardly mobile' (*The Guardian*, 4 October 1989) and 'typically more at home in pinstripes than leathers'. However, the core part of the business was still American bikers, who remained loyal partly as a result of rallies, newsletters and the efforts of the Harley Owners Group (HOG).

In 1983 the management of HD, after intensive lobbying of Congress and Senate, secured a protective tariff of 45 per cent. This declined gradually to 10 per cent in 1987. During this period efficiency measures were taken to improve stock control and the quality control of components, to develop staff and to introduce computer-aided design techniques, so that the number of defective bikes fell and the break-even point for the manufacture of bikes fell considerably. HD's superbike market share in the USA went from 25 per cent in 1983 to 33 per cent in 1986 and 50 per cent in 1989, and 25 percent of output was exported to Japan.

In October 1989 the company was subject to the attentions of a takeover raider. Malcolm Glazer launched a $350 million bid for HD, following his policy of investing in companies 'significantly under valued, (which) are leaders in their field, have strong brand name recognition and exhibit tremendous future growth potential'.

Triumph's last stand

In 1981, with no source of working capital and few professional managers left, the TMM cooperative decided to look for backers. As a result of a report by Price Waterhouse they produced a five-year plan which provided ▷

financial projections for the introduction of a new model and a resumption of production. At this time TMM had no real UK competitors: Hesketh was producing (in 1982) 20 bikes a week before the appointment of a receiver later in the year; Armstrong Equipment was making replicas of racing bikes; and NVT was assembling light motorcycles and mopeds from imported parts under the BSA name and was continuing to develop its 1970s promise of a Wankel-engined superbike under the Norton Villiers name.

TMM's new model was to be positioned in the mid-price band but the costing had not been done in detail. The preliminary costings on the new range suggested a break-even production level of between 6500 and 7000 units per annum. The superbike market segment was estimated by Arthur D. Little (ADL), the management consultants employed to comment on the five-year plan, to be in the mature or early mature stage in the UK and TMM were considered to be in a weak competitive position in that segment. Moto Guzzi was considered to be in a tenable position, BMW in a favourable position and the Japanese in a strong position. ADL felt the critical factors for success were:

- low cost position relative to the competition;
- product differentiation;
- distribution and after-sales service;
- reliability.

The superbike market in the USA was estimated by ADL to be at the mature stage, with TMM in a weak competitive position, BMW and HD in a tenable position and the Japanese in a strong position.

TMM had problems with its site, which was too large for the projected output. It was in a scheduled residential area and mortgaged to the bank. TMM's plan required an injection of around £2 million and they approached the newly formed West Midlands Enterprise Board (WMEB) for funding. The WMEB responded by saying that the venture was too risky to undertake by itself but, given ADL's favourable comments, they would search for other backers. This helpful response to an almost impossible situation was typical of the reaction TMM engendered. Both Price Waterhouse and ADL executives promised help on a personal basis. There was considerable support from the Labour Party councillors who set up the WMEB and were on its board of directors. However, the plan had to be commercially viable. Conventional backers were sought but unsuccessfully, although backers could be found if other backers become interested. Several senior figures in the City approached successful entrepreneurs with personal fortunes who expressed an interest. It seemed at the time of the 1983 election that a backer had been found but the result, a return of the Conservative government – which had not been predicted by the polls – led ▷

to the withdrawal of the backer and without the chance of a restructuring TMM was forced to call in the receiver.

A new beginning

John Bloor, a multi-millionaire whose wealth is based on a privately owned building group, bought the assets of Triumph from the liquidator. He has invested 'tens of millions of pounds' (*The Independent*, 14 July 1990) because he wants to 'make a fine piece of equipment that appeals to people'. The proposed production throughput is 10 000 units a year at a new factory in Hinckley, Leicestershire. Costs are to be reduced because of the modular concept, unique in motorcycling, which utilizes the same engine parts, clutch and gearbox, but by the use of different crankshafts gives alternative engine capacities. A range of six Triumphs was to be launched in September 1990.

Such was the plan. In fact, the Trophy 1200 and Daytona 1000, both with four-cylinder engines and plastic bodywork, were introduced. Some claimed they were too similar to rival Japanese machines, although performance and quality were excellent; strong sales, however, justified Triumph's decision to compete head-on. In the autumn of 1991 the Trident 900 was launched. This third and most basic model has three cylinders but still uses most of the same components as the previous two models. It was described by Roland Brown in *The Independent* (5 October 1991) as having 'a personality of its own'.

Meanwhile, in Staffordshire Norton has launched a rotary-engined motorcycle on a cottage industry basis – five units a week. In 1990 it launched a model (the F1) based on the winner of the 1989 British championship. Time will tell whether either of these ventures will be successful.

References

1 D. R. Schoen and P. A. Sprague, 'What is the case method?', in *The Case Method at Harvard Business School*, M. P. McNair (ed.). McGraw-Hill, New York, 1954; pp. 78–9.
2 J. Argenti, *Systematic Corporate Planning*. Nelson, Sunbury-on-Thames, 1974; 103.
3 J. F. Weston and E. F. Brigham, *Managerial Finance*, 2nd UK edition, Cassell, London, 1988.
4 C. Gore and K. Murray, 'The development of enterprising personnel', *International Journal of Manpower*, 1990; **11**(6): 17–19.
5 R. T. Pascale, 'Perspectives on strategy', *California Management Review*, 1984; **26**: 47–72.

6 Small-Firm Decision-Making

It is now time to apply some of the ideas of the previous chapters. The remainder of the book uses these ideas and concepts to analyse the strategic decision-making process that determines the future direction of a business. Basing decisions on rational principles is as important in strategic decision-making as in other areas and many of the issues that will be addressed in the next few chapters apply across a wide spectrum of firms irrespective of size.

Nevertheless, there are considerable differences between firms in the decision-making process and perhaps some of the most distinct of these occur with relation to the size of firm. Even though, as Robinson and Pearce[1] point out, there is woefully inadequate knowledge of strategic management in small firms, they should not be treated as though they were subject to the same forces as large firms. It is useful, therefore, before examining the tools that are of particular help in large firms, to pay some attention to the issues of decision-making that arise in small to medium-sized enterprises. Using decision-making concepts that have already been established, this chapter examines these issues. Its objectives are to:

- identify the distinguishing characteristics of small-firm decision-making;
- consider which environmental factors are of particular importance to the sector;
- examine the use of strategic management in such firms;
- identify factors affecting strategy formulation and implementation.

The environment

Definition

Like the proverbial elephant the small firm is one of those things that is recognized when seen but difficult to define. Even the Bolton Committee,[2] which was set up to examine the small-firm sector, made heavy weather of finding a definition and there has been little agreement on the issue since. Nevertheless, perhaps the most widely accepted definition is still one based on the ideas of the Bolton Committee. They identified three important characteristics that are likely to have a strong effect on management and decision-making within a small firm. This is useful as it enables the identification of firms with similar decision-making conditions as a separate group from large firms. The committee suggested that small firms:

1 Have a relatively small market share and cannot affect the market price.
2 Are managed in a personalized way by their owners.
3 Are independent and do not form part of a larger company.

The committee went on to give operational form to these criteria in terms of the levels of employment, turnover, output and capital that were typical of firms with these characteristics. Subsequently, the Wilson Committee[3] updated some of these, such as the turnover requirements. The 1981 Companies Act, when providing size exemptions to its requirements that companies adopt a particular format for account presentation, provided yet other levels of these variables beneath which firms qualified as small firms.

For our purposes it is the management characteristics that are of importance. While it is recognized that even with respect to this the Bolton definition is clearly limited – for example, a one-man business such as a stained glass window repairer may have a large market share – it does identify characteristics with wide applicability and is a suitable basis for analysis.

Market dynamics

There are three forms of business through which small firms may progress. These are:

1 Sole trader – a business owned and operated by one individual, who is personally liable for all the debts of the business.
2 Partnership – two or more individuals join together to do business and each partner has unlimited liability for the debts of the partnership.
3 Companies – a company registered in accordance with the Companies Act is a separate legal entity and the liability of the shareholders is limited to the amount paid or unpaid on issued share capital.

Even within the small-firm sector there is a growth pattern for small firms. Many writers have suggested that this growth of a firm passes through the stages of development shown in Figure 6.1. The process starts with the initial development of the idea into the concrete form of a new venture, and the activities associated with the start-up of the company, which involve management implementation plans. Once the business is up and running the issue of growth arises. This is likely to be associated with changes in management and organizational structure, expansion of market area and movement into other market areas. After a period of time there may be a stabilization as markets become saturated. At this stage the firm will have to examine pastures new and/or innovation in order to

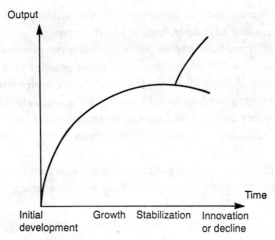

Figure 6.1   Life cycle of a firm.

stabilize or grow further, or it will face a decline as its products come to the end of their life cycles.

Ganguly[4] has analysed some of the features of this life span using VAT registration/deregistration statistics, and concluded that 40–45 per cent of businesses can be expected to be trading after ten years. However, about 9 per cent can be expected to deregister each year, with deregistrations higher in the first three years of a business's life. A study by Storey[5] of the Cleveland area from 1965 to 1978 showed that out of the 1200 firms started only 774 survived and he concluded that most firms stay small or die.

According to the Bolton Committee[2] the number of small firms in the economy was declining in 1971. However, since then information such as that provided by the Economic Intelligence Unit[6] suggests that this trend has been reversed, with a growth of 0.2 per cent per annum in the number of firms between 1975 and 1980 and an increase in employment levels in the sector of 2.2 per cent per annum over the same period. Clearly the small-firm sector is extremely dynamic in the sense of being associated with a high rate of births and deaths. In terms of the overall size of the sector and changes in that size, once again opinions differ.

Government policy

The size and growth of the small firm sector are of concern to the government because of problems of economic recession and the apparent decline of UK industry, where large firms predominate. The view that the bureaucratic management of large firms may have impeded the flexibility of response necessary in today's dynamic environment has led to an appreciation of the role of small firms. In addition, they continue to represent a large portion of economic activity. In some industrial sectors, such as leather goods, fur, timber and furniture, they account for the majority of the employment in the sector.

In the past small firms have had to face very much the same rules and regulations as large firms. More recently, however, some policies have been designed with the needs of small firms in mind. They are made exempt from some of the statutory requirements placed on larger firms in the areas of employment regulation, health and safety at work and planning controls, and they are allowed to present simpler annual accounts and to benefit from value added tax exemption levels.

In addition to this there are also policies designed specifically to alleviate some of the problems in the sector. These cover three problem areas.

Information

Counselling to new and small firms is provided by enterprise agencies, and this is backed up by the specialist help provided by the Small Firm Service, which acts as a consultant to the enterprise agencies.

Investment

Assistance with investment projects has been provided in a number of forms, ranging from grants and special loan schemes to tax incentives for equity investment. There is a national scheme to encourage start-ups, the Enterprise Allowance Scheme. This provides a cash subsidy of £40 per week for the first year of trading if certain conditions are met, and within regions of high unemployment extra help is often available.

To help existing businesses there is quite a wide range of loan schemes, sometimes with interest rates below market rates. Perhaps the best known of these is the Small Business Loan Guarantee Scheme of 1981. In addition, all companies are eligible for export advice, some financial help to enter new markets and guarantees to insure exporters against the risk of not being paid for their export sales.

The availability of such assistance means that an awareness of government policy is important to the decision-maker, with regard not only to legal and tax obligations but also to the various forms of assistance available.

Market conditions

Another environmental factor that considerably affects the decision-making of small firms is the market conditions within which they operate. The definition of a small firm identifies it as having a small market share. This has several implications.

Small firms are at the margin of market forces. They have little market power and this, combined with the fact that they have a very limited portfolio of products that could offset the effect of changes in demand in one market, means that they are exposed to considerable risk from economic fluctuations. Survival in such an environment demands considerable flexibility and rapid response when conditions change.

With regard to their customer base another point was raised by Lydall[7] and Adams,[8] who identified three types of small firms: specialists, which produce a limited product range for just a few customers; jobbers, which produce a wider range of products for a few customers; marketeers, which produce their own designs and products for a wider customer base. However, according to Storey[9] there are few marketeers. Small firms usually have the problem of a limited customer base, and because the small firm will have a relatively small output it will be vulnerable to the decline or bankruptcy of a major customer, and the loss of a major customer to a competitor is likely to be of very considerable significance.

On the supply side the labour market presents difficulties for the small firm. According to Curran and Stanworth[10] small firms find it difficult to recruit more able staff. Given the limited prospects for promotion and the general lack of provision for training this is not surprising. Many surveys show that a large proportion of small firms cannot get labour, premises or capital to exploit the markets open to them.[11] They are restricted by a lack of resources, whereas large firms are restricted by a lack of demand.

Distinct factors that affect the decision-making of small firms

Ownership and control

According to Birley and Norburn[12] one of the most important features that distinguishes small- from large-firm decision-making is that small firms are managed by their owners. The Bolton Committee stated that 85 per cent of small firms were controlled and owned by one or two people.[2] In such firms decision-making is more heavily affected by the personal characteristics and motivations of the owner-managers. Empirical studies of these motivations find that they are rather different from those of any of the stakeholders in large companies. The findings in this area, such as those of Golby and Johns,[13] suggest that the main motivation is independence. The need to be 'one's own boss' is placed above maximizing profit or growth.

The personal characteristics of the owner also have a strong effect on the decision-making process. First there is the issue of lack of expertise. Because of the size of the firm there is little scope to employ specialists in functional areas, and studies of the background of entrepreneurs suggest poor educational background. Ket de Vries[14] suggests that the management style of the owner-manager tends to be autocratic and that there is a reluctance to delegate operational decision-making. Although the Bolton Committee showed that a significant minority had some accountancy or technological qualification most entrepreneurs have learned through experience, and that experience is often narrowly based on the single firm. This means that the management is likely to be particularly weak in areas that benefit most from specialization. The advantages of good marketing, for example, are often given little attention by the entrepreneur immersed in the intricacies of production engineering.

Secondly, there is the question of the relationship with employees and the degree of informality present. The organization structure of a small firm is of a simple nature and is usually characterized by a high degree of informal interaction between the owner-manager and the employees. Writers such as Ingham[15] suggest that industrial relations in small firms are conflict-free and seen by both employers and employees as mutually satisfying. Even though such views are criticized by Curran and Stanworth[16] for providing too romantic a view, the nature of industrial relations is necessarily more informal in such firms.

The financial resources of the owner also have a strong effect on decision-making because owners are often the only or main source of capital. The availability of finance is often mentioned as one of the most substantial problems the entrepreneur has to overcome.

Burns and Dewhurst[17] analysed liquidity, gearing and balance sheet structures. Using business monitor data they found that small companies were less liquid and more highly geared than large companies and a far smaller proportion of the gearing was represented by long-term loans. They also found that small businesses were heavily financed by creditors, which explains the low liquidity, but relying heavily on credit from suppliers is risky and unreliable, because terms of credit may change, even if it is cheap. In addition, small firms can have problems in collecting their debts, particularly from their large-company customers. So small firms are exposed to considerable risk in terms of market fluctuations, and the pattern of finance itself involves high risk.

The main source of outside non-creditor finance is borrowing from joint-stock banks. The first port of call for such loans is the branch manager. As such his or her attitude is crucial to the success of the application for finance, particularly because he or she can exercise discretion in the amount of security required as the basis for the loan. As the Wilson Committee[3] showed, there is considerable variation in this with typical security ratios of net assets to borrowing ranging from 2:1 to 4:1.

The main forms of borrowing from a bank are overdrafts and short-term loans and both types of loan can be expected to be well secured. This security may sometimes be based not only on the assets of the business but also on personal assets. There are other methods of outside financing, but access to the stock market through the unlisted securities market is only suitable for the large end of the small business spectrum, because the cost of a listing is not likely to be much less than £100 000, and companies should have been trading for three years and have signed an undertaking providing for a minimum standard of regular disclosure of the company's affairs.

Even though there may be little shortage of financial facilities, available finance is still regarded as one of the major environmental problems by entrepreneurs. Perhaps, however, the real problem lies with the lack of financial expertise present in the small business. The small business may be at a disadvantage because the management time taken to arrange a loan falls as a proportion of the size of loan obtained,[18] but even more important is the lack of expertise, which presents additional obstacles to the entrepreneur in search of capital. Without such expertise there may be no knowledge of potentially suitable sources of funding. Furthermore, to overcome such problems it is essential to formulate the requirements in the form of a properly presented plan that identifies the needs of the business and the means for eventual repayment.

The lack of strategic decision-making

An important characteristic of many small firms is a lack of rational long-term decision-making. This stems from various aspects of operation.

When a business is very small it may have the simple structure shown in Chapter 4. This means that the entrepreneur is likely to be heavily involved in the operating decisions of the company. It would be hard, for example, to imagine the owner of a local grocery store not becoming involved in its operation. Even if a functional structure has developed, because there is no divorce of ownership from control the owner is likely to be very involved in the operation of the business. Because of his or her personal stake in and commitment to the business the owner may find it very difficult to delegate responsibility for operational and administrative decision-making to other individuals. Even when other individuals are given tasks and responsibilities, many such entrepreneurs continue to intervene in all areas of operation to ensure that decisions are taken in line with their own views and perceptions. Under such conditions the functional specialists are frequently in a position to operate only in line with past practices and the owner requires that all new problems requiring new decisions are referred to him or her. So, even in a functionally arranged company, the entrepreneur may be bogged down with deciding which new supplier to use if the established supplier cannot meet an order, or how to obtain additional capacity to distribute a large batch order. There is, in other words, short-term decision-making and problem-solving.

Both the simple and the functional structure can lead to problems in this situation. First, there is little time available for the consideration of strategic issues. One of the things that can easily be crowded out is an adequate scanning of the environment. Such scanning does not seem as important to the owner as the resolution of short-term problems but without scanning, opportunities will be lost and threats may develop to such an extent that short-term problems appear insignificant. Ignoring signs that a major customer is getting into difficulties may mean that credit is extended rather than reduced to such a customer, thus putting the small business in an extremely vulnerable position. Furthermore, continual involvement in operational matters may affect perception. A concentration on minor problem-solving may crowd out perception and an awareness of major issues. It is the old syndrome of not seeing the wood for the trees.

Another reason for the apparent dearth of strategic decision-making stems from the background of the owner-managers. Their limited experience and education contributes to a lack of appreciation of the importance of strategic decision-making. As they have had little in the way of formal business education they may not only lack the skills necessary to undertake such decisions but even be unaware of the existence of concepts and tools associated with such decision-making. Decisions are based on a response to problems as they arise: they are merely reactive. The lack of awareness of strategic decision-making methods means that they are unaware of the need to be productive and of management methods to enable them to become productive by taking strategic initiatives.

Because they do not perceive the valuable role of rational long-term decision-making they are also unlikely to pay for advice in this area, even if they have the funds. They probably will not even be prepared to have the benefit of discussion of the issues with employees because many small business owner-managers are extremely cautious about disclosure of what they consider to be sensitive information. In addition, if the mission objective is one of maintaining independence, as long as they feel their independence is secured there will be little pressure to address issues of improved management.

Nevertheless, strategic decision-making is of undoubted value. The life cycle ideas demonstrate quite clearly the need for some type of planning. To continue in existence the entrepreneur must take account of and plan for market changes. Financial plans must be found to ensure adequate financing throughout the life cycle, because different periods have different financial implications. At the start-up the owner will have to spend money in researching the market and developing the product and methods of production, and at maturity further funds may be needed for new areas. External sources of funding will expect to have evidence that a close analysis of the long-term situation has been undertaken.

Only with an explicit attempt to address strategic issues can the entrepreneur become proactive, take the initiative and ensure the firm's long-term health. Studies such as that by Bracker and Pearson,[19] who examined the revenue growth and net profits of 265 entrepreneurs in dry cleaning, have shown that firms that had undertaken strategic decision-making for five years or more had outperformed other firms. A study by Ackelsberg and Arlow,[20] using a sample of 135 small businesses spread across six industries, also suggested that the use of strategic management tools leads to increased sales and profits. Even the study by Orpen,[21] who found the extent of long-range planning to be unrelated to company performance, found that when such factors as attitude to planning and content of plan were taken into account, the data strongly suggested that firms involved in planning had a better performance.

Characteristics of small firms' strategic decisions

The characteristics of small firms discussed above have a considerable effect on the strategic decision-making process. First of all there is the effect of the owner's need for independence rather than, say, growth. Gallante[22] suggests that because of this aspect of motivation there is a significant difference between the small business owner and the entrepreneur. The entrepreneur is seen as orientated toward growth and his or her decision-making involves planning for that growth. The small business owner, on the other hand, will remain with just a single product, and be less likely to undertake strategic decision-making. Firms that do not adopt any form of planning are classified by Mintzberg[23] as being in the adaptive mode, in which they just muddle through, adopting reactive policies to changes in the environment and internal problems. However, even for this group long-term issues are important and a lack of consideration of such issues can result in business failure.

Another factor affecting the strategic decisions of small firms is that some alternative lines of action are not possible because of size limitations. The low-cost strategies that a large company can follow because of its advantageous economies of scale are frequently not available to small firms, and strategies that depend on the development of market power, rapid market penetration and growth are also out of consideration. To concentrate on this, however, would be a very negative approach. The other side of the coin is that the unique strengths of small firms in terms of flexibility and low management overhead costs can enable them to take advantage of market niches and specialized products denied to the large firms, which are better suited to the production of standardized units.

The type of personnel relationships and the dominance of the informal structure mean that strategic management operates far better if it is conducted in a more informal way than in large firms, which is the conclusion reached by Robinson and Pearce.[1] In a more recent article[24] they went even further and suggested that if the strategic decision process is too formalized performance may be reduced. In such an organization the imposition of some formalized written plan may well be detrimental and alien to the management style and reduce the advantage that small firms have in terms of good employee relations. Furthermore, the market conditions facing small firms demonstrate considerable change and the firm above all else needs to remain flexible. For example, the vulnerability of the small firm to a loss of one of its customers or a non-payment of an account is acute and must be a major factor in the decision process. Formal written plans are too vulnerable to such major change and it is therefore important that the firm maintains a flexible responsible approach. This flexibility is facilitated, according to Woo and Cooper,[25] in the production process. The ability to change its length of production run, tailor products, modify products at short notice and meet unanticipated changes in order size is undoubtedly one of the small firm's strengths and the existence of a formal written plan to be adhered to would reduce this. Because of this Schuman *et al.*[26] suggest that strategic decision-making in small firms is necessarily more short-run-orientated than that in larger firms.

In the small business, therefore, attention to long-term decision-making does not necessarily mean that the outcome should always be a written detailed formal plan. The need for formal plans will vary with the nature and type of market and the size of the business. A venture that is growing rapidly within a complex market area where there is, perhaps, strong competition may need more formal planning. Very often, however, what is needed is the process of strategic decision-making rather than the formulation of a written plan. For example, it is the process of the SWOT analysis that ensures that the manager adopts a rational framework and it is this that is beneficial to the decision-maker. The very act of assessing internal strengths and weaknesses can prove vital; for example, many companies fail because of an entirely foreseeable cash flow problem. Even though environmental scanning may be a great deal less sophisticated and formal than is possible in a large firm it is essential. For example, proposals to change parking restrictions or a plan for a town bypass can have a crucial effect on the success of a small retail store. However, not only do small firms have less resources for the formal scanning but their personal involvement may prevent them from perceiving an action as a threat or prevent them from perceiving the extent of the threat. A fast-food restaurant may know when McDonald's intends to open a branch in its area but the owners may be reluctant to recognize the extent of the threat to their market share that this represents. Even if a formal plan is not written, therefore, the process of consideration of such factors is vital and will help to offset biases of perception. This form of strategic planning has been referred to by Mintzberg[23] as the entrepreneurial mode of planning, where the focus of the decision is the single decision-maker with an objective of growth.

The extent to which it may be desirable to construct a formal long-term plan will vary from firm to firm. What is not in question, however, is the desirability of undertaking a process of strategic decision-making, whether or not it results in a formal written plan. The next stage is to examine such a process.

Stages of strategic decision-making

There are two major issues in small-firm strategic decision-making. One is the question of start-up and the issues arising from that. The second is to do with growth and survival. In each of these circumstances – even though in practice strategic decisions may emerge from a series of incremental operational decisions, with each action taken in isolation without an awareness of its consequences – a rational and explicit approach to strategy formulation is advantageous.

Objectives

The start-up and continuation of a business are very much responses to personal motivation and the need for independence. It is relatively clear that the needs of different stakeholders have less relevance in determining the mission than they do in a large firm. Nevertheless, an objective of maintaining independence as the driving force of the business needs further analysis. For that vision to be achieved there might need to be subsidiary objectives and targets similar to those in a large firm. For example, at least a certain level of profitability will have to be achieved.

Problem recognition and search

In the case of a start-up problem recognition is a particularly important stage of the decision. The first issue is to decide upon the area of operation. Although the traditional view of entrepreneurship has been to assume in-born characteristics of owners, Gibb and Ritchie[27] have argued that these 'can be wholly understood in terms of the types of situation encountered and the social groups to which individuals relate' (p. 183). Further support for the view that environmental factors are important in the start-up decision comes from Bannock,[11] who suggests that the number of start-ups increases in times of high unemployment and recessions. This increase may also result from 'technological pull' when the development of a new technology requires the setting up of a small firm. This is particularly important in areas such as electronics. On other occasions the firm may start up as a result of a buy-out by the existing management of a part of a larger company.

In other cases the issue of the area of operation can be tackled as a problem in its own right using decision techniques. Once the objective has been decided, a systematic approach can be applied to the generation of possible areas of operation.

The particular variables that are of importance to the entrepreneur are the degree of risk, finance and the growth potential involved in a start-up decision. Bearing this in mind, possible areas of entry can be classified with regard to the state of maturity of the market and product, because this is associated with particular characteristics of these variables. This will then enable the entrepreneur to choose to start up in an area of operation associated with the levels of risk, finance and growth that he or she finds acceptable.

Table 6.1 helps to correlate risk, growth and the degree of difficulty in obtaining finance with the product and market. It suggests that entry is most hazardous with a new product and new market. In such a proposal good market research is essential but risk is high because it is an untried product. Finance may be difficult to obtain and expensive. However, one of the advantages of entering into a relatively new market is that mistakes may not be crucial because demand is strong and, of course, the possibility for growth is substantial, particularly if the industry as a whole is in a state of change.

Table 6.1   Risk, growth, financial implications

	Risk	Growth	Finance
New product and new market	high	high	high
New product and old market	medium	high	medium
Old product and new market	low	high	low
Old product and old market	?	low	low

Another strategy is to enter with a new product in an old market. This is rather less risky because at least there is knowledge of the market conditions for the existing product. Once again, however, some market research is important to ensure that the new product is likely to be preferred, and a careful market analysis must be conducted of the likely response of the producers of the existing product. Care must be taken not to underestimate the extent of customer loyalty to the existing product, and to consider the issue of complementary goods that may have been purchased to facilitate the consumption of the old product. If these difficulties can be overcome the growth potential is high.

Perhaps the safest form of entry is with an established product in a new market. It is in this area that franchises are important. Market research should ensure that the characteristics of the market are not significantly different from those of areas where the product is known to be successful. Risk is then minimized because customer response, and the costs of operation of the business, can be estimated fairly accurately. As a result of this, finance is more easily available and at a lower cost. Because it is a new market there will be potential for growth but in estimating this factor consideration should be given to the potential for entry. Even a relatively short delay in the entry of competitors can be an advantage in creating a customer base. If you are setting up the first fast-food restaurant on a high street, the lack of availability of premises to other potential restaurants for a time is a considerable advantage.

The final possibility is to enter an established market with an established product. The stimulus for such an entry is usually that excess profits are perceived as accruing to existing businesses operating in the area. The risk under such circumstances depends on the extent of entry. While the profitability of the first video shops served to induce entry, in many locations this occurred to such an extent that too many entered the market, profits were reduced and some of the entrants went out of business.

Another helpful piece of information comes from PIMS (profit impact on market share; see Chapter 9) data, which show that entry is more successful in a market with a dominant firm that has more than 50 per cent of the market share and therefore is not too hostile to fringe activities by marginal small firms. The monopolistic pricing practices of the large firm may provide an umbrella to shelter the small firms. In such markets the small firm may serve a niche by providing a more specialized version of the generic product and thus be perceived by the large firm as of little potential threat. This ability to create a market niche is important to the chances of success for the small firm. Such a niche is often easier to find or create if demand is for differentiated products.

A final factor that could affect the determination of the area of operation arises from the ideas of information analysis as applied to the consumer. Where a good is technical in nature there is asymmetrical information. The producer has an understanding of the intricacies of the product but the consumer can only learn about quality from experience. If it is a consumer durable good the consumer is operating with very limited information on quality because of the infrequency of repeat purchases. In such circumstances factors such as branding and reputation are of considerable importance. Such markets can be very difficult for a new small business to become established in.

For the existing business the stage of problem awareness is perhaps the weakest part of the decision process. Problem diagnosis requires a detachment of view that is difficult for the entrepreneur to obtain because he or she is so deeply involved in the operation of the business. In addition, in a strategic sense, it is at this stage of the decision-making process that scanning the environment is vital and, as has been shown, the entrepreneur neither has the time nor perceives the importance of this activity. In addition, in a search for alternative strategies the single-manager business is at a tremendous disadvantage because without group interaction the generation of possible alternatives will be limited.

Evaluation of alternatives

Once a business area has been identified the next stage is a careful investigation of alternative strategies. This is similar for a start-up and for an ongoing business. Time is scarce and an assessment should be made of the asset base in terms of capital, abilities, experience and manpower in order to identify strengths and weaknesses. Then the external environment must be considered for potential threats and opportunities. In practice, time constraints frequently limit this procedure. Experience of past methods may play a strong part at this stage of the decision.

One of the features that makes evaluation particularly difficult in the small firm is a problem with the use of financial ratios as indicators of the state of the company. According to Levin and Travis[28] this is because:

1 An entrepreneur may enter a sum of money as a loan rather than equity because of the fear of loss if the firm fails, even though the entry should be regarded as equity.

2 The taxation system may encourage rewards to be taken in a form other than profit so that it may be a rational strategy for profits to appear to be low. The asset base may include assets devoted to the use of the owner, such as country cottages. In addition, high salaries may be paid to members of the owner's family so that costs are inflated and standard profit measures such as return on investment (ROI) are of little use for evaluation.

3 Dividend ratios are not particularly useful either. Dividend decisions are not based on stock price, because shares are not traded, but on the owner's decision of the form in which to take the profits.

Choice

The mission of independence means the choice of strategies may well be dominated by the need to keep control over the firm and to ensure future security. In as much as risk is associated with new markets, practices and products the owner-manager will tend to be cautious and the safety provided by experience and incremental change will dominate the decision-making process. In practice the process is likely to have been rather more incremental than it may seem. Rather than several possible strategies being identified, developed and investigated equally through to the choice stage, it is more likely that as search takes place on the initial proposals some will be shown to be unfeasible and discarded. Thus by the choice stage the decision may well be whether to agree to a particular scheme or to do nothing. This is particularly the case with regard to a start-up decision, where the proposal is often refined through a series of feasibility considerations that are gradually modified from an initial idea generated on the basis of experience.

Implementation

The implementation of the decision is concerned with giving operational form to the strategy chosen. In the case of a start-up decision this is probably the most difficult stage because with little operational experience it is difficult to foresee implementation problems. Nevertheless, a careful analysis of similar operations and of supply markets and labour markets may mean that possible problems and the possible advantages of some policies can be anticipated.

In an existing company at this stage of the decision process the small firm has certain advantages over large companies. Too often in a large company the strategic decision-making process takes place in a vacuum. When decisions are made it is assumed that the adoption of appropriate management techniques can ensure successful implementation. Such an approach can underestimate the effect of implementation problems and lead to the failure of the policy. In small firms, the fact that the owners are involved in operation and administration ensures that they are aware of operational problems. They will have had an impact within the decision process. Owner-managers will, for example, be more able to predict whether a proposal such as shift working would be so strongly opposed by the working staff as to make it unviable and thus they can eliminate that policy from consideration before the choice stage. The most severe implementation problems are likely to have been taken into account in the determination of the feasibility of a policy.

While it has been argued that undergoing this type of rational decision process is valuable in itself, if the business is to raise capital to finance a project or to cover set-up costs the process must be completed by the formulation of a business plan, feasibility study or loan proposal.

The business plan

A formal business plan is necessary for financial backing, but it has several other advantages. Committing the plan to paper actually helps to clarify many of the issues and to create a greater sense of objectivity. Threats in the environment, for example, are less likely to be ignored when they are identified in writing. The allocation of events to a time schedule serves to ensure the feasibility of the strategy. Unless a written plan is formulated this time-planning approach is unlikely to be undertaken. A written plan also requires the entrepreneur to consider implementation issues that might otherwise be disregarded, so this approach means that expensive mistakes can be foreseen and avoided.

The form that such a plan takes follows the form of the decision-making process very closely. It should start with details of current status and the proposed venture. It should identify the future market trends and the opportunities available. Good reasons should be provided for the choice of strategy, along with an assessment of its potential. In short, the main issues that have emerged as a result of the decision-making process should be outlined.

After this discussion of the strategic issues, the implementation issues must be addressed. These can be divided into sections representing the main functional areas of marketing, finance, personnel and management.

Marketing

It is useful if the marketing section starts with an introduction to the marketing philosophy of the firm. This can be explained in terms of the kinds of customer groups that will be targeted and the pattern of change in this targeting that will take place over time. This is also the point at which special or important features of the product should be identified as the basis for the creation of the product image.

The next step is to address the nature of the market. This can start with an assessment of market size and include characteristics of the population in terms of income, education, unemployment, age distribution and so on. Changes over the past few years should be identified and predictions made of any future changes. Estimations should be made of the number of potential customers from these data and an assessment should be made of market trends and the state of demand in terms of the product and its life cycle. Even though a product may be new, it must be remembered that if, for example, it is a fashion product the life cycle may be relatively short.

The state of competition in the market must also be assessed. Direct and indirect competitors must be identified, along with as much information on exit and entry over the past five years as it is possible to obtain. The policies that are followed by competitors are also very important. These can be noted in terms of pricing practices, promotions, advertising and services offered, and conclusions may be offered about the extent to which retaliatory action is likely.

The plan should identify the actual marketing policies to be adopted, the form of the marketing mix, the type of pricing and credit policies, and the methods and means of distribution.

Production

The consideration of operational issues should start with a review of location issues. An optimal location minimizes labour and other costs, is close to suppliers and customers and has a good provision of services. While it may be difficult to establish a location as optimal these factors should be considered in the location decision.

The production section should also identify potential suppliers and examine the stability of supply. It would be advisable to consider the vulnerability of production to the failure of a major supplier or changes in the supply conditions.

A consideration of the physical facilities is of course very important. This should include a determination of work flow and the layout of equipment, and an assessment of the type of access available and of loading and unloading facilities.

Personnel

Given that the nature of the operation has been explained and an estimate has been made of the operational level of the business, a consideration of personnel issues is essential. The manpower section of the plan must contain a review of the expertise and numbers of staff employed, along with an estimate of the salaries necessary and a realistic assessment of recruitment possibilities.

At this stage the provision of an organizational chart, showing the formal structure and identifying roles and areas of responsibility, would help to ensure that the issues had been thoroughly thought through.

Finance

If the proposal is for a start-up the plan must include a projected income statement showing the expected financial position over a time period and a profile of projected cash flows, so that the break-even point can be easily identified. The finance section shows the potential viability of the proposal. It should be in the form of four basic financial statements constructed on the basis of expected costs and revenues, which have been worked out from the results of the previous stages of investigation in the plan. The statements are:

1 *A balance sheet* This details the assets required to support the expected level of operations and shows how these assets will be financed. It is from this that investors can work out ratio analyses.
2 *An income statement* This gives projected operating results based on profits and losses. It depends crucially on the sales forecast made in the marketing segment, because this is taken as the basis for working out production costs and provides projected earnings.
3 *A cash flow statement* This sets out the amounts and timing of expected cash inflows and outflows. It will show the need for and the timing of additional finance and the peak requirements for working capital. It will also show the sources of the finance: equity, bank loans and short-term lines of credit.
4 Finally, *a break-even chart* shows the level of sales needed to cover all costs.

After these functional areas have been examined one of the last sections of the plan should incorporate all the factors into a dated profile. This should provide a schedule for the implementation steps and identify particular milestones in the process.

Conclusion

The cultural characteristics of small firms involve a high degree of personalized management and informality. While this has some advantages, it is important that the entrepreneur does consciously address the issues of decision-making and long-term planning in order to reduce risk and become proactive.

At start-up the entrepreneur's source of finance is likely to require an explicit plan, but that should not be the end of the process. Even though a high degree of formalized planning may not be appropriate, objective reviews should be made of the current situation of the firm and possibilities for future action.

Case study 6.1
A business start-up

This case illustrates factors affecting the start-up decision at the level of the entrepreneur.

Part I

On leaving a sixth-form college in Leicester, where she had studied English, history and music, Amrita Kaur decided not to pursue her academic studies any further. For the previous two years she had been building a career as a singer of Asian music at weddings and other social occasions at weekends in the local community. On leaving college she decided to try her luck at similar events in the London area, in the hope of gaining nationwide recognition. She made considerable headway in this career and found that she was very busy with engagements in most of the major cities in England. After a few years, however, she decided that the travelling involved and the unsocial hours of work were too demanding. She had by this time acquired enough capital to have bought outright a large house in Leicester for her family and herself, and she decided that the time had come to return to Leicester to set up a business.

Part II

Amrita decided that she would set up a record store selling Asian music film sound-tracks and bhangra music. She identified the area of the town with the highest concentration of people of Asian origin and conducted market research in the area to find out about the availability of cassette recorders, the size of the population and, as bhangra music mainly appeals to people between the ages of 14 and 25, the age distribution of the population.

She then chose a site for the store in the centre of an area devoted to the specific needs of the Asian population. She chose a corner location next to a sari shop. Finance was a particular problem. She was able to raise some of the necessary finance in the form of a mortgage for her property and she was able to call on the resources of her family and friends to participate in the venture. However, further finance was necessary. Her only contact with a bank manager had been in London and in view of the fact that she had already mortgaged her property the manager of the local bank was not helpful. Eventually she was introduced to a manager of a branch of another bank in another part of the town and obtained sufficient finance.

The business has been a success and she is now considering plans for future expansion.

Case study 6.2
Alpine Foods

This case illustrates the importance of strategic decision-making at stages in the life cycle of a small firm.

Alpine Foods was a small company producing health nut bars called Raw Bars. Production was started by a housewife in the kitchen of the family home using family labour in 1980, and then moved to a shop that had low rent. Initially only family labour was used but as production expanded friends were also used as a source of labour. The work involved mixing, baking, wrapping and packing. As the business grew, second-hand machinery for these procedures was used. This machinery increased volume and enabled reductions in the number of people employed. In 1985 new premises were taken. The result was increased growth and an emergent partnership between husband and wife.

The corporate strategy pursued can be divided into three phases.

Phase I

In 1980 the corporate objective was mainly to grow as rapidly as possible, because through growth production costs could be reduced and profitability could be ensured. Cost reduction was to be achieved by more efficient use of labour and machinery, and through bulk purchases, which reduce cost per unit bought. However, the formulation of strategy depends on information and very little was known about the market. This was a new industry and a new product market with no history. So the information was mainly impressionistic. For example, changing consumer tastes towards healthy foods were evidenced by people's desire to avoid pesticide residues. The trend was thought to be in the right direction for an increasing market size, but little in the way of market research was done.

The search for opportunities to meet the growth objective was limited mainly because of financial constraints. Thus, the company was unable to take advantage of some opportunities, such as improved packaging equipment, because sufficient finance was not available. Alpine Foods was unable to provide any security and received no government funding. Government grants were not available and banks would provide working capital for existing turnover but not for further expansion. There was also a reluctance on the part of the owners to risk borrowing large sums of money.

Phase II

In 1985 production was in an old factory that met basic requirements, such as washing up and services. The objective had been refined from general ▷

growth into a desire to grow as quickly as the market. Jordans, a large food company, was entering the market (it is now market leader). Alpine Foods aligned prices with Jordans, and ensured that it distributed through many health food wholesale distributors. The company manufactured only under its own label.

During this period the company introduced new products (muesli bars, cereals and so on), all made from the same ingredients using similar processes and packaged and presented in similar ways. At this time the company hoped to expand into new markets, especially into supermarkets, as opportunities arose.

Phase III

In this phase previous strategies came under threat.

Significant environmental change occurred for two reasons. There was increased competition in the market, arising from Jordans's corporate strategy and that of other food companies. There was a dramatic increase in the size of the market, from about £8 million in 1984 to £50 million in 1988.

Manufacturers in related food lines realized the potential of the large market. Changes in attitudes were significant. For example, in 1978 Unichem (wholesalers for pharmacists) said that the market was not big enough. However, competition since 1980 has increased with the launch of new bars – from Quakers with 'Jump Bar' and Mars with 'Tracker Bar'. These products were heavily advertised.

Alpine Foods had a strategy of getting into supermarkets, which sell 60 per cent own-label goods. So Alpine Foods investigated the possibility of making for own-label products. There were difficulties with this, because the production conditions were not acceptable. To meet supermarkets' requirements would involve expensive modification of equipment, but with no guarantee of a contract.

By 1986 Alpine Foods was squeezed in its own market by new entrants and unable to move into an allied market – the production of own-label products – and profit margins were under pressure. It was anticipated that it would be entirely squeezed out of the market if these trends continued.

What happened?

In 1986 Wilson Kings, a flour miller based in Merseyside, sold part of its business to Spillers, which generated cash. A division of Wilson Kings was based in Warrington and produced wholemeal flour. This was scheduled for closure because a condition of the sale to Spillers was that this plant should not compete with Spillers. So the owners had a great deal of money and a plant they could not mill flour in. Wilson Kings already produced sugar-free jam for wholesale, using apple juice concentrate produced by Whole Earth ▷

which had a 70 per cent sugar content. Apple juice appeared on the label instead of sugar.

Wilson Kings asked Alpine Foods to make a sugar-free bar to sell to Whole Earth. The bar was not a success. Subsequently Wilson Kings made an offer for Alpine Foods' production process and this was moved into the redundant mill at Warrington. There is now an ability to produce own-label and own-product goods, and Alpine Foods is now a marketing company.

References

1 R. B. Robinson and J. A. Pearce, 'Research thrusts in small firm strategic planning', *Academy of Management Review*, 1984; January: 128.

2 Bolton Committee, *Report of the Committee of Enquiry on Small Firms*, Cmnd 4811. HMSO, London, 1971.

3 Wilson Committee, *Interim Report on the Financing of Small Firms*, Cmnd 7503. HMSO, London, 1979.

4 P. Ganguly, 'Business starts and stops: regional analysis by turnover size and sector 1980–83', *British Business*, 1984; **13**: 240–3.

5 D. Storey, 'Entrepreneurship and new firms', in *Applied Economics*, 2nd edn, Griffiths and Wall (eds). Longman, Harlow, 1986.

6 Economic Intelligence Unit, *The European Climate for Small Business. A 10-Country Study*. EIV, London, 1983.

7 A. Lydall, 'Aspects of competition in manufacturing industry', *Bulletin of the Oxford University Institute of Statistics*, 1958; **20**: 319–37.

8 A. Adams, 'Barriers to product innovation in small firms', *European Small Business Journal*, 1982; **1**: 67–86.

9 D. J. Storey, 'Small firms' policies: a critique', *Journal of General Management*, 1983; **8**: 5–19.

10 J. Curran and J. Stanworth, 'The spatial dynamics of the small manufacturing enterprise', *Journal of Management Studies*, 1981; **18**: 141–58.

11 G. Bannock, *The Economics of Small Firms*. Basil Blackwell, Oxford, 1981.

12 S. Birley and D. Norburn, 'Small vs. large companies: the entrepreneurial conundrum', *Journal of Business Strategy*, 1985; Summer: 81–7.

13 C. W. Golby and C. Johns, 'Attitude and motivation', *Bolton Committee Research Report No 7*, 1971.

14 M. F. R. Ket de Vries, 'The entrepreneurial personality: a person at the crossroads', *Journal of Management Studies*, 1977; **14**: 34–57.

15 G. K. Ingham, *Size of Industrial Organization and Worker Behaviour*. Cambridge University Press, Cambridge, 1970.

16 J. Curran and J. Stanworth, 'Worker involvement and social relations in the small firm', *The Sociological Review*, 1979; **27**: 317–42.

17 P. Burns and J. Dewhurst, *Small Business Finance and Control*. Macmillan, London, 1983.

18 P. Johnson, 'Policies towards small firms: time for caution', *Lloyds Bank Review*, 1978; July: 129.

19 J. S. Bracker and J. N. Pearson, 'Planning and financial performance of small mature firms', *Strategic Management Journal*, 1986; 503–22.

20 R. Ackelsberg and P. Arlow, 'Small businesses do plan and it pays off', *Long Range Planning*, 1985; October: 61–7.

21 C. Orpen, 'The effects of long range planning on small business performance: a further examination', *Journal of Small Business Management*, 1985; January.

22 S. P. Gallante, 'Counting on a narrow market can cloud a company's future', *Wall Street Journal*, 20 January 1986; 17.

23 H. Mintzberg, 'Strategy-making in three modes', *California Management Review*, 1973; Winter: 44–53.

24 R. B. Robinson and J. A. Pearce, 'The impact of formalized strategic planning on financial performance in small organizations', *Strategic Management Journal*, 1983; July–September: 97–207.

25 C. Y. Woo and A. C. Cooper, 'The surprising case for low market share', *Harvard Business Review*, 1982; November–December: 106–13.

26 J. C. Schuman, J. D. Shaw and G. Sussman, 'Strategic planning in smaller rapid growth companies', *Long Range Planning*, 1985; December: 48–53.

27 A. Gibb and J. Ritchie, 'Influences on entrepreneurship: a study over time', paper presented to the 1981 Small Business Policy Research Conference 20–21 November, Polytechnic of Central London.

28 R. I. Levin and V. R. Travis, 'Small company finance: what the books don't say', *Harvard Business Review*, 1987; December: 30–2.

7 Strategic Decision-Making – Defining the Strategic Problem

With a framework for decision analysis having been established, Chapters 7 to 9 apply the ideas to strategic decision-making within a business. First there is an examination of the nature of strategic decision-making (Chapter 7), then a discussion of environmental influences and the generation, analysis and evaluation of strategic information (Chapter 8). It is then explained how models can be used as tools to help in the choice part of the decision process.

The study of strategy begins, as in the decision process in Chapter 1, with objective-setting and problem diagnosis. The nature of the generic strategic problem and the issues it addresses have to be identified. This chapter surveys the divergent opinions about what strategy is and provides a framework that can reconcile these ideas.

The objectives of this chapter are to:

- show that adopting a rational reasoning approach facilitates the understanding of strategy;
- define strategy;
- identify the nature of strategic decision-making;
- classify types of strategic decisions;
- provide an integrated model of strategy.

The rational reasoning of strategic decision-making

The theory of strategy is defined by Mintzberg[1] as a 'field of study concerned with the management of the total organization with particular emphasis on its decisional behavior' (p. x). A major part of this has a very rational orientation towards the improvement of management decisions. As was explained in Chapter 2 an important task has been to develop and publicize the general models that are representative of or helpful to real management situations, for managers seeking to make successful situation-specific decisions and working in a world that allows only partial rationality.

In the main the theories and models of management strategy do not indicate preferred, rational, courses of action. Instead they are an aid to the process of strategic decision-making and act as sensitizing concepts – they indicate areas for thought and investigation in arriving at 'better' decisions. Rather than providing prescriptions of what to do or what to see, many of the models of management strategy 'merely suggest directions along which to look'.[2] The strategic decision-maker is usually left with the job of operationalizing these concepts in ways that fit and make better sense of his or her decision-making situation. Invariably, the strategist is left to perform the choice stage of the decision. Nevertheless, the use of models is vital to improved decision-making.

A major aim of the theory of management strategy is to stimulate a more systematic, model-underpinned approach to decision-making practice. As explained in Chapter 1, we are dealing with partial rationality. In this sense strategy-making is more to do with the achievement of the best outcome that is possible practically. It does this by providing insight and a good situational fit (as perceived by the decision-maker). Pre-prescribed objectives such as profit maximization are currently out of favour. Peter Drucker[3] speaks for many of today's strategic thinkers: 'The attempt to replace judgement by formula is always irrational' (pp. 82–3). Rationality, from theory's perspective, is less to do with decisional outcomes and more to do with the effectiveness of the types of decision processes identified in Chapter 1. 'Commitments to action' (Mintzberg's[1] definition of decisions) are thus assumed to be more rationally based (and hence more appropriate) if they are made by following the stages of the rational decision-making cycle. In the context of this rational decision-making, models of decision strategy are primarily concerned to:

- enhance the decision-maker's understanding of the decision to be made;
- give rise to useful decision-making information;
- stimulate creativity in the search for possible solutions to the problem(s) identified;
- aid the evaluation of alternative courses of action;
- help the strategist think through the problem of how to implement more effective activity.

What is strategy?

Problems over definitions of strategy

Glueck[4] has noted that 'Business Policy, Long Range Planning, Strategic Management are terms which may have as many definitions as there are experts' (p. 6), and other writers have discussed the lack of consensus over what strategy is. The multivariant nature of 'strategy' definitions reflects the nature of strategy-making itself. In practice strategies are created and implemented by their propagators to provide pertinent ways forward. Unique situations perceived by individual strategists produce unique strategies.

Given the plethora of strategy definitions and the customized nature of strategy-making, students of strategy should not be surprised to find that strategy teachers often dodge the question of what strategy is. Despite recent growth in MBA, business studies and in-house management development and consultancy type programmes of learning, each of which revolves around the concept of strategy, few students address the issue of how to define strategy.

Despite this vagueness an implicit assumption underlying the literature, study and practice of business is that business success is born from the design and implementation of effective strategy. If 'strategy' is a vague term then strategy-making is likely to be an imprecise *practice* – we should not assume that 'natural strategists' are able to recognize successful strategy when they see it despite having been unable to define it beforehand.

Towards a more explicit concept of strategy

A more explicit concept of strategy therefore provides a basis for more successful strategic management. This section of the book provides a contribution to the development of a clearer, more explicit concept of strategy. The view proposed is derived from and supported by a synthesis of the many different definitions and perspectives available in the theory of management strategy, including the growing body of strategy-in-practice case study literature, and is supported by our own experiences in a number of managerial and consulting strategy-making roles in a range of businesses and professions.

The series of propositions that follows, therefore, draws on this basis to provide a logically sequenced, interrelated and integrated framework for bringing together the many different models of what strategy is.

An integrated model of strategy

This model (see Figure 7.1) unifies writings in different branches of strategy. For each sector of the 'strategy wheel' there is a considerable literature – each part has its proponents. Accordingly, it is argued that the theory and practice of strategic decision-making are about the following things.

The organization as the fundamental strategy

Henry Mintzberg[1] and Igor Ansoff[5] support this view. Thus

> Individuals may also find it in their interests to share voluntarily common goals which are not intrinsically their own. The most obvious case of this is where the individuals benefit from the very existence of an organization – as

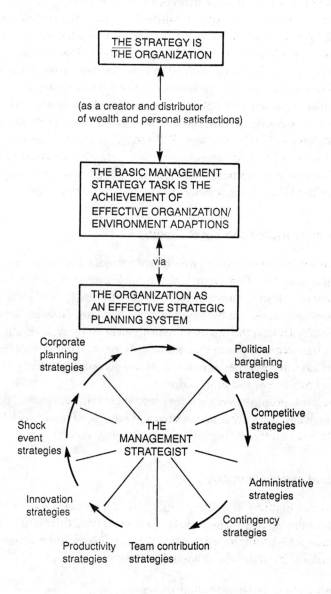

Figure 7.1   An integrated response to the question, 'So what is strategy?'

a system independent of what mission it happens to pursue (ref. 1, p. 610).
... The one goal all the players may share is the need for a common playing
field (ref. 1, p. 250).

For over one hundred years, the firm has been the principal and successful
instrument [strategy] of social progress . . . it [is] a breeder of wealth (ref. 5,
p. 139).

This basic proposition therefore sees strategy as being fundamentally concerned
with the achievement of successful organization as a mechanism for creating and
distributing wealth. This wealth sustains the organization and provides satisfaction to its people.

Effective adaptation by the organization to its environments over time

Quotations from Hofer and Schendel[6] and Harrison[7] support this proposition:
'Strategy is the basic characteristics of the match an organization achieves with its
environment (ref. 6, p. 10), and 'In essence the term strategic management refers
to the fit between the internal capabilities of a given organization and the attractive opportunities and significant threats in its external environment' (ref. 7, p. ix).
If the organization is to continue to act as a strategy for the fulfilment of personal
aspirations then it must continue to negotiate and create wealth from its changing
environments. The organization as a system unto itself will survive and grow
through efficient control of its wealth creating interactions with its environment.

The organization as a multi-decision-making system

A system of plans, decisions and actions is seen as the means for achieving
successful organization – environment adaptations. This view of strategy is
expressed by Andrews:[8] 'Corporate Strategy is the pattern of decisions in a
company that determines and reveals its objectives, purpose or goals, produces
the principal policies and plans for achieving those goals'. It is further supported
by Mintzberg[9] – 'Strategy is a pattern in a stream of decisions' (p. 936) – and by
Glueck[4] – 'Strategic planning involves all those sets of plans, decisions and actions
which lead to the development of an effective strategy' (p. 6). This view of
strategy provides a basis for theorists to express the functional orientation that
underpins management strategy. In the main they seek to help practising strategists to make 'better' plans and decisions. The strategist, of course, has the
responsibility for making better decisions (and for deciding, in each decisional
situation, what 'better' means). The theorist's role is to stimulate improved
decisional processes to facilitate better decisions.

Particular sets of plans for particular types of problems

The literature of management strategy can be categorized into attempts to help to
provide particular sets of plans to address particular types of problems. These are
responses to environmental changes and aim to promote better decisions by

paying greater attention to critical strategic decision-making problems as they arise or intensify. The study of management strategy, therefore, might proceed through a series of related sub-studies, shown on the wheel in Figure 7.1, which deal with particular problems or which view the strategy problem in a particular way. The subject has many areas, which are listed below.

1 The making of plans and decisions related to human aspirations (the design and implementation of political bargaining strategies). Ansoff[5] and Mintzberg[1] describe this view of strategy. 'If the firm is to play a more effective role in the shaping of its future (it must develop a societal strategy).... In bargaining processes, which involve mutual give and take ... the firm needs to formulate a bargaining strategy' (ref. 6, pp. 131–2). 'Strategic decisions of large organizations inevitably involve social as well as economic consequences, inextricably intertwined – and, thus the orientation of basic strategies to suit personal interests is the ultimate pay off, reserved for the most powerful of influencers' (ref. 1, p. 249). Theory and practice are here concerned with organizations as political arenas. They are about 'stakeholders' and the employment of effective political bargaining strategies to achieve beneficial exchanges.

2 The making of plans and decisions related to major longer-term organizational developments (corporate planning activities). Tom Cannon[10] expounds this view:

> The firm's strategy outlines broadly how management sees the firm achieving its overall objectives and goals. It emerges from an appraisal of the best way of taking the company forward to achieving these in a coherent way.... Once embarked upon, a particular strategy will establish the position of the firm in the market. It should lead clearly into specific tactics for execution (p. 58).

Kast and Rosenzweig[11] concur: 'Strategic planning involves management considering internal and environmental information in the process of establishing objectives and comprehensive planning. Plans are then transmitted to the operating system' (p. 101). This world of strategy-making is one of product/market-related developments, of systematic analysis and of anticipation of longer term future scenarios. It is a world of top–down management, corporate planners and systematic, sequential planning approaches. This model of strategy-making underpins a major approach to the study of strategy, but it currently provides an inappropriately large portion of the basis of the teaching of strategy. While this view of strategy may deserve a prominent position in the modern strategist's 'bag of tools' (and the next two chapters draw heavily from this branch of theory), it is considered that the generally accepted view of strategy-making is too exclusively rooted in the corporate planning approach. It is essential that it is recognized that a more holistic view of and approach to strategy is now called for.

3 The making of plans and decisions to enhance organizational competitive-

ness (via competitive strategies). Michael Porter is the most famous competitive strategy protagonist.[12, 13].

> Essentially, developing a competitive strategy is developing a broad formula for how a business is going to compete (ref. 12, p. xvi).
>
> Two central questions underline the choice of competitive strategy. The first is the attractiveness of industries for long term profitability. . . . The second central question in competitive strategy is the determinants of relative competitive position within an industry (ref. 13, pp. 2–3).

A major paradigm underpinning modern approaches to strategy-making equates greater competitive prowess with greater wealth-creating capability (usually expressed as profit). This paradigm is based on a 'Darwinian' notion of survival of the fittest.

4 The making of plans and decisions that take account of risk and uncertainty (contingency strategies). In changing environmental situations a major task for the strategist is the design of strategies that reduce or negate the potentially harmful effects of particular developments. Strategic writers like David Hussey[14] emphasize the importance of contingency planning:

> This key use of assumptions in strategy has further relevance in another area – contingency planning. However much work a company has put into its assumptions . . . there is still an element of uncertainty. In ideal circumstances every strategy should have a portfolio of alternative or contingency plans which can be swung into action in the event of the failure of an assumption (p. 61).

5 The making of effective administrative plans and decisions (administrative strategies). Associated with the corporate planning paradigm referred to in point 2 is the concept of the administration of product/market strategy from plan to action, through the sequencing, scheduling, motivation and control of activity down through the organization's structure via a hierarchical ends–means chain. Vancil and Lorange[15] provide a quotation that is representative of those available from the body of theory that adopts this view of strategy making: 'Strategic thinking and the resultant strategy formulation occurs at three levels in the organization. These levels are corporate, business and functional.'

6 The making of plans and decisions for the creation of organization-wide team effort and of ongoing incremental contributions by all personnel to the organization's task of incremental adaptation (team contribution strategies). The importance of culture was emphasized in Chapter 3. As environments become more and more dynamic, turbulent and competitively hostile, so too the team culture paradigm is growing. A major strategy for getting ahead of the competition today is the harnessing of 'people power'. Tom Peters, for example, says[16] 'Executing the business strategies . . . means we must: involve all personnel at all levels in all functions in virtually everything [and] be guided by the axiom "There

are no limits to the ability to contribute on the part of a properly selected, well trained, appropriately supported, and, above all, committed person"' (p. 284). Gareth Morgan makes a similar call:[17]

> Much of the literature on corporate planning and strategy formulation uses the basic metaphor in this way, viewing the process of strategic management and control as equivalent to the brain and nervous system of an organisation. In contrast it is far less common to think about organisations *as if they were brains,* and to see if we can create new forms of organisation that disperse brain like capacities throughout an enterprise, rather than just confine them to special units or parts. This is the challenge for the future (p. 79).

7 The making of plans and decisions designed to improve significantly the wealth-producing productivity performance of the organization (productivity strategies). The view of strategy expressed in this chapter is founded firmly on the notion of the organization as a wealth breeder. One major function of each of the planning activities described above, therefore, is wealth creation. Team culture planning, for example, is predominantly concerned with the management of people and their indoctrination in the idea of achieving incremental improvements on an ongoing, daily basis. However, the management literature also contains a body of work more concerned with the achievement of management-inspired, large productivity improvements. This provides a more systematic, quantitatively orientated and assisted approach to strategy-making. Turn-of-the-century productivity planners, such as Frederick Taylor with his 'scientific management' methods, have their modern counterparts. Paul Mali[18] is one:

> The era of the casual manager who uses trial and error methods until the work is completed began disappearing about a decade ago. Casual performance results in a waste of resources, heavy expenditure of time, and low levels of performance. To compete in the 1980s and on into the future, efficiency processes that accomplish productivity gains are needed. (p. 286) ... We've moved into an era in which productivity must clearly and deliberately define the results wanted, allocate carefully the resources needed, set up effective and efficient work processes, and provide the day to day surveillance and control needed for accomplishment of the intended results. We've moved into an era in which productivity must be managed. (p. 255)

This 'major productivity drive' aspect of strategy theory assists practising strategists in their searches for cost-saving and benefit-increasing opportunities.

8 The making of plans and decisions to enhance creativity and innovation (innovation strategies). No longer, it seems, can organizations rest on their past laurels content to employ traditionally proven ways of organizing. The innovation planning perspective of strategy is growing and emphasizes with increasing strength and vigour the importance to strategic success of doing new things

(evolutionarily or revolutionarily). Theorists and practitioners working in this area of strategy seek to improve organizational creativity (thinking up new product and process ideas), and innovation (putting new ideas, successfully, into practice). John and Snelson[19] are just two of the researchers providing inputs into this aspect of strategy making: 'In fact, only a small number of British and American companies practice state-of-the-art product innovation.... Leading product innovators – at present clustered in the electronics industry . . . pursue a balanced product innovation strategy.'

9 The making of plans and decisions to anticipate what might otherwise have been major shocks or surprise opportunities and to respond effectively to them when they happen (shock event/sudden opportunity strategies). This shock event planning element of 'complete strategy' has only recently emerged into main-stream strategic thinking. It is evolving in response to what is seen to be a growing incidence of Bhopal, Chernobyl and Hillsborough type disasters. Theorists and practitioners are paying attention to the problem of how to plan for the unplannable. Ian Mitroff,[20] in seeking a rational approach to the minimization of the shock events problem, asserts: 'The principles governing crisis manage-ment resemble those applicable to other strategic planning activities.'

The above discussion portrays strategy as being about the theory and practice of:

(a) Organization in its role as a breeder and distributor of wealth and a fulfiller of personal aspirations.
(b) The achievement of effective adaptations of the organization to its environ-ment – the placing or maintenance of organization in a wealth-producing position.
(c) The achievement of (a) and (b) through the making of effective plans, decisions and actions in a range of critical problem areas and/or from a range of different 'planning strategy' perspectives – the achievement of organization as a productive decision-making process.

It also provides a basis for a more integrated and holistic approach than is pres-ently generally employed for the teaching and practising of management strat-egy. This model of strategy-making is presented pictorially in Figure 7.1. Note how the management strategist (practitioner, consultant, teacher, researcher or writer) has been placed in the middle of 'the organization as a strategic planning system'. It is he or she who works in, with and around the components of this 'what is strategy?' framework. Student and practitioner readers should by now have picked up a key message of this book. Success is born from better decisions. The theory of management strategy helps us to achieve better decisions. Princi-pally, it does this by guiding us towards, and through, more effective decision-making processes.

The nature of strategic decision-making

The model of 'what strategy is' put forward in this chapter is author-specific but it is not dissimilar to views expressed by other writers.[21-23] Placed in a wider setting, the 'what strategy is' model fits into a generally prevailing perception of strategic decision-making, as described by Harrison.[7] Thus, the model illustrated in Figure 7.1 fits into a view of strategy-making as having many aspects. According to this view, strategy-making is evolving – the underlying theory and practice are in a constant state of flux and development. It is eclectic, being based on and using knowledge from a range of disciplines. It is generic, applying to all types of organizations. It is both global (it regards an organization as a sub-system of a larger system, namely the external environment) and holistic (concerned with the management of total systems, or complete sub-systems). It is synergistic (it creates additional wealth). Often it is unstructured, but it is purposeful in that it is concerned with the achievement of objectives and the resolution of problems. Despite this chapter's very prescriptive approach to the question of 'what is strategy?', management strategy will remain a user-specific or situation-specific concept. Readers are thus invited to use the model here (to debate, modify, reject or replace it) as a springboard towards a clearer understanding and articulation of their own preferred model(s) of strategy.

Linear sequential and incremental adaptive strategic decisions

Words like holistic, global, rational and unstructured describe strategic decision-making. These terms point to a picture of strategy-making that has top managers making major resource-committing decisions that shape the long-term destiny of their organizations. The traditional view of strategic decision-making takes this perspective. Top managers are seen to deliberate with their corporate planner specialists over resource strengths and weaknesses, environmental opportunities and threats, and product/market and financial objectives. Once the big decisions are made they are formulated into more specific objectives and more structured tasks for the administrative and operating hierarchies of the organization to perform. Vancil and Lorange express this view of strategy-making. Chaffee[24] describes it as the linear sequential model. Figure 7.2 illustrates the linear sequential approach to strategy. Typically this model emphasizes:

- major 'one-off' developments;
- extended futures;
- anticipation of future situations;
- top management positions and inputs;
- the importance of organization owners;

- corporate planning specialists;
- top-down, linear sequences of plans and activities;
- a separation of planning and doing.

The model is clear and unambiguous. 'A strategic decision ... is substantially different from an operational or administrative decision. This is the outcome of a way of thinking rather than an application of decision rules' (ref. 25, p. 78). 'Strategic decision making is about the determination of the basic long term goals of an enterprise and the adoption of courses of action and the allocation of resources necessary for carrying out these goals' (ref. 26, p. 5).

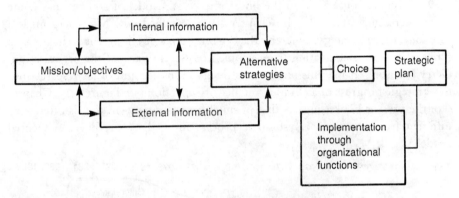

Figure 7.2   The linear sequential approach to strategy-making.

How the linear sequential model is actually operationalized into decision-making behaviour varies from firm to firm. Goold and Campbell,[27] for example, report how large, diverse British organizations adopt one of three types of linear sequential planning styles depending upon the corporate centre's basic business philosophy (see Table 7.1). *Strategic planners*, such as BOC, BP, Cadbury Schweppes and Lex Service, use a style that has the corporate centre participating in and influencing business unit strategy. *Strategic control* companies believe in greater autonomy for business unit managers. Unit plans are reviewed by the centre but the centre does not become involved in advocating business strategies. Control is maintained by the use of financial targets and strategic objectives, which are agreed by the centre. Companies operating in this mode of linear sequential decision-making include Courtaulds, ICI, Imperial Group, Plessey and Vickers. *Financial control* companies, such as BTR, GEC, Hanson Trust and Tarmac, do not use long-term planning systems or strategy documents. Here control is maintained by approving budgets and investments, setting targets and monitoring performance. This form approximates to the management approach identified in Chapter 3 as the 'M form'. The model examined in that chapter shows how this form of control can operate.

Table 7.1 Three types of linear sequential strategic decision-making

Core business philosophy	Diverse business philosophy	Manageable business philosophy
Strategic planning	Strategic control	Financial control
Centre participates in, and influences business unit strategies, requires demanding planning processes; flexible targets set and reviewed in context of long-term progress	Requires demanding planning processes but focuses on reviews and critiques of proposal rather than influencing, initially; tight control of strategic and financial objectives	Primarily control organizations; centre sanctions expenditure, monitors financial performance against annual targets

Over the past decade or so the linear sequential model of strategy has come under increasing attack.[28–33] In Chapter 1 we described how Mintzberg made a case for *emergent* strategy, whereby the organization's development is shaped by a series of decisions emanating from people in different parts of the organization. Gerry Johnson[34] paints this picture of strategy in his account of his research into the strategic progress of a clothing retailer organization (see Figure 7.3). Chapter 6 of the present book suggests that in small firms strategy-making is often very different from the formal systematic process implied by the linear sequential model.

1960s 1970 1971 1972 1973 1974 1975 1976 1977 1978 1979 1980 1981 1982 1983

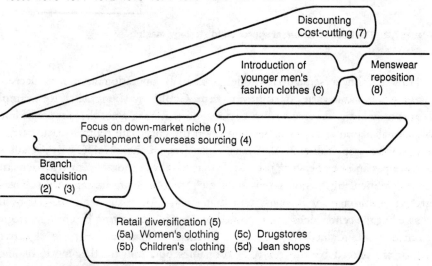

Figure 7.3 Emergent strategy at a clothing retailer.
Source: G. Johnson, 'Re-thinking incrementalism', *Strategic Management Journal*, 1988; **9**: 75–91.

Bill and Roy Richardson[35] refer to the 'strategic shortcomings of systematic corporate planning' (pp. 165–6) (see Table 7.2) and infer that the linear sequential approach to strategy-making might be the exception rather than the rule. Along-side these criticisms of the linear sequential approach new models of the strategy-making process have been developed. The adaptive and interpretive models of strategic decision-making[24] have now joined the linear sequential model to provide supplementary and complementary views of how strategy-making takes place. These newer models emphasize:

- openness of the organization and its environment to each other;
- organization changes to fit environmental changes;
- continuing adaptations;
- complex strategic decision-making;
- a range of stakeholders and political activities;
- social contracts between stakeholders;
- mutually beneficial exchanges;
- wider distribution of planning and of contributions to strategy;
- motivation stimulation, culture creation and perception modification.

Just as the conclusion of Chapter 4 was that aspects of design should fit together and be consistent with each other to provide a holistic approach, so too these newer models of strategic decision-making emphasize the creation of 'all-round organization fit'. Strategists are advised to redesign their organizations so that all aspects of their systems are internally harmonious and collectively congruent with the nature and demands of the organization's environment. In this way the organization gets ahead through being effective across a multitude of ongoing decision-making processes, which collectively and incrementally adapt it to its changing environment (which the organization itself helps to shape (see Figure 7.4).

The linear sequential style of strategic decision-making most readily 'smacks of rationality'. However, it is important to understand that the theory of management strategy contains contributions designed to make us more rational and effective linear sequential planners and also contains contributions more concerned to enhance our effectiveness as incrementally adaptive planners.

Conclusion

In this chapter it has been emphasized that help is available from theory for the generation of more rationally processed management decisions. It is important to understand that even the sternest of the critics of the 'rational approach' are not criticizing rationality itself. Rather, these critics attempt to make us question decision-making processes that are based on the irrational assumptions that formulas can replace judgement and that a quantitative approach to strategy-making should always be feasible and is always preferable. Peters and Waterman[32] are arguing the case *for* rationality when they say, 'Above all, we deplore the unfortunate abuse of the term "rational". Rational means sensible, logical, reasonable, a conclusion flowing from a correct statement of the problem. But

Table 7.2   Strategic shortcomings of systematic corporate planning

Corporate planning perspective offers:	Environment requires:	Example
Strategic creativity as a top management and specialist planner function	People at all levels get involved in the strategic process; the environment calls only for somebody to make decisions and take action	Sensing and communicating strategic information, e.g. the buying department clerk who is the first to spot a major supplier bankruptcy or the sales assistant who is the first to hear about a competitor price or product change

Contributing operational knowledge and expertise to the decision-making process

Creating strategy through action (e.g. the enterprising sales rep who, against the odds, captures an important new customer) |
The primacy of shareholder/owner objectives	Attention to the range of stakeholders and continuous stakeholder ranking order changes	Note the potentially adverse effect on customers' (and hence owners') interests from a dissatisfied workforce
Clear, precise, objectives to provide a blueprint for future actions	Broader, long-term objectives that allow for flexibility in achievement and quickly made, subjectively decided and expressed responses	Much 'merger mania'-type decision-making made 'off the cuff' but related to broader, long-term power, profitability and security objectives
Major 'one-off' decisions	Experimentation and modifications to ideas and plans. 'Bet hedging' and contingency planning	Trial and error pilot tests in sample stores before decisions on mass production/distribution of a new product
Mid- to long-term resource commitment project	Many short-term developments	Consider, for example, the new product innovation record of the IT industry
Clean sheet into the future	Modified approaches moulded in the light of the recipes, values and power structure in and around the organization	The difficulties encountered in the 1980s by Fleet Street strategists in the implementation of preferred strategic developments
Separation of planning from doing and the sequential nature of doing following planning systematically	Many planning/doing on-the-spot decisions/actions, the involvement of doers in planning and the iterative interaction as plans are tested, checked and reconsidered/modified	On-the-spot negotiations with customers

Quality circles

Re-modifications of products based on post-launch monitorings |

Table 7.2   Strategic shortcomings of systematic corporate planning (*continued*)

Corporate planning perspective offers	Environment requires	Example
Projection into the future via the use of formal, often quantitatively based, computerized planning models	Incremental adaptation, often necessitating 'gut feeling' subjectivism	The everyday business of organization
		Research findings, which suggest that many firms do not plan formally
		The requirement for major fashion retailers to anticipate next year's fashion trends

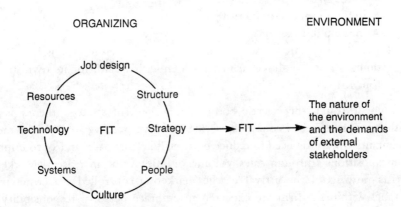

Figure 7.4   The organizing fit relationship.

rational has come to have a very narrow definition in business analysis. It is the right answer, but it's missing all of that messy human stuff' (p. 31). Paradoxically (at face value), by providing us with models to help us take better account of 'all of that messy human stuff' the anti-rationalists are actually seeking to help us to achieve greater rationality in organizational problem-solving.

What is the strategic problem that the theorists seek to help us solve? When help is given in an investment appraisal situation, for the solving of a workforce motivational problem or in a decision on which markets to serve, what underlying problem is being addressed? The answer to this question is wealth creation. Practitioners and theorists alike are ultimately concerned with organizational success – and this demands the capability of the organization to adapt to its environments through time. In turn this process, for profit-making and 'not for profit' organizations alike, requires that the organization generates more wealth than it consumes. Igor Ansoff[5] describes the fundamental 'wealth breeding' rationale for organizations:

For over one hundred years, the firm has been the principal and successful instrument of social progress. . . . In recent years much interest has been excited by the atomic breeder reactor which appears to violate the law of conservation of energy by producing more fuel than it consumes. But the firm, an invention of the mid-19th century, was a similar breeder 'reactor' except that instead of breeding fuel, it was a breeder of wealth. . . . It has several impressive features:

1 It generates both goods and the buying power for the goods.
2 It supports the expansion of the social infrastructure, and provides a return to the investors [and 'investors' can be interpreted to mean all stakeholders who contribute to the organization].
3 It creates jobs in three ways
   • in the firm itself
   • in the suppliers to the firm
   • in the public sector.
4 But the most impressive feature of this breeder reactor is that, while doing all of the above, it generates enough wealth for its own growth (pp. 131–2).

Running through the eclectic body of management strategy theory is this wealth-creating theme. Economists seek to achieve positive benefit/cost ratios. Accountants talk of the need to reduce bottom-line (cost base) and/or to improve top-line positions (through sales volume or sales value increases). Marketing theorists now extol the arrival of the marketing-controlled era (wherein all personnel within the firm are expected to embrace personal responsibility for improving their contributions to customer satisfaction *and* profitability).[36] Competitive theorists advocate least-cost producer positions and/or focused, differentiated market positions for the gaining of competitive advantage (which in turn has been defined as the ability to earn above industry average profits).[13] Political theorists talk of the organization's own-systems goals of efficiency and control of the environment.[1] Practitioner Marcus Sieff demonstrates his central concern of managing a wealth-creating enterprise:[37] 'Last year we spent £57 million on welfare benefits. . . . Of course, everyone must understand that none of this can happen unless the company is profitable, that without profits there cannot be progress.' Figure 7.5 provides a pictorial representation of the wealth-producing prescriptions of management strategy.

Thus, while profit maximization might be out of fashion in management strategy circles the pursuit of wealth for the organization and for its people does take prime position as the fundamental strategic problem to be addressed. If the organization fails to be a wealth breeder then it fails to survive and for one eminent strategist, at least, 'it is the first duty of a business to survive' (ref. 3, p. 50). If the organization fails to create wealth then it cannot grow and its people cannot expect any opportunity of receiving from it an improving personal wealth package.

The next chapters demonstrate how some of the models of management

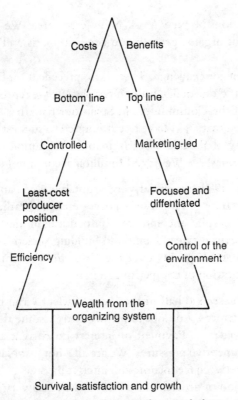

Figure 7.5   Management strategy's productive growth prescriptions.

strategy can be used to stimulate more rationally derived decisions to solve what are, ultimately, 'wealth breeding' problems.

Case study 7
An interview with Lord Alexander and Tom Frost of National Westminster Bank

Question: How do you see the National Westminster in the context of the global financial services business?

Responses: Essentially building from where our core strengths lie. Our principal strengths are mainly in the UK: in retail franchise with its 3100 branches; and our corporate banking. From there we see ourselves increasingly developing services in this country which . . . were not always linked with the conventional high street banks . . . by way of example, not by way of priority – mortgages, insurance advice, stockbroking and our role as a savings institution. Outside this country we believe that business in the north-east US is a very strong asset. It is extremely well managed and ▷

highly regarded in the New York/New Jersey area. We foresee expansion by a mixture of organic growth and acquisition, as and when the opportunity arises.

Europe is a major challenge. There is no precedent for the enlargement of the UK market to one of 320 million people. We are represented in 10 of the 12 countries of the Community. In Spain our bank has 183 branches. We hope to build on that. . . . I have not attempted to suggest that we are going to seek to be a global bank . . . each financial institution is going to have to choose its priorities. . . . We have 14 million account holders, worldwide.

Question: In the 1980s the underlying profitability of banking – the rate of return on assets/rate of return on equity – increased rather than decreased. This occurred despite the intense competition in the financial services sector, particularly between banks and building societies. How do you see the outlook for bank profits over the 1990s in what must be a period of further intensification of competitive pressures?

Responses: In the second half of the 1980s efficiently run banks managed to improve their returns. I do not think any of us assume this will be the case during this decade. . . . Payment of interest on current accounts is a clear example of competitive pressures. We are all – not just NatWest – hoping to alter the ratio between fee income and interest income. . . . There will not be as strong a period of growth . . . the 1990s will be a very challenging time. . . . There are lots of opportunities. We are not at the top of the cycle. The prosperity of the 1980s is going to stay. Individuals still want to borrow; companies to invest. . . . One can move down the high street and see the number of players. The weak will be exposed and the strong will gain the competitive advantage that they thought they were building up in the 1980s. . . . Profitability is there providing it is profitability you are after and not size. . . . We shall need to choose where we fight in that battle. . . . Banks are increasingly customer-driven . . . good institutions have built their profitability as well as giving the customer a better service. That is a very positive development for the community generally. . . . Profitability with growth. Going forward, but not hell for leather with size as the king.

Question: What can be done to make it cheaper for the small private investor to buy and sell securities?

Responses: We have more small investors than ever before in this country but, following Big Bang, the percentage of shares held by small investors has dropped sharply. . . . The market is there. We pioneered the touchscreen system which we now have in 270 branches. That makes dealing easily accessible and payment easy. NatWest Stockbrokers now has 7 per cent of all equity transactions on the international stock exchange. . . . The introduction of Taurus will also be important. Once the first fright of not getting ▷

a piece of paper that can be deposited in your bank has worn off, and a computerized record is substituted, people will realize that dealing is not so difficult. . . . We need more volume . . . screen-based facilities is a great incentive. . . . If you go to a branch, touch a screen and receive instant confirmation of an investment . . . people will say: 'I can hold it the way that I can hold property or a piece of silver'. . . . You have to have surplus income, too; and a propensity to invest.

Question: Will personal sector lending growth of the 1980s be sustained in the 1990s?

Responses: In the 1980s . . . the personal side of the balance sheet had probably gone from something like 17 or 18 per cent to just over 25 per cent. A lot of that was . . . mortgage business – £7.5 billion. . . . We would like more mortgage lending on our books . . . because of the profitability over time and the 'locking' in of the private customer. It is a very good cross-selling opportunity. It will grow. I am not sure that the total market will grow at the same rate . . . we would like our share to grow greater than the market might grow. . . . We are strongly committed towards prudential policy in lending and advertising.

Question: Your distribution system. Can you expand that beyond just offering shares . . .?

Responses: Mortgages, pensions, insurance . . . the range of services associated with people's financial needs, in which we can offer expertise. . . . You could characterize it as one-stop financial services. Phrases like that can be used too glibly. You cannot offer expertise in all areas in every single branch. That would detract from specialization. We are seeking to provide increased specialization as we have more sophisticated consumers. . . . The key is access to all our services – some 300 of them. It has to be done on a cost effective basis. Technology is the key . . . instant quote for a best-value life policy. We can do that now through more than 1000 of our terminals. . . . I am sure that if you have a property between Marks & Spencer and John Lewis, then if you do not make money out of it, there is something wrong with you. I do not think that everything is going to be done at home for a long, long time.

Question: What are the major opportunities for the UK clearing banks in the 1990s?

Responses: The main opportunity is to give leverage to our strengths which are immense. . . . We can use ourselves as a base for Europe – to take advantage of that tremendous market. We can exploit our competitive advantages . . . our major technology investment with which no one else can compete. . . . There is our relative market share. Somebody has to come ▷

and get it. . . . Capital is king. Under the BIS rules and the new level playing field that is emerging, we are strong in terms of capital. We have the people. We spend £60 million a year training our people. I do not know any other bank in the world that can say that. There is also our historic position and customer base . . . a tremendous strength – a base for fending off European competition and for launching further into Europe. . . . Home banking is in its infancy but 10 years ago credit cards were in their infancy. . . . In general, the use of technology to assist people is something which will increase. Getting the technology right, as well as judging where people will want the technological benefit, is the key to success . . . we have committed over £1 billion to technology over the next five years. The more one can use technology for mechanistic processes, the more one can free staff to create relationships . . . the concepts of small business advisers, and business centres. Banks seek to get closer to their customers; to understand their needs; build better relationships. . . . I firmly believe there are further opportunities for deepening relationship banking over the next decade. It will not only be profitable but satisfying. . . . NatWest is a relationship banker not a transactional banker . . . others do that well. . . . Probably, too, there will be an increase in the number of people who prefer taking cash from ATMs. Some 65 per cent of cash now goes that way. . . . The cost base is undoubtedly a key challenge. I do not regard it as an opportunity, I regard it as a necessity. Fortunately, we do not have to make the sort of pruning that would destroy our income base. We have to cut costs without, in any way, damaging the service we give. . . . It has to be the lowest-cost producer that comes through at the end of the day. That is purely textbook stuff. We are unbundling all the time; we are segmenting our markets and we know our cost profiles better. Nothing can hide under stones.

Question: Your strategy on North American regional banking appears to be on hold . . .?

Responses: We have our strategy. We are talking about tactics and timings. The strategy is to build a super regional bank . . . in the north-eastern states of America. That is on line. Nothing has altered. What has happened in the past year or so is that there is a little bit of heat in the economy, and in New Jersey it is a little bit hot. It is controlled. It is looked after by a very good management team that we have in North America. They are Americans running the American bank. . . . We have been successful so far. We . . . feel very comfortable in using our present management team to make proper acquisitions in North America which will be in their market area or adjacent thereto, and we shall not be going beyond that. It is a question of when, there is no rush; no push. It is quite encouraging. We are getting £129 million pre problem-country debt profit from Bancorp. If you add together ▷

NatWest's wholesale profits in North America, it comes out at about £180 million at the bottom line, which is where we set out to be 11 years ago.

Question: What opportunities do you see for the major clearing banks ... following the recent political changes across ... eastern Europe?

Responses: It is one thing to welcome the political changes on a personal level; it is another in terms of commercial and investment decisions. ... I do not see immediate scope for a massive, broad-scale assault by a bank from this country. East Germany is likely to have an economic recovery of a different order from the rest of Eastern Europe. ... That is recognized by the German banks who are going back to eastern Germany – Deutsche Bank, Dresdner and Commerzbank. It does not necessarily raise good opportunities for western banks outside Germany.

Question: Has the balance between competition and cooperation in the development of the UK payment systems swung too far towards competition ...?

Responses: Of any country in the world the payment system we have here is probably as near to being right as we can make it. Our history is one of cooperation; and this is why we have the best system in the world. ... There have to be standards when dealing with so much paper. ... If there is competition, I suppose it is: can you meet the required standards? if not you cannot be part of the team. ... The feeling among some is that the smaller, newer players should come in on the same basis as the established clearing banks. It does not work just like that. ... I think we get together better than anybody I know.

Question: Are there international economies of scale which can arise?

Responses: I doubt there will be pan-European retail banks and I doubt the idea of international economies of scale. There may be a situation where, because of its competitive skills, a bank from a particular country can successfully manage a bank in another country. ... You will not get real economies of scale until you can get the processing done in one point in the world ... (say) Iceland for everywhere in the world. No doubt that will come. It will be electronically based.

Question: Banking is a mature industry. ... The UK is clearly a limitation on your growth?

Responses: I do not believe it is a mature industry. Elements of it are: if you want to borrow £10 there is not much new about that. But with product definition and the availability of distribution systems you have a young industry at the cash point or on the telephone. ... Our bank has 14 million customers. That is mind-blowing if you think of it in a marketing sense – to ▷

find out what your customer wants and to know that you are going to make a profit out of it. You have the power – this is the most exciting thing about it.

Question: What has been the thinking at NatWest on the issue of student loans and the banks?

Responses: Quite simply we had to look at our valuable commercial relationships, our ultimate accountability to our shareholders. We have a very large share of the student market. We have a very large number of branches on campus built up over many years. Clearly we had to take account of the weight of opinion that was directed against the scheme.

Question: What positive steps can banks take on environmental issues?

Responses: There is what we do internally: at NatWest we have unleaded petrol in our cars; we conserve energy in our rooms; we seek to recycle paper; and we seek to maximize the use of waste paper. We have to be careful about the use of CFCs in air conditioning. . . . In terms of our business approach it can operate in terms of public opinion. . . . We see some banks standing back from projects that might, for example, cause deforestation in South America. . . . In environmentally developed countries . . . a bank will have to take into account regulations (when evaluating projects). . . . What can a bank do? It can do a great deal. It should join the Tidy Britain group with me and sponsor 1990, which is Tidy Britain Year.

Question: With so many rapid changes in technology and other aspects of the banking environment, how will you ensure that your staff update their knowledge and skills?

Responses: It depends on constantly keeping our training courses under review to make certain that what we offer matches need. . . . Where increased technology frees people for more sophisticated relationship banking, we must make certain that they get the training. . . . We have 17 000 staff who received off-job training in the past year. . . . This is linked to demographic changes. If you want the best people, you will have to offer attractive packages – not just in remuneration, but opportunities for self-development . . . we have taken positive action to enable women to return to work . . . we are looking more and more to the possibility of part-time staff. We have 7000-plus part-time employees at the moment.

Question: What is the effect of retail strategies on older members of staff who are having to change their traditional approach to customers?

Responses: Most people realize that changes have to be made and they have contributed positively towards them. . . . Clearly, where appropriate we have to be flexible in our retirement policies. . . . Performance-related ▷

reward system is undoubtedly a very helpful catalyst.... I do not think that sensible cost control prevents you motivating staff ... banking is a much more exciting job than it used to be ... getting into the market, as do corporate business advisers, to meet clients, means they are engaged in the very positive act of giving customer service ... staff are fiercely loyal and dedicated to the success of the organization.... Equally, when you are asking more of staff in terms of customer relationships ... it is not unreasonable to reward them, as we are increasingly doing, on an incentive, performance-related basis.... We try to involve people in the business.... We train people, challenge them, and respect them.... Involvement is fairly new, I suppose, although the good manager always did it. We have the biggest quality action programme that has ever been done in Europe. ... We divide staff into quality service action teams, in which they say how they can serve the customer better. They run these themselves.... Thousands of ideas have already been put into effect – even things like moving a mat six inches to stop people from tripping up.... Some 7000 management cadres and the appointed staff on top of that – perhaps another 10 000 to 11 000 – will have the potential to share in the profits of the business in proportion to their input as defined by their bosses and if performance exceeds the broad objectives of the bank then, depending on seniority, they can get bonuses of up to 10, 15 or 20 per cent.... I am currently travelling the country speaking to the managers – at 30 meetings. Now part of income is at risk through performance and commitment to the business. It is not just that there is prospect of more money, but the realization that they can help influence the future. And that goes for all our staff. It is very exciting. It is like electricity going through the place.

Source: Adapted with permission from *Banking World*, 1990: June: 24–33.

Notes and References

1 H. Mintzberg, *Power in and around Organizations*. Prentice-Hall, Englewood Cliffs, NJ, 1983.
2 See M. Bulmer (ed.), *Sociological Research Methods: An Introduction*, 2nd edn. Macmillan, London, 1984, for a discussion on sensitizing and definitive concepts.
3 P. F. Drucker, *The Practice of Management*. Pan Books, London, 1968.
4 W. F. Glueck, *Business Policy: Strategy Formation and Management Action*. McGraw-Hill, New York, 1976.
5 H. I. Ansoff, *Implementing Strategic Management*. Prentice-Hall, Englewood Cliffs, NJ, 1984.
6 C. W. Hofer and D. Schendel, *Strategy Formulation: Analytical Concepts*. West Publishing, St Paul, MN, 1978.
7 E. F. Harrison, *Policy, Strategy and Management Action*. Houghton Mifflin, Boston, MA, 1986.

8 J. G. Smith, *Business Strategy: An Introduction*. Blackwell, Oxford, 1985, p. 10, quoting K. R. Andrews, *The Concept of Corporate Strategy*. Richard D. Irwin, Homewood, IL, 1978.

9 H. Mintzberg, 'Patterns in strategy formation', *Management Science*, 1978: 934–48.

10 T. Cannon, *How to Win Profitable Business*. Sunday Telegraph Books, London, 1984.

11 F. E. Kast and J. E. Rosenzweig, *Organization and Management*, 4th edn. McGraw-Hill, New York, 1985.

12 M. Porter, *Competitive Strategy*. Free Press, New York, 1980.

13 M. Porter, *Competitive Advantage*. Free Press, New York, 1985.

14 D. E. Hussey, *Corporate Planning: Theory and Practice*, 2nd edn. Pergamon, Oxford, 1984.

15 R. F. Vancil and P. Lorange, 'Strategic planning in diversified companies', *Harvard Business Review*, 1975; **53**: 81–90.

16 T. J. Peters, *Thriving on Chaos*. Macmillan, London, 1988.

17 G. Morgan, *Images of Organisation*. Sage, London, 1986.

18 P. Mali, *MBO Updated*. Wiley Interscience, New York, 1986.

19 A. John and P. Snelson, 'Innovate or die', *Management Today*, 1987; November: 133–8.

20 I. I. Mitroff, 'Crisis management: cutting through the confusion', *Sloan Management Review*, 1988; Winter: 15–20.

21 H. I. Ansoff (6), for example, traces the evolution of 'what strategy is' and uses his book to consider 'how to do' different types of strategic planning.

22 G. Margon (18) provides a synthesis of management strategy metaphors.

23 H. Mintzberg is currently working his way through 'what strategy is' via his collection of volumes on the theory of management policy.

24 E. E. Chaffee, 'Three models of strategy', *Academy of Management Review*, 1985; **10**: 1.

25 S. S. Mathur, 'Strategy: framing business intentions', *Journal of General Management*, 1986; **12**: 1.

26 A. Chandler, *Strategy and Structure*. MIT Press, Boston, MA, 1962.

27 M. Goold and G. Campbell, 'Managing diversity: strategy and control in diversified British companies', *Long Range Planning*, 1987; **20**(5): 42–52.

28 C. Stubbart, 'Why we need a revolution in strategic planning', *Long Range Planning*, 1985; **18**(6): 68–76.

29 R. V. Emmerson, 'Corporate planning. A need to examine corporate style', *Long Range Planning*, 1985; **18**(6): 29–33.

30 J. Robinson, 'Paradoxes in planning', *Long Range Planning*, 1986; **19**(6): 21–4.

31 M. A. Carpenter, 'Planning vs strategy – which will win?', *Long Range Planning*, 1986; **19**(6): 50–3.

32 T. J. Peters and R. H. Waterman Jr, 'The rational model', in *In Search of Excellence*, Harper & Row, New York: Chapter 2.

33 H. Mintzberg, 'Planning on the left side and managing on the right', *Harvard Business Review*, 1976; July–August: 49–61.

34 G. Johnson, 'Rethinking incrementalism', *Strategic Management Journal*, 1988; **9**(1): 75–91.

35 W. Richardson and R. Richardson, *Business Planning: An Approach to Strategic Management*. Pitman, London, 1989.

36 See, for example, T. Gardener, P. Feeney and P. Molyneau, 'Strategic marketing', *Banking World*, 1987; October: 12–15.

37 M. Sieff, Gold medal award acceptance speech, British Institute of Management, London, 1984.

8 Strategic Decision-Making – Gathering and Analysing Information

We have emphasized the importance of the development of a holistic view of strategic decision-making and the essential role that adopting a rational approach takes. This chapter now uses the linear sequential view of decision-making as an organizing framework for the development of such an approach. The objectives of this chapter are to:

- introduce models for the generation of information for situational analysis;
- demonstrate how these models improve the information-gathering and analysis stage of the strategic problem-solving process.

The corporate planning view of strategic decision-making

In order to set the context for what follows readers are reminded of the nature of corporate planning. Two quotations will help:

> Strategy is an explicitly rational type of management process which stresses the long term future and the external environment. The focus is firmly on analytical approaches. . . . The approach stresses getting the strategy right first because it determines appropriate structure and systems.[1]

> Random planning activity is similar to buying a Lottery ticket. . . . The only way to compete successfully is through a sound qualitative strategic planning sequence that begins with a rigorous environmental evaluation, continues with an internal source assessment, and concludes with the selection of the appropriate generic strategy.[2]

This view of strategy-making is encapsulated in Figure 8.1. It portrays a systematic and sequential decision-making process that begins with the strategic analysis

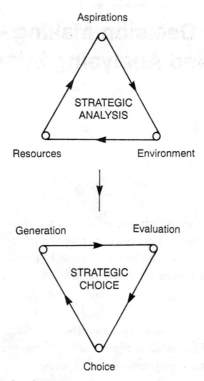

Figure 8.1 **The corporate planning process.**

of organization resources, stakeholder aspirations and environmental situations and then moves on to the generation, evaluation and choice of strategic developments. A third stage, that of strategic implementation, has not been included in the diagram. Chapter 10 deals with this important aspect of strategy-making. Because Chapter 2 has dealt with organization stakeholders, their aspirations and power situations, this chapter will largely ignore this aspect of strategic analysis. This section concentrates on environment and resource analyses.

While this approach to strategy-making takes no account of informal activities and emergent and surprise-handling approaches to strategy,[3] it does give a basis that can be modified to include these as responses to rationality constraints. It also provides

1 A framework for the adoption of a more proactive and rational attempt to improve organizational success.
2 A means for developing greater understanding of the 'whys' and 'hows' of the stimulation of more effective emergent and surprise-handling strategic processes.
3 The most fertile source of analytical models to demonstrate their roles in the decision-making process.

The next task is to examine some of these models using the framework for analysis established in Chapter 6.

The objectives of environmental analysis

Environmental analysis has a number of related objectives. The importance of relating the organization's position to its wider environmental setting was stressed in Chapter 4. Environmental analysis helps to reveal future wealth creation opportunities, and drawing on insights from other areas of strategic analysis it provides a more rational basis for decisions about the changes needed to take advantage of wealth-creating opportunities and to avoid threats. This process of analysis is based on a number of related conceptual models which, when used together in a systematic manner, generate more comprehensive and meaningful information for the strategy-making task. These models assist, progressively, in the location, analysis and evaluation of information. They help us to find relevant data, to sort them sensibly and to gain understanding of the information gleaned in terms of its significance to the future of the organization.

The models to be discussed are summarized in Table 8.1. Their use can encourage a way of thinking about the organization as a wealth producer that interacts with its environment. First, they generate insight into the *nature* of the environment and the implications it has for strategy; secondly, they identify the most important factors likely to affect the organization. Systematic use of these models should enable the strategist to develop an increasingly *specific* view of the implications of the environment for strategic development decisions. Planning has been described as 'the design of a desired future and of effective ways of bringing it about'.[4] These models are expected to help us locate and earn our desired futures.

Table 8.1 Summary of environmental appraisal models

The organization as a wealth-creating, open system

Nature of the environment models
    the placid/turbulent model
    the general/specific model
    nature of the environment models

Environmental analysis and evaluation models
    the PEST model
    market segmentation models
    an attractive market model
    the market life cycle model
    the competitive structure analysis model
    competitor and key player analysis models
    the opportunities and threats concept

The organization as a wealth-creating, open social system

This model identifies the major task of an organization and shows the importance of the environment.

In Chapter 7 we discussed a model of the organization that portrayed it as a planning system: moving through time in a manner shaped by environmental forces *and* by all the plans, decisions and activities undertaken by the people of the organization. This view owes much to the open-systems model of organization,[5] which in essence sees the organization continuing to exist through a process of ongoing wealth-creating interactions with its environment. The open-systems interaction process is modelled in Figure 8.2. Resource inputs are shown to be attracted from the environment, converted inside the organization and then released back into the environment in the form of goods, services, information and waste.

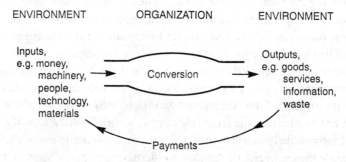

Figure 8.2   The open social systems model of organization.

Theorists have labelled some organizational aims that are implied by the open systems model:

- the quest for *homoeostasis* – the ability to move forward, because of a self-regulatory capability, in a more or less balanced, steady state;
- the quest to achieve *negative entropy* – because they are open, organizations can continue to import energy and can thus maintain survival, the opposite of entropy.

For many organizational theorists, the concept of the open social system has been internalized. However, for many strategists, who still bring a 'closed, inside the organization' perspective to their work,[6] an introduction to the model can lead to a new way of thinking about the nature of their jobs and the role and objectives of their organizations. Its value to strategic decision-making lies in its ability to stimulate a view that places the organization clearly in an environmental context.

The model reminds us forcibly that the survival of the organization depends upon effective interactions with environmental variables. It implies that the organization must satisfy environmental interests if it is to survive,[7] but it also suggests that the environment does not entirely determine outcomes.

In a world of environmental turbulence and hostility the open-systems model of organizing seems to provide a basis for a sensible and safer understanding of organizations.[8, 9] Critics, however, point to its over-emphasis on the organization as a medium transacting its way, as an independent force, *through* an environment, rather than acknowledging the organization as an interactive *part* of a wider total system. Certainly a wider view, which sees organizations as contributors to (or detractors from) a more comprehensive life system, raises for consideration the issue of collaboration between all environmental systems as a potential way forward for the ecosystem in general.[10]

Nature of the environment models

Models dealing with this topic identify the reasons why decision-making in today's environment must be more proactive and rational.

Turn-of-the-century organization theorists such as Henri Fayol[11] and Frederick Taylor[12] proposed classical, one best way, principles for organizing work. Because they were working in an era when change was comparatively slow, competition was less fierce and work was a basic necessity for many, it is not surprising that those interested in revealing and promoting the secrets of organizational success should conclude that the basic problem was one of applying best principles to order the internal workings of the organization. The theory of management strategy, of course, changes to reflect the needs of 'today's' management. In 1965 Emery and Trist published an influential article, 'The causal texture of organisational environments'.[13, 14] In this work the authors alert us to the need to adopt a wider view of organizational environments. They provide a four-category classificatory model to help us think about and investigate the nature of environments. *Placid–randomized* environments exhibit little change and comprise easily understood transactions with non-powerful environmental players. In such circumstances treating the organization as a closed system and concentrating attention on internal efficiency is likely to be a useful approach. *Placid–clustered* environments comprise more powerful, but still well-understood, external players. Change is again slow and predictable. In such circumstances planning for organization success remains comparatively easy but it does make sense to gather information from the organization's arena of activity and to monitor events happening there. *Disturbed–reactive* environments are more complex and contain numerous powerful 'others'. In such environments the organization has to try to make sense of slowly unfolding futures through the development of an understanding of how the interactive presence of government, competition, technology, etc. will affect the organization. This, of course, can be seen to be the task of the corporate planning function, which looks outward and onwards to anticipate. *Turbulent fields* are environments in which significant forces for organizational change develop in the firm's general environment. Initially unconnected, these general forces gather momentum as they roll into the organization's task (or specific) environment. Once inside the task environment, these forces combine to create a massive collective force for change. British textile, cutlery, motorbike and car industries have been decimated by a failure to take early account of developments in materials, technology, competition, consumer aspirations, distribution channels and free-market governmental policies. Triumph, as shown very clearly in Case study 5, provides one example of this type of planning failure. Turbulent fields require greater sophistication from strategic decision-makers in their monitoring of long-term developments, wider environmental horizons and the potential interconnections between environmental variables. Turbulent environments inevitably create confusion and are characterized by rapid changes, and so demand the creation of an organization form that is effective at handling emergent and surprise strategies. Over the course of this century environmental natures have shifted progressively from the placid–randomized type to the turbulent fields type.

In drawing attention to the nature of modern environments by means of this general classification, Emery and Trist help strategic decision-makers in a number of ways. First, they alert strategists to the need to appreciate the organization in a *universal* environmental setting. Secondly, they indicate the need to monitor *general* environments as well as *specific* environments. Thirdly, they stimulate thought on the issue of what changes might be made to the organization's form so that it can be a more effective emergent/surprise handler. A major drawback of the Emery and Trist model, however, is one that appears in many management strategy conceptual models. It is too general. Strategists working with the model have still to make sense of general and specific environments particular to them. However, Emery and Trist can take credit for pointing out the need to adopt a wide socio-economic view of the organization, and for emphasizing the different planning problems associated with different environmental natures. A socio-economic view is essential to the solving of the basic positioning and processing problems of strategy-making.

> An understanding of the nature of business environments is essential if management strategists are to make effective change choices. Such understanding helps strategists to make informed choices about the product/market/competitive positioning most appropriate for future success. . . . It is also useful for considering and making planning process changes (changing the ways the enterprise picks up and uses important information).[15]

If the model provided by Emery and Trist stimulates our first thoughts about the nature of our business environment, Richardson and Richardson[16] and Miles[17] provide further 'nature categorizations' to help strategists in a practical sense to 'locate' their organizations on 'nature continuums'. These models are illustrated in Figure 8.3(a) and Figure 8.3(b), respectively.

Models such as these point strategists along useful lines of enquiry and engender more comprehensive and cogent understanding of the environmental situation within which the organization operates.

Environmental analysis and evaluation models

Political, economic, social, technological (PEST) analysis

Having been alerted to the need to cast the environmental analysis far, wide, and into the future, strategic decision-makers require an investigatory framework. In providing a framework, such as PEST, theory assumes that strategists will be stimulated by its general headings to seek out significant trends and future events.

David Hussey[18] extends the PEST framework to incorporate legal, ecological and demographic classifications. He points out some of the limitations of this model, for although it is easy to consider factors in general terms, 'it is very, very difficult to weave them into the fabric of plans. . . . Only a general overview is possible: every business must estimate for itself its own individual situation. In addition it is important to remember that the factors are mutually inter-dependent. What happens in, for example, the economy will also affect social attitudes.'

In the higher education (HE) sector we can see important demographic trends (a reduction in numbers in the traditional HE student population of 18–22-year-olds), economic trends (the recession of the early 1990s is likely to reduce company spending on higher education), legal trends (the new corporate status for polytechnics), technological trends (the growing importance of information technology to organization processes and distance learning products) and sociological and ecological trends (the range of 'green' issues in which HE institutions might be expected to take a lead, e.g. a reduction in the volume of paper consumed in such organizations).

Systematic applications of a PEST-type model might have improved the performances of many traditional British industries. Certainly, the problems encountered from the 1960s by such UK industries as cars, steel, textiles and rubber were instrumental in bringing environmental forecasting to a more prominent position in the theory and practice of management.

Market segmentation models

'Any market with two or more buyers is capable of being segmented. . . . Each buyer is potentially a separate market because of unique needs and desires.'[19] Case study 8.2 illustrates this.

Market segmentation involves the subdivision of the customers who buy, or

(a)   The move from '4S to 4D' environments

Static ◄——————► Dynamic
(little or no   (rapid rate
change)   of change)

Single ◄——————► Diverse
(well understood,   (more complex,
clearly defined   turbulent-field
area of product/   situation and/or
market operation)   many product/market
                                    operations)

Simple ◄——————► Difficult
(easily understood,   (difficult to make
planned for,   sense of and to plan
environmental   for; a consequence
situation; a   of dynamic, diverse
consequence of   marketplaces)
static, single
marketplaces)

Safe ◄——————► Dangerous
(strong,   (hostile, competitive,
unthreatened   survival-threatening
marketplace   marketplace situation)
position)

Figure 8.3(a)   Environmental nature classification continuum.
Source: Richardson and Richardson.[16]

might buy, a product and service into sub-groups of similarly characterized customers. This exercise, performed during the strategic analysis process, should help to answer questions about the potentially attractive markets the organization might serve and about those which are likely to be worthy of special differentiated attention. Market segmentation exercises tend to require that a closer examination is made of the special needs of different types of clients. In highly competitive markets, where homogeneous products and services are the norm, theory advises that success is earned through paying closer (compared to competitors) attention to satisfying customer needs. Market segmentation exercises, therefore, should help to furnish insight-generating information on the whereabouts of environmental opportunities and on how to realize the opportunities perceived. The Next organization of the early 1980s provides a well-used example of how market segmentation and an associated focus of organization effort can create a new market structure and a winning strategic position. However, the segmentation exercise is a creative one. It requires the strategist to stand above his or her marketplaces and to look down at them, utilizing a range of perspectives. Market segmentation concepts range from the view that each additional customer extends the size of our market share (already 100 per cent),[20] through to a series of like-buyer focusing models (geographic, demographic and

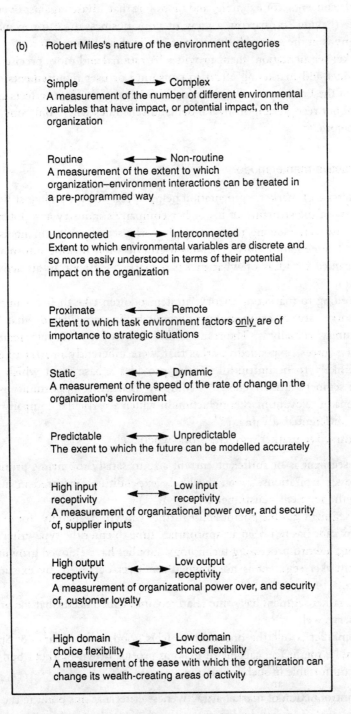

(b)   Robert Miles's nature of the environment categories

Simple   ←——→   Complex
A measurement of the number of different environmental
variables that have impact, or potential impact, on the
organization

Routine   ←——→   Non-routine
A measurement of the extent to which
organization–environment interactions can be treated in
a pre-programmed way

Unconnected   ←——→   Interconnected
Extent to which environmental variables are discrete and
so more easily understood in terms of their potential
impact on the organization

Proximate   ←——→   Remote
Extent to which task environment factors only are of
importance to strategic situations

Static   ←——→   Dynamic
A measurement of the speed of the rate of change in the
organization's enviroment

Predictable   ←——→   Unpredictable
The exent to which the future can be modelled accurately

High input   Low input
receptivity   receptivity
A measurement of organizational power over, and security
of, supplier inputs

High output   Low output
receptivity   receptivity
A measurement of organizational power over, and security
of, customer loyalty

High domain   Low domain
choice flexibility choice flexibility
A measurement of the ease with which the organization can
change its wealth-creating areas of activity

Figure 8.3(b)   Environmental nature classification continuum.
Source: Miles.[17]

life style concepts, for example) and on to one that advises against over-focus and myopia (having too narrow a view of your business area; for example, an oil company is in the energy business, not just in the oil business).[21]

Market segmentation, then, provides 'A rational and more precise adjustment of product and marketing effort to consumer or user requirements. In the language of the Economist, segmentation is disaggregative in its effects and tends to bring about recognition of several demand schedules where only one was recognised before.'[22]

An attractive-market model

The exercise of market segmentation helps to provide the strategist with a better overview of the structure of his or her company's industry and potential industries. However, viewing the market place as a set of sub-segments is, by itself, useless. Segmentation only generates useful decision-making information if it is accompanied by ideas of what makes a market segment an attractive area for operation.

According to marketing theory, strategists often take their organizations into new market areas of opportunity without having considered what 'an area of opportunity' actually is. The result is that many of these development decisions waste resources, expended in areas that were inherently unattractive and were always likely to be unfruitful. Kotler provides a base from which to explore market segment attractiveness: 'A company marketing opportunity is an attractive arena of relevant marketing action in which a particular company is likely to enjoy a differential advantage.'[19]

An attractive market segment is one where:

1 The segment is of sufficient current size to satisfy the firm's profit and sales turnover aspirations, given the likely expenditures incurred in 'negotiating' with the segment's customers.
2 The segment has the potential for further growth. Generally, for example, the past decade has not been an appropriate time to enter the typewriter industry – although word processing technology supplies have enjoyed growing sales.
3 The market segment is not 'owned' or 'over-occupied' by existing competition.
4 The market segment has some relatively unsatisfied needs that the organization can serve well.
5 The market is one the organization feels good about. Marks & Spencer, for example, might feel capable of making profits 'down-market', but would not feel comfortable in such a situation.

The introduction of market attractiveness criteria at this point in the process of strategic *analysis* raises doubts about the sequential, step by step, process prescribed by the linear sequential model of strategic decision-making. These 'attractiveness' criteria take us into the stage of strategy *evaluation*. This reminds us that the strategy-making process, like the general decision-making process modelled in Chapter 1, is often iterative: attention to one part of the decision-making process often promotes recycling between stages.

Other models associated with the general concept of 'attractiveness' can also be used to generate meaningful information appropriate to the analysis stage of the strategic decision-making process.

The product/market life cycle

In Chapter 6 a life cycle model of a firm was introduced in relation to its importance in financial planning. This life cycle approach can be applied to a product or market to analyse the current and potential size of a market segment. Every product in a particular market setting appears to go through a life cycle. A typical sequence is shown in Figure 8.4.

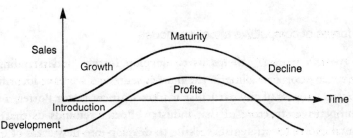

Figure 8.4   The 'standard' product life cycle model.

This 'typical' sequence suggests that the development stage incurs increasing costs. The launch and introduction stage develops sales volume and begins to accumulate sufficient profitable sales to work towards a break-even position. The growth stage is associated with additional sales and growing profits. Market maturity sees sales volumes at their highest levels and, proportionately, costs at their lowest levels, so this is the period of peak profitability. Decline eventually sets in and, according to the general model, produces declining sales and worsening profitability. Consideration of the product/market life cycle model in the context of the organization's present or potential market segments, therefore, concentrates attention on the inherent attractiveness of each segment in terms of its current size and of its growth potential.

It is important to understand that not all products go through the traditionally modelled cycle. For example, a 'craze' for quickly sold, short-life products, such as the hula hoop of the mid-1950s or the Rubik cube of the early 1980s, can produce a product life cycle more accurately modelled by a triangular shape. And even the decline stage can be profitable. Decision-makers, therefore, should customize the life cycle model to the product they are considering. Products should be seen in the context of their markets. The traditional product life cycle model does not take into account the possibility of a company extending a product's life through, for example, its sale to new markets. Firms engaged in asbestos removal, for example, might have in mind the inevitability of eventual total market decline. In the meantime, however, they might continue to grow through a series of growth/maturity/growth/maturity forays into new market segments. The traditional product life cycle seems inherently to show that mature and declining markets are to be avoided. However, some organizations make higher than average returns from appropriate strategies, such as the creation of a monopoly, in market life stages that the model suggests are unattractive.

It should be apparent that meaningful market segmentation exercises are based on measurement. Analysts need to be able to quantify in some meaningful way the size and growth of the market segments under review. However, measurement is often a difficult job that keeps market researchers busy locating and analysing governmental and commercially generated sources of data and conducting their own pieces of field research.[23]

The five forces of competitive structure model

Michael Porter's work[24, 25] helps us to develop further understanding of the competitive situation prevailing in the market segments we have identified. The inherent attractiveness of any particular market segment is, for Porter, a function of the competitive structure of that industry. Porter reminds us that the first fundamental choice for strategists seeking to develop into new areas of operation is 'which market?' For him the answer to this question should be based on an understanding of the 'five forces of competition' at work in any industry segment (inter-firm rivals, buyers, suppliers, new entrants, substitute products). 'All industries are not alike from the standpoint of inherent profitability. In industries where the five forces are favourable ... many competitors can earn attractive returns. But in industries where pressure from one or more of the forces is intense ... few firms command attractive returns despite the best efforts of Management.'[25]

The value of Porter's five-forces model in the strategic analysis process is derived from how it answers, in the context of particular market segments, the following types of questions, raised by the model itself and by Porter's associated prescriptions:

1 Which segment are we analysing?

2 Who are the inter-firm competitors?
   - how intense is rivalry now and what is it likely to be like in the future?
   - are market rivals seeking dominance?
   - is the market mature and subject to 'shake out' activity?
   - do high fixed costs provoke users to maintain capacity?

- are products/services homogeneous?
- have new influxes of capacity created excess capacity, or will they do so?
- do high exit barriers exist?

3 Who are the industry consumers and what are or would be their power *vis-à-vis* our organization?
- is there a concentration of buyers?
- are there attractive alternative sources of supply available to customers?
- is product/service information easily available?
- do customers shop around, and can they afford to?
- do customers have bargaining 'will and skill'?
- is there a threat of backward integration if customers do not obtain satisfactory supplies and prices?

4 Who are or would be the suppliers to our organization and what is the extent of their (potential) power?
- is there a concentration of suppliers?
- are the costs of switching from one supplier to another high?
- is a supplier likely to integrate forward if it does not obtain the price, profits and performance it seeks from us?
- what is or would be the extent of any countervailing power we might be able to employ?

5 What is the threat of entry by new inter-firm competitors into the market segment?
- is the customer base, present and potential, sufficient to support new entrants?
- how heavy is the capital investment requirement in the industry, and is finance available?
- is there a strong brand image to overcome?
- how costly would be access to distribution channels?
- what operating cost advantage might existing competitors hold (experienced staff, patent protection, etc.)?
- is there governmental/legislative protection for existing players?
- how vigorously will existing operators be expected to react against entry attempts?

6 Where are the present or potential substitute product/services located and what is their impact or likely impact on the industry?
- do customers perceive other products/services to perform the same function as ours?
- do substitutes offer higher value for money?
- do substitutes offer higher profits?

Porter thus makes a significant contribution to the analysts' job by drawing attention to the notion that competition is more than inter-firm rivalry alone. Many strategists are unused to thinking about their marketplaces as 'wealth cakes', from which five categories of players seek to take their 'bites'. Porter's competitive-structure model does, however, tend to push us towards a shorter-term, task environment orientated 'snapshot' view of the organization in its environment. Furthermore, it is based on a 'rational economic' view of the nature of organizational–environmental interactions. Recent research[26] suggests that, in the Irish clothing industry at least, a greater ability to shop around on the part of customers does not necessarily make a difference to the profit earned by the supplying organization. This research undertaking also found that greater information for the customer on the organization's operations produced higher organization profitability. Thus, Porter's model might not take sufficient account of social influences, non-rational (economically speaking) activity and collaboration as a strategy for earning greater wealth overall. The five-forces model also leaves the decision-maker to define 'the market' under review.

Of course, Porter's model does not provide any direct answers to the strategists' environmental analysis problem. Rather, in keeping with most management strategy models, it offers indications as to the most pertinent areas for enquiry. Despite these comments, Porter's model, used in conjunction with the other models referred to in this chapter, is an important analytical tool for the generation of more comprehensive, detailed and pertinent information.

Competitor and key player analysis

The models presented in this section so far can be seen to address, in increasingly greater detail, some of the important areas for analysis raised by the earlier models. A key determinant of market segment attractiveness and of the success enjoyed by an organization in its marketplace will be the moves and counter-moves of its 'five force' players. In very competitive marketplaces, therefore, it makes sense to analyse closely the positions and attitudes of significant competitors. Theory is not as well formulated here as in other areas of strategic analysis. Most texts, for example, concentrate on competitor (inter-firm rival) analysis even though for many organizations key customers and key suppliers deserve at least as much attention.

The aim of competitor analysis is to 'get into the minds' of the strategists who occupy key decision-making positions in other organizations in the marketplace. This is no easy task. Many organizational strategists do little in the way of competitor analysis other than absorbing titbits of information picked up piecemeal. This leads to an often inaccurate 'gut feeling' that the organization understands its competitors and knows what is going on in the marketplace. Increasingly, however, theory is prescribing a very systematic response to the problem of understanding environmental players, their moves and their potential moves. The aim of this systematic approach is to introduce or develop organization systems that accumulate competitor information over time. The need is extolled for organizational restructuring to create posts of responsibility for competitor monitoring and profiling. Information is to be systematically gleaned through the soliciting of information from:

1 Third parties (financial analysts, former employees of the competitor, and published accounts of competitor situations and activities, for example).
2 Own company personnel (the introduction of forms and systems that formalize the process of competitor monitoring). Inevitably competitor monitoring will have been undertaken by salespeople and other colleagues, informally, over the years.
3 From competitors themselves (in annual reports, company newsletters, conversations, press interviews, etc.).

Ian Gordon[27] prescribes a very systematic approach to the generation of competitive intelligence. The model advanced by theorists such as Gordon prescribes the adoption of strategic analysis processes applied to competitor organizations. A full strategic analysis of competitor organizations is expected to provide insight into their aspirations, assumptions, strengths, weaknesses and competitive positions.[24, 27] This in turn is expected to provide a realistic understanding of the likelihood, intensity and effectiveness of any offensive or defensive moves from these competitors.

Opportunities and threats

As was shown in Chapter 4, a major outcome of the environmental appraisal process is a ranked list of major opportunities and threats. At this stage, recommend the theorists, the analyst sitting on a mountain of information needs to 'sort out the wood from the trees'. Johnson and Scholes[28] advise: 'The aim should be to arrive at a list of key changes or influences on the organization. Whilst there is no fixed number which should be agreed upon, it is helpful if the list does not exceed seven or eight key points.'

A further refinement to this approach is suggested by Argenti,[29] who recommends that major opportunities and threats should be evaluated according to: (a) the significance of the potential impact of the environmental factor; and (b) the likelihood of the event occurring. Low-impact/low-probability events can be ignored. High-impact events whether of high *or* low probability become

> the crucial ones . . . but of these countless billions of occurrences only a handful are of strategic importance. . . . If we think we have identified one, we should be prepared to spend much time and money in examining it, its possible impact and the probability of it happening. We should search for

possible 'lead indicators' for it – trends or events whose occurrence may herald the event itself and which we should therefore watch carefully and continuously.

Opportunities and threats analysis and the associated ranked list herald the end of the environmental analysis activity. As explained in Chapter 4, the strategist must next turn his or her attention inwards, to resource analysis.

Understanding the resource position and the aims of resource analysis

After environmental scanning the strategist next needs to conduct a formal and systematic internal appraisal of the organization itself. Resource analysis is the second stage in the three-pronged quest to develop a comprehensive understanding of the organization's strategic position (aspirations analysis, covered in Chapter 2, is the third).

Resource analysis is intended to provide a clear picture of the organizations' resources in the context of their potential contributions to, or detractions from, organizational success.[30] The aim is to generate knowledge about the firm's resource positions for use in combination with assessments of stakeholder aspirations and understandings of future environmental situations. This facilitates strategic choices that fit the strategic analysis triangle. Outcomes of the resource analysis process are intended to include:

1 A list of major strengths to be built on and of major weaknesses to be reduced, removed or avoided through appropriate choices of strategic developments, thus enabling the completion of the SWOT analysis suggested in Chapter 4.
2 Understanding of any distinctive competences that the company enjoys. These give the company a particular competitive advantage over competitors who cannot match them.
3 Identification of organizational areas which need improvement as part of an all-round incremental approach to improving organizational productivity.

In this section some management strategy resource analysis models are considered. These are designed to help strategists to generate useful and more comprehensive information. There are two types of resource analysis aids. First are models that help to identify organizational resources and evaluate their significances. These models will be referred to as *resource identification/evaluation* models. Second are models designed to progress the analysis by stimulating a more rigorous evaluation of the resources identified. We will call these models *resource evaluation* models. Table 8.2 summarizes the models discussed in the next two sections.

Table 8.2 Summary of resource analysis models

Resource identification and evaluation models
    Drucker's key performance areas
    resource analysis checklists
    Porter's value chain

Resource evaluation models
    productivity ratios
    the concept of flexibility
    resource balance models
    ● balanced management team models
    ● balanced product portfolios
    ● organizing components and organization fit
    strategic standing
    strengths, weaknesses and distinctive competences

Resource identification/evaluation models – the key resource concept

A series of models is available for the identification of resources and the strategic significance of each resource. This section provides a review of some of these. While it is difficult to think about a particular resource without also beginning an evaluation of its strong and weak points, our discussion is structured to take us through a 'mainly identification' to an 'identification with much evaluation' process of analysis. Many of the models discussed are based on a key-resource concept – the idea that particular resources or resource categories are highly significant to the level of success the organization achieves. Indeed, it will be seen that a primary objective of resource analysis is to understand strategically vital resource areas.

Peter Drucker's key performance areas

In 1955 Peter Drucker[31] insisted on the need for improvement targets to be set in key resource areas:

> Objectives are needed in every area where performance and results directly and vitally affect the survival and prosperity of the business. . . . Objectives in these key areas should enable . . . practising businessmen to analyse their own experience and, as a result, improve their performance. . . . At first sight it might seem that different businesses would have entirely different key areas – so different as to make impossible any general theory. . . . But the areas are the same, whatever the business, whatever the economic conditions, whatever the business's size or stage of growth.

There are several key resource areas identified by Drucker:

Market standing calls for analysis of the firm's competitive position. Market share and competitive advantage positions need to be recorded as resource areas of strength or weakness. This involves looking inwards from Porter's industry environmental analysis.

Innovation reminds us that survival depends upon the organization's ability to meet new situations effectively and to perform and make successful new operations, products and services. Innovatory capability analysis might lead, for example, towards recording the resource situation in terms of new product development and the organization's capacity to change its way of thinking to deal with new situations.

Productivity is obviously important. A productivity audit requires an analysis of the firm's general ability to create wealth and of the productivity of its different departments, functions and personnel. This requires the use of *measurement* models, as discussed in Chapter 6.

Drucker treats *profitability* as a concept distinct from productivity. For him, profit 'records the net effectiveness and soundness of a business's efforts. It is indeed the ultimate test of business performance.' Drucker argues that returns on money within the business should be equal, at least, to the capital market rate of return. This key performance area calls for an identification and evaluation of the firm's profit performances by product and market area.

The resource analyst also needs to evaluate *manager quality*. This should take the form of a skills assessment and include knowledge-based skills, managerial competencies, team-building approaches, responsiveness to change and enterprising characteristics. Analysts should be seeking to assess whether the team as a whole provides a balance of required skills that interact in a harmonious fashion. *Financial strength* (liquidity and access to financial resources) and *physical resources* (land, machinery, buildings, etc.) should also be assessed.

Public responsibility provides a categorization that might have been less enthusiastically received as a 'key performance area' 35 years ago. These days, however, as the firm becomes more clearly viewed as an instrument of society, each organization needs to review its performance record and organizational arrangements for the achievement of a cost-effective socially responsible stance.

Worker performance and attitude is the last of Drucker's key objective-setting areas. Here, the task for the strategist is to record strong and weak points relating to workforce size, skills, attitudes and performance. This should be an audit of the firm's approach to managing the workforce. Many autocratic, 'them and us' management approaches have been amended in recent times to achieve greater team spirit and better workforce productivity. At Pedigree Petfoods, for example, everyone is an 'associate' and everyone is paid weekly. Increasingly, workforces are being given greater responsibility, via quality circles, for example, and are being measured on their tangible outputs-to-inputs records.

Drucker's general theory provides a helpful first indication of what strategists should be seeking to include in their resource audit. He also provided a major stimulus for incorporation of the less tangible and quantifiable resources in analysis exercises. These include manager performance and development, public responsibility and worker performance and attitude. His views on the importance of these 'softer' areas were published in an era when the profit maximization based classical economist's model of the firm provided our major theoretical understanding of organizations. Drucker has thus been instrumental in the development of a wider, more rational approach to strategy-making. In a 1990s era of 'productivity through people' a hard *and* soft approach to making management decisions continues to gain favour.

Despite these seminal qualities Drucker's general model of key resource performance areas suffers from its intended nature – it is too general. Drucker himself acknowledges a problem for the individual strategist: 'It is indeed true that different key areas require different emphasis in different businesses – and differing emphasis at different stages of the development of each business.' This reminds us again of a basic problem created by the very purpose of strategy-making, which is the making of specific sense of unique situations. Practising managers can use Drucker's key performance area model but only as a stimulator of thought and enquiry. Ultimately they must identify and evaluate the specific resources. However, strategists can also turn to other theoretical contributions in order to develop their theoretical underpinning for the making of situation-specific decisions.

Resource analysis checklists

In attempts to be more specifically prescriptive over the resource analysis process, numerous writers have provided their own versions of resource audit checklists.[32, 33] An example of one such pre-prepared audit checklist is shown in Table 8.3. Such devices often help strategists new to the analysis process to generate a more comprehensive view of their strategic resource situation than might otherwise have been possible. However, whereas more generalized categorization models leave too much to the imagination and creativity of the analyst a detailed checklist of the type shown in Table 8.3 creates the danger of 'false security'. The analyst equipped with a seemingly comprehensive and 'expert prepared' list can forget to look beyond the list. Many standard checklists, for example, neglect intangible resources such as manager contacts and company image. A failure to examine these aspects of the resource situation means that, often, vitally important resources are not being taken account of. The need, therefore, is to use resource checklists in modified, customized ways.

Michael Porter's value chain

Michael Porter's efforts to help managers create competitive advantage have also given us a general resource identification/evaluation model based on an underlying concept of key performance areas. Porter's central thesis is that resources should be arranged to reduce organizational costs of operation and/or to make the

Table 8.3 Some resource strength–weakness questions

Resource area	Some evaluatory questions
Owners and management	Does management have sufficient skill and management motivation?
	Does management have a *balance* in terms of skills, attitudes and experience?
	Is there any over-dependence on particular managers?
	Is there any chance important personnel might be leaving?
	Do the organization's systems require attention in order to improve information and communication flows and to improve monitoring, control and motivation? Are the top managers successful planners?
Personnel	Has the organization enough/too many personnel? Is absenteeism and/or turnover high?
	Where is the organization strong and/or weak in personnel terms?
Marketing and market standing	Does the organization have marketing/markets expertise?
	Does it know its customers and competitors?
	Is its product/service range successful?
	Does it have a useful product innovation record?
	Which markets does it serve?
	Does it compete favourably with competitive offers? If so, why? If not, why not?
	Does it have a secure, loyal customer base?
	What is good, bad or indifferent about the firm's prices, products, promotional efforts, distribution channels and customer reception and service?
	Is the organization over-reliant on one customer?
	Is its customer base spread too thinly?
Finance	Is the capital structure in balance?
	Has the organization an improving profits record?
	Is it sufficiently liquid?
	Does it have too much idle cash?
	Does it enjoy good relationships with bankers and other financiers?
	How efficiently are resources contributing to financial strength?

Table 8.3 Some resource strength–weakness questions (*continued*)

Resource area	Some evaluatory questions
Production	Is production efficient?
	Are stock levels too high?
	Do bottlenecks occur?
	Is purchasing effective?
	Any problems with suppliers?
	Any over-reliance on particular suppliers?
Premises and equipment	Are premises/equipment adequate?
	Are they too old? Inefficient?
	Do they present a poor image?
	Is there room for expansion?
	Are premises/equipment badly located?
Organization	Does some restructuring seem necessary?
	Is the organization top heavy, short on middle management?
	Do existing jobs need redesigning?
	Do new jobs need to be created?
	Is there a need for new or improved communication links?
Image	How would the planners like the organization to be perceived?
	How is it perceived by customers; the community; suppliers; the workforce; the local authority?
Contacts	Do personnel have particularly useful contacts with other important stakeholders?
	Should some of these contacts be shared with other personnel?
Others	No checklist is all-embracing. Introduce other questions as and when they appear pertinent.
Finally	What are the major strengths of the organization . . . and the major weaknesses?

organization more profitably attractive to its customers. Strategists can use Porter's value chain model to consider, in detail, their own value-creating resource activities. The model groups organizational activities into five main areas.

Inbound logistics are the activities concerned with receiving, storing and distributing the inputs to the organizing system. *Operations* convert inputs into the final products/services of the organization. *Outbound logistics* are concerned with the collection, storage and distribution of these products/services to the customer. *Marketing and sales* activities attract customer purchases. *Service* activities ensure that customers enjoy their purchased goods/services by providing installation, product use training, product maintenance and breakdown assistance. These primary activities are linked to support activities, which Porter classifies under four headings:

- procurement is the process whereby each primary activity obtains its own resources;
- technology development is concerned with 'know how', and with improvements to the way in which each activity performs its functions and to the quality of each activity's own system outputs;
- human resource management recruits, trains, develops and rewards people working in primary and support activities;
- management systems plan and control activities throughout the organization.

Porter's value chain model has provided us with a framework for classifying organizational activity into primary and support activities and for thinking about how these interrelate and contribute to competitive standing. Importantly, his value chain concept takes us outside the organization to the linkages that exist between the organization and external stakeholders. This reminds the resource analyst to incorporate in the analysis aspects of the resource base of suppliers, distributors and customers that affect the way the organization does business. Access to TOPS (Thomson's Open Line System), for example, has been a major strength and selling point for travel agents. The value chain becomes an additionally potent strategy-making tool when it is used in conjunction with Porter's models for understanding competitive situations and for thinking about the changes that should be made to key performance areas to enhance *generic* competitive strategy.

Resource evaluation models

The models discussed above perform two tasks. First, they set us thinking about which resources we have. Secondly, because we are identifying resources as a preliminary step in an evaluation of their significance for strategic development choices, they lead us into evaluation processes. At this level, however, evaluation might be insufficiently rigorous.

A range of models exists to help us perform more comprehensive and detailed evaluations than are likely to be produced by our key performance area based analysis. Quantitatively and/or qualitatively these resource evaluation models demand an attempt at measurement. The emphasis at this stage of the strategy-making process is on the measurement of past and existing performances. However, because of the iterative nature of strategy-making, measurement of resource performances has to be undertaken with 'half an eye', at least, on the future. The basic problems being addressed are 'how productive have we been?' and 'how productive are we likely to be?' Some of management strategy's productivity measuring and resource evaluation models are referred to below. This section provides a brief discussion of each of these models.

1 How productive is our resource utilization?
- productivity ratio models.
2 How flexible are our resources?
- the concept of flexibility for productivity.
3 How productively balanced are our resources?
- Belbin's balanced management team model;
- the Boston Consulting Group's balanced product portfolio model;
- the concept of organizing components and organization fit.
4 How productive is our strategic standing?
- Porter's market power model (again).
5 Which are our major strengths, weaknesses and distinctive competences?
- The concepts of strengths, weaknesses and distinctive competences.

Productivity ratios

Productivity ratios are essential aids in resource analysis. They calculate how productive the organization has been in utilizing its resources. Ratios have been covered in Chapter 5, so students are advised to return to that chapter to read the appropriate section again. Productivity assessments require measurements of effectiveness over efficiency or, put another way, of output over resource input or, put yet another way, of benefits over costs. It is important that analysts have a clear measurement of their organization's productivity performances.

The concept of flexibility

Flexibility refers to the effectiveness with which resources can be re-arranged and redeployed to meet new situations. Today's environments are dynamic and often bring frequent changes in direction. In such situations new organizational approaches and/or resource deployments need to be implemented quickly. Items on the resource audit, therefore, should be considered in the light of flexibility questions. Is management too set in its ways and too prone to follow older, out-of-date success recipes? Is the workforce sufficiently multi-skilled and motivated to handle change effectively? Is the organization locked into particular industries, particular products or particular methods because of heavy investment in specialist plant and machinery, and a shortage of finance?

The resource analyst should find and consider areas where a lack of flexibility might lead to a loss of competitive position.

The concept of balance

Belbin's balanced top management team model

Consultants often report of finding situations where, for example, 'that firm is led by good engineers, they have some useful products, but they are hopeless at marketing', or 'he is exceptional at selling but desperately needs an administrator to sort out the operating systems'. Research has suggested that the person who rose to the top in the 1980s had gained experience with several companies and in a number of different disciplines (most commonly including marketing and pro-duction). Top management balance questions should therefore attempt to estab-lish whether too narrow a view, in a functional sense, is being adopted at the top of the organization.

Top managers are spending more of their time on external matters than their predecessors of 10 or 15 years ago but some can still be too inward-looking. Owners of smaller businesses, particularly, can become engrossed with internal operations and – because of pressure of work – embroiled in day-to-day detail. In strategic terms top management might be spending too much time on short-term internal operations and too little time on longer term, external, strategic issues.

Belbin (see Table 8.4) suggests that management teams are more successful decision-makers when they comprise a balance of complementary roles. Further, in terms of management style, theory prescribes a balanced approach. On the one hand this approach is extremely inflexible and autocratic in insisting that subordi-nates adopt the core organizational values of concern for quality, productivity and customer satisfaction, and work strictly within guidelines set for these purposes. On the other hand this balanced approach offers a looser, more interac-tive and supportive management style, as long as core values are held.

Asking the question, 'are we achieving appropriate balances?', in the context of the firm's different resources stimulates additional insight into resource strengths and weaknesses and into appropriate resource changes.

The Boston Consulting Group's balanced product portfolio concept

In the context of the organization's products or (in the case of a divisionally structured firm) its business sub-units, the balance question is designed to reveal whether the organization has, for example:

- too many declining products/services or sub-units;
- too few units, or products/services, with growth potential;
- insufficient profit generators to maintain, at least, present organization per-formance and to provide investment funds for the nurturing of tomorrow's successful ventures.

A useful model to aid this analysis of products or services has been provided by the Boston Consultancy Group. Assumptions underlying this model equate high

Table 8.4 Group decision-making – a range of roles

Type	Symbol	Typical features	Positive qualities	Allowable weaknesses
Company worker	CW	Conservative, dutiful, predictable	Organizing ability, practical, common sense, hard-working	Lack of flexibility, unresponsiveness to unproven ideas
Chairman	CH	Calm, self-confident, controlled	A capacity for treating and welcoming all potential contributors on their merits and without prejudice; a strong sense of objectives	No more than ordinary in terms of intellect or creative ability
Shaper	SH	Highly strung, outgoing, dynamic	Drive and a readiness to challenge inertia, ineffectiveness, complacency or self-deception	Proneness to provocation, irritation and impatience
Plant	PL	Individualistic, serious-minded, unorthodox	Genius, imagination, intellect, knowledge	Up in the clouds, inclined to disregard practical details or protocol
Resource investigator	RI	Extroverted, enthusiastic, curious, communicative	A capacity for contacting people and exploring anything new; an ability to respond to challenge	Liable to lose interest once the initial fascination has passed
Monitor-evaluator	ME	Sober, unemotional, prudent	Judgement, discretion, hard-headedness	Lacks inspiration or the ability to motivate others
Team worker	TW	Socially orientated, rather mild, sensitive	An ability to respond to people and to situations, and to promote team spirit	Indecisiveness at moments of crisis
Completer-finisher	CF	Painstaking, orderly, conscientious	A capacity for follow-through; perfectionism	A tendency to worry about small things; a reluctance to 'let go'

Sources: R. M. Belbin, *Management Teams: Why They Succeed or Fail.* Heinemann, London, 1981, and R. M. Belbin *et al.*, 'Building effective management teams', *Journal of General Management*, 1976; **3** (3).

market share with higher profitability and competitive advantage and prescribe that growing markets are more commercially attractive than static or declining ones. The model categorizes organizational products and services as:

Dogs These are low-market-share products or services in markets with low growth rates. Thus they seem to have little to offer the organization for the future and might be best divested or otherwise discontinued.

Question marks These offerings occupy a low market share position in a growing market. Additional expenditure, in an effort to achieve a more lucrative market share position, might be the way forward for such products or services.

Stars These are high market share products and services occupying positions in high growth markets. According to the theory, these commodities deserve heavy investment support so that they will develop into cash cows.

Cash cows These organizational products and services have leading positions (earned by heavy investment previously extended in their development) in markets that have peaked. Little investment is required to sustain these leading positions and so cash can be 'milked' from these products and services, and organizational activities.

The concept of organizing components and organization fit

We considered the open social system model of organization in the earlier section on environmental appraisal. The resource analysis exercise should attempt an assessment of how harmoniously aspects of the organization interact – with each other and collectively with the environment. Theorists have referred to the need for organizations to integrate internally and to adapt externally. Figure 7.4 (p. 151) describes the organization's internal and external 'fit' relationships.

This model describes an ongoing 'organizing' process. Greater strategic success is to be earned through attention to the job (the organization's technical and decision-making duties), the structure (the way the jobs are linked to each other), the product/market strategies, the people, the communicating, motivating, controlling and recruiting systems, the technology (the machines and methods employed) and the resources of the enterprise. These components of organizing should be designed and implemented in such a way that they are congruent with each other and are, in totality, congruent with the nature and needs of the organization's environment. Together they create the culture of an organization.

Analysts can use this model as a basis for investigating the source and nature of any strategic 'misfits'. Readers will note that this theme of 'fit' appears in different parts of this book, and is an important concept for strategists to grasp and implement.

Porter's market power model and strategic standing

Strategic standing is about power in the market place. Analysis here requires another look at the strength of the organization's competitive position. Questions to be answered under this category of investigation include:

- How powerful are we *vis-à-vis* our customers (are they tied to us in some way, or can they shop around)?

- How powerful are we *vis-à-vis* our competitors (do customers prefer our offerings to those of our competitors)?
- How powerful are we *vis-à-vis* our suppliers (do they need us more than we need them)?
- In each of the above situations what is it about our resource situation that is responsible for the answers we have given?
- Is our strategic standing changing (are we becoming more or less powerful market place players, and why)?

A consideration of strategic standing should generate insights into the types of resource changes that need to be made if success in the market place is to be maintained. It should also seek to measure the urgency with which such changes need to be made.

Porter's forces of competition model, in the context of resource analysis (as well as in the process of environmental analysis), emphasizes a building block approach to systematic corporate planning. The internal perspective adopted at this stage of the analysis will feed from and work with the previous externally orientated appraisal. It also reminds us to consider again key resources in the value chain in the context of their significances as strategic success 'drivers'.

Strengths, weaknesses and distinctive competences

The information generated by the previous ideas can be evaluated to uncover the few really significant resource strengths and weaknesses, as discussed in Chapter 5, or the distinctive competences that differentiate the firm attractively, in the eyes of customers, from its competitors. This provides the information for the first half of the SWOT model, the strengths and weaknesses. The point of using this model to organize the material is that future product/market strategies should seek to build on the major strengths and distinctive competences identified and to avoid or reduce resource problem areas.

Conclusion

The way in which resources are deployed to generate wealth from environmental interactions is fundamental to the maintenance of strategic success.

The discussion in this chapter and the discussion on organizational stakeholder situations in Chapters 2 and 3 have provided a systematic 'journey' through the concepts and techniques of situational analysis. These tools and concepts enable a more rational undertaking of customized, organization-specific analyses. Appropriate models generate better information on the strategic position of the firm in terms of its resources, environment and aspirations. This information provides a platform for thinking about the most appropriate ways forward for the organization. It also provides criteria for evaluating the strategic development choices that might be made.

Resources need to be considered in terms of the changes that might be made to them, so that the organization is more in tune with its environment (strategic fit) and enjoys greater power in the marketplace (strategic standing). One key to attaining greater marketplace power is the employment of strategic developments that build on strengths and avoid weaknesses to gain competitive advantage. Another is to make sound choices about the environments in which the organization will locate itself. Organizational success is attained by adding value to the organizing system – through new resource deployments that reduce the costs of organizing and/or through similar changes that attract more profitable exchanges from customers and other stakeholders. All these changes have to take account of the political dimension within which the organization exists.

Strategic analysis thus provides a major input into strategic choice – the subject matter of the next chapter.

Case study 8.1
How the mighty have fallen

This case study indicates important longer-term environmental trends.

If John Major wants evidence that the British economy is indeed slowing, he should read this year's *Management Today* 250 Growth and Profit league tables. The spectacular gains of the mid- to late-1980s appear to be a thing of the past. The star performers then – those angels who dominated the financial pages with their derring-dos in takeover battles – are now fallen and largely forgotten.

But it is not all doom and gloom. In the higher reaches of both the growth and profit leagues, we find a whole range of industrial companies producing the very goods needed to whittle away the £15 billion annual trade deficit. It may be early days yet but if the 1980s was the decade of the niche retailer, advertiser, designer, not forgetting the stockbroker and merchant banker, maybe the 1990s will be the age of industry yet again.

What is amazing is how British industry has actually survived and in parts flourished in recent years – given the appalling British infrastructure (roads, rails and airports), training and education levels that are woefully behind those of our trading rivals and above all the complete U-turns in various governments' policies since the 1960s. Industry has had to cope with nationalization and then privatization, continued tinkering with union legis- ▷

lation, wildly fluctuating exchange rates and the debilitating stop–go policies.

How a British industrialist must look on enviously at his German or Japanese rivals who have enjoyed years of stable and consistent support from their governments.

The wild Rover workers

Are they mad? Many people must be wondering that of Rover's Long-bridge car workers after their curt rejection of a radical new working programme. Those millions condemned to the drudge of a fixed five-day week will have looked on enviously at Rover's offer of a $31\frac{1}{2}$ hour week and 17 days off in any 35-day period.

A good old British compromise may eventually be cobbled together, but it seems the Rover workers wanted to keep the traditional weekend, rather than accept a long seven-day and another five-day break from Sir Graham Day, the Rover chairman. The deal, welcomed by pragmatic union leaders like Jack Adams, would also have created 1200 new jobs as Rover built up production of its new 200/400 series. Longbridge's decision is symptomatic of the growing sclerosis in Britain's labour market in 1990. Gone, it appears, are the heady productivity increases of the mid-1980s. Now, with the spectre of stagflation and its twin evils – no growth and high inflation – stalking the economy, Britain's workforce has forgotten that brief virtuous period, settling instead for a re-run of the late 1970s.

It is as if the Thatcher revolution had not occurred. Pay claims are rising to double figures, ballots move in favour of industrial action though few union members are yet prepared for full-scale strike action. Despite the economic slow-down, a growing skills shortage and the demographic revo-lution are giving unions a muscle and confidence not seen for some years. All we need now is a good old-fashioned demarcation dispute, and someone returning to Britain after a ten-year absence would feel quite at home.

At the root of the problem is Britain's sheer inability to develop the sort of flexibility in attitudes and mobility in jobs that characterizes the Ameri-can labour market. The government has a role here: to increase the miserly spending on training and education. British firms spend just 0.15 per cent of turnover on training, compared to the 1–2 per cent spent by Japanese and German companies. Worse still, the numbers of British youngsters at the higher reaches of the education ladder falls far short of our economic com-petitors. Some 40 per cent of Britain's 16–18-year-olds remain in full-time education. In Japan and America, the figure is nearer to 90 per cent.

Little wonder that in examining Britain in his compelling new work, *The Competitive Advantage of Nations*, Harvard's Professor Michael Porter rightly savages the British education system for producing a workforce ▷

'well behind in education and skills compared with that of many other advanced nations'.

The government also needs to sweep away the last vestiges of red tape in the housing and other markets, particularly for rented accommodation, to increase labour mobility. Perhaps, bearing in mind the Longbridge workers, it also needs to lift restrictions on Sunday trading to change attitudes to the sacred British weekend.

Capitalism versus altruism

Caring capitalism? A year ago, many on the left and even the not-so-left would have laughed at the notion. But now with Marxism and communism so completely discredited as a political and economic force, capitalism uniquely has a chance to prove itself as the only viable economic system for the twenty-first century.

But will it have to be a capitalism with a difference – a capitalism with a human face? There may be signs that this is happening already, as explored in this issue of *Management Today*. Firstly, the green revolution appears to be swept along every bit as much by companies such as Tesco as by the Friends of the Earth. True, there is a large element of marketing hype in the conversion of many companies to a green stance, but the likes of Tesco's Richard Taylor are responding to growing public pressure for better and safer products, and more importantly, they see that money can be made out of it.

This is fine as it goes, but the real test of their new green colours will come when governments start to introduce (as they inevitably will) more draconian laws which will directly hit the bottom line. These will include tightening up on packaging laws, recycling of plastics, the banning of a wider range of materials which are increasingly in short supply and probably, in the long run, some restrictions on the use of private cars in cities. It will be a test of business patience if they can accept these growing restrictions, but it will be a better world in the long run.

As important to capitalism's image is the way it responds to deprivation. . . . It is not often that an industrialist admits openly that the sight of beggars in central London makes him feel ashamed. The private initiatives being carried out by business in deprived inner-city areas are laudable, but they are only scratching the surface.

The real test of business commitment to helping the inner cities will come when the demographic revolution really bites. Can we expect the likes of IBM, ICI and other blue-chip companies then to make a determined effort to mop up the underclass in Brixton and turn them into computer programmers?

Source: Editorial, *Management Today*, June 1990, p. 5.

Case study 8.2
We shopped till we dropped then we stopped

This case study illustrates the different market segments that retailers might target in the 1990s.

Retailers trying to keep up the appearance of good cheer this anxious Christmas will not find their gloom alleviated by visions of the future of shopping. A noxious combination of boom-time hangover, lack of fore-sight and consumer ennui are likely to produce a persistent headache even if interest rates eventually fall. To compound the current economic misery, there is a long-term fear that those who threw themselves into the spending jamboree of the mid-eighties will emerge as changed people in the next decade: older, wiser and a lot more discriminating.

Already, though times have only just begun to get tougher, the fortunes of the retailing successes of the eighties have tumbled one after the other, and so, so easily. The fate of Next, Storehouse, Dixons, Sock Shop, Tie Rack and the others who are suffering has been sealed partly by shaky financial structures, partly because they were aimed at the 25–45-year-olds who are now suffering most from mortgage increases.

Worse, for retailers who have targeted the affluent, independent young, are that demographics are changing the market out of all recognition. There are already the beginnings of a sharp increase in families, rising to 6.9 million in 2001. As 16–24-year-olds dwindle, there will be 41 per cent more 45–54-year-olds in the population by the year 2016. The implications are that large sections of the retail trade will have had to switch from making a fast buck out of Margaret Thatcher's vanishing free-spending yuppies, into catering for the more complex psychology of modern parents and affluent over-60s – the 'new-old'. Many are hopelessly unprepared.

Richard Hyman, managing director of the retail consultancy Verdict, blames a 'sheep mentality' amongst retailers which has prevented them from seeing rather obvious opportunities developing. It is 'absurd and perverse' he says, 'that there are only two well-known chains, Mothercare and Adams, in children's wear, and that nobody is providing for the over-60s who are spending money in quite staggering quantities. Those markets are wide open.'

The Henley Centre for Forecasting calls the nineties 'the era of the young family' – but they will be very different families from the stereotypes of the past. Henley predicts that, provided there are two working parents, these new families are likely to be older, choosier and more affluent than their predecessors, not about to trade down just because they've had children, and unwilling to bring them up on cheap, inferior goods and foods. . . . ▷

A survey by Verdict found 75 per cent of respondents bored with modern shopping centres, voicing a sense of loss that the variety and choice of the traditional high street has given way to a dull uniformity of facias and merchandise throughout the country.

The paradox of Next – commonly accepted as the most acute example of over-proliferation and uniformity in the eighties – is that George Davies had it half right. His idea – to offer exclusive designer imagery rather than palming people off with yet more anonymous chainstore fare – identified the individualistic aspirations of the children of Thatcherism.

Aside from the impulse to individualism, consumer fussiness has two other important components. The desire for pleasant shopping environment is one; convenience the other.

Because of the decline of the high street into a dirty, run-down and difficult place to shop, convenience has come to mean packing the kids into the car and going to the trouble of making a journey out of town to be able to park in a vast retail centre where at least the children won't get run over and you buy in bulk in order to postpone the next trip as long as possible. The new-old understand this definition of convenience least, resent being forced to shop by car and would rather be able to pop round the corner for necessities.

The environmental cost of all these people getting cars to escape city centres has not gone unnoticed by Chris Patten, Secretary of State for the Environment; increasingly, it is bound to weigh with the public. There are rumblings from the Department of the Environment that planning permission for out-of-town shopping centres may be more difficult to come by in the future; but for the moment projects for centres planned in the mid-eighties are going on apace. Verdict estimates that there will be 4285 super-stores by 1992, an increase of 1985 since 1987.

The Henley Centre, reckoning that women will outnumber men in the workforce by the year 2000, foresees that they will want to spend at least some of their incomes on pampering themselves.

There has been much talk over the years of the openings for mail-order shopping, and lately for the developing of shopping via TV, but given the current state of marketing and distribution, the prospects seem pretty dismal. Home shopping by catalogue has always been a downmarket activity in this country and has been hit hard by current economic conditions.

With the next decade upon us, imaginative initiatives may be sorely needed for the future of shopping, but are particularly hard to come by at a time when many retailers are barely holding on. Everyone in retail analysis is expecting a shake-out at any moment, forcing the closure of many of the shops that reflected the self-indulgent, easy-spending character of the eighties.

Source: The Independent, 19 December 1989.

Notes and references

1 R. Stacey, *Handling Strategic Disturbance*, referred to by F. Martin, Business strategy unit, MSc in Entrepreneur Studies, University of Stirling, 1989; 14.
2 R. Hoffman and D. Becker, *Confrontation – A Strategic Management Simulation*. Irwin, Homewood, IL, 1989.
3 See our discussion in Chapter 7.
4 R. Ackoff, *A Concept of Corporate Planning*. Wiley, New York, 1970.
5 G. Burrell and G. Morgan, *Sociological Paradigms and Organisational Analysis*, Heinemann, London, 1982. Chapter 5 provides a discussion on the history of and contribution to open social systems theory.
6 Classical organization theorists of the first part of this century adopted a closed-box view of the organization and paid little attention to the environment.
7 A. K. Rice, a 'father' of the systems movement, says, for example, 'The *Primary* task of the organisation is to survive', *The Enterprise and Its Environment*. Tavistock, London, 1963; 13.
8 For a discussion on the advantages and disadvantages of systems theory see G. Morgan, *Images of Organisation*. Sage, London, 1986; 74–6.
9 H. Interhuber and P. Wolfgang, 'Strategy as a system of expedients', *Long Range Planning*, 1988; **21**(4): 107–20.
10 H. I. Ansoff, writing in *Implanting Strategic Management*. Prentice-Hall, Englewood Cliffs, NJ, 1984; 472, on future strategic challenges, heralds the era of 'new forms of co-operation among firms, which used to be unthinkable under the historical competitive rules of the game'.
11 H. Fayol, *General and Industrial Management* (trans.). Pitman, London, 1949.
12 F. W. Taylor, *Scientific Management*, Harper, New York, 1947.
13 F. E. Emery and E. L. Trist, 'The causal texture of organisational environments', *Human Relations*, **18**(1): 21–32.
14 C. Stubbart, 'Why we need a revolution in strategic planning', *Long Range Planning*, 1985; **18**(6): 68–76, provides one recent example of how Emery and Trist's 'environment type classification' model has continued to underpin much strategy debate.
15 W. Richardson and R. Richardson, *Business Planning: An Approach to Strategic Management*. Pitman, London, 1989.
16 Richardson and Richardson (15), pp. 13–23.
17 R. E. Miles, *Macro Organizational Behaviour*. Sutt Faresman & Co., Glenview, IL, 1980.
18 D. E. Hussey, *Corporate Planning: Theory and Practice*, 2nd edn. Pergamon, Oxford, 1984.
19 P. Kotler, *Marketing Management Analysis, Planning and Control*, 4th edn. Prentice-Hall, Englewood Cliffs, NJ, 1980.
20 B. D. Henderson, 'The origin of strategy', *Harvard Business Review*, 1989; November–December: 139–43.
21 T. Levitt, 'Marketing myopia', *Harvard Business Review*, 1965; September–October: 26–44.
22 W. R. Smith, 'Product differentiation and market segmentation as alternative marketing strategies', *Journal of Marketing*, 1956; **21**.
23 P. M. Chisnall, *Marketing: A Behavioural Analysis*, 2nd edn. McGraw-Hill, New York, 1985, provides information on market segment data sources available to researchers.
24 M. E. Porter, *Competitive Strategy*, Free Press, New York, 1980.
25 M. E. Porter, *Competitive Advantage*, Free Press, New York, 1985.
26 P. McNanamee and M. McHugh, 'Competitive strategies in the clothing industry', *Long Range Planning*, 1989; **22**(4): 63–71.

27 I. Gordon, *Beat the Competition*, Blackwell, Oxford, 1989.
28 G. Johnson and K. Scholes, *Exploring Corporate Strategy*, 2nd edn. Prentice-Hall, Englewood Cliffs, NJ, 1989.
29 J. Argenti, *Practical Corporate Planning*, George Allen & Unwin, London, 1980.
30 In Chapter 7 we identified wealth creation for survival and for growth, through efficiency and control of the environment, as the organization's goals for itself as a system unto itself.
31 P. F. Drucker, *The Practice of Management*, Pan Books, London, 1968.
32 For example, L. L. Byars, *Strategic Management: Formulation and Implementation*, Harper Collins, London, 1991; Chapter 3.
33 W. Richardson and P. Jennings, *Both Sides of the Business Plan*, BMDP, Sheffield, 1987.

9 Generating, Evaluating and Choosing Strategic Developments

Introduction

Chapter 7 identified wealth creation as *the* strategic problem. Chapter 8 was concerned with the analysis of strategic situations as a systematic stage in the process leading to the choice and implementation of strategic developments. This chapter examines the choice stage of the strategic decision-making process. The objectives of this chapter are to:

- demonstrate the richness of management strategy's contributions to the choice stage of the decision-making process;
- provide a discussion of concepts and models that are concerned to:
  — generate strategic development ideas
  — assist the evaluation and choice of strategic developments
  — help with decisions on *who* should be involved in the strategic decision-making process;
- help develop understanding of how the above-mentioned concepts and models might be employed to produce more rationally taken strategic development decisions.

Table 9.1 categorizes these concepts and models and illustrates the structure of this chapter. Concepts and models designed mainly to stimulate thought processes leading to a wide consideration of potential strategies are considered first. These models deal with the general developments that *can* be undertaken and the theoretical prescriptions of the types of developments that *should* be undertaken. Next will be considered a range of techniques designed primarily to enable decision-makers to test the pertinence of a strategy as an adequate and acceptable wealth creator. Finally, there is a discussion of some models that are most concerned with helping the central decision-makers to think through the issue of whether other organizational personnel should be involved in the strategy-making process.

Table 9.1 Concepts and models to enhance the rationality of strategic choices

Concepts and models to generate strategic development ideas
  development directions
  development methods
  wealth producing developments
  tactical competitive strategies
  key resource changes
  brainstorming

Concepts and models to assist the evaluation and choice of strategic developments
  financial and risk appraisal models
  suitability and the TOWS matrix
  a stakeholder support evaluatory model
  fit with emerging wisdom and research findings
  strategic fit ranking matrices

Models to assist with choices over whether to involve other personnel
  the classical approach to choice
  decision-making styles for different situations
  prescriptions for participative decision-making

Models to generate strategic development ideas

The stage of the decision-making process that leads directly to choices of organizational developments needs to be a creative one. In terms of the linear sequential model of strategy-making the choices made will be of medium- to long-term effect and will have major resource-committing consequences. Rationality requires an extensive consideration of potential developments.

This comprehensive approach theoretically enables consideration of *all* choices and avoids commitments being made to inappropriate developments. The major difficulty to be overcome at this stage of the corporate planning process is introversion, whereby only developments relating to existing strategies are chosen. This behavioural problem arises because management relies on its own experience. To overcome this there are a number of models designed to help the strategist think through a wide range of potential developments. The aim of these 'strategy generation' models is to stimulate thought about situation-specific developments that the organization might actually undertake. They achieve this by providing general concepts that are intended to provoke a wide list of particular potential developments (see Table 9.2). For example, development direction and development methods concepts and models aim to open up the strategist's thought processes to all the general ways in which the organization might move forward. The wealth-producing concepts and their associated models offer prescriptions for the general ways in which the organization can create wealth from the environments into which it might choose to move. Competitive tactics models describe shorter-term moves that might be adopted. Key resource models help decision-makers to become prescriptive about the sorts of organizational changes that will be necessary if the organization is to deploy effective wealth-producing strategies in chosen environments. The brainstorming technique aims to ensure that a comprehensive list of potential strategies is developed before the decision-makers move on to the evaluation and choice stages of this part of the decision-making process. Used together, systematically, these concepts and models help in the production of an extensive list of potential developments. As is the style of this book, these models are presented in an order that moves from the more general to the more specific and from purposes of 'generation only', through 'generation with evaluation', to 'evaluation and choice'.

Table 9.2   Concepts and models to generate strategic development ideas

Development directions
   the product/market growth vector

Development methods
   internal development, joint venture and acquisition

Wealth-producing developments
   market growth, size and market share strategies
      (the attractive market model, the experience curve, the Boston Consulting Group
      growth/share matrix)
   quality achieving strategies
      (the PIMS research, Garvin's 'productivity from quality' model)
   focused effort strategies
      (the customer profitability classification matrix, close to the customer, 'sticking to
      the knitting', focus strategies)
   synergistic strategies
      (the concept of synergy and the 'better off' test)
   generic competitive strategies
      (Porter's integrative generic competitive strategies model)

Competitive tactics
   offensive, collaborative and defensive moves

Key resource area changes

Brainstorming

Development directions: the product/market growth vector

If wealth creation is the basic problem for strategic decision-makers then a model that identifies the directions organizations might take to locate new wealth-creating areas is useful. In 1968, Igor Ansoff[1] provided a product/market growth vector model based on the assumptions that:

- a basic task of the management strategist is to seek productive growth;
- productive growth is to be earned for *any* organization through changing its products and/or its market places and positions.

Subsequently, writers have extended Ansoff's strategies for growth, to include changes to the *processes* whereby products are made available to markets, and to include the wealth *maintenance* objective (rather than the wealth *generation* objective) of strategic decision-making.[2] A modified version of Ansoff's product/market growth vector matrix is illustrated in Figure 9.1.

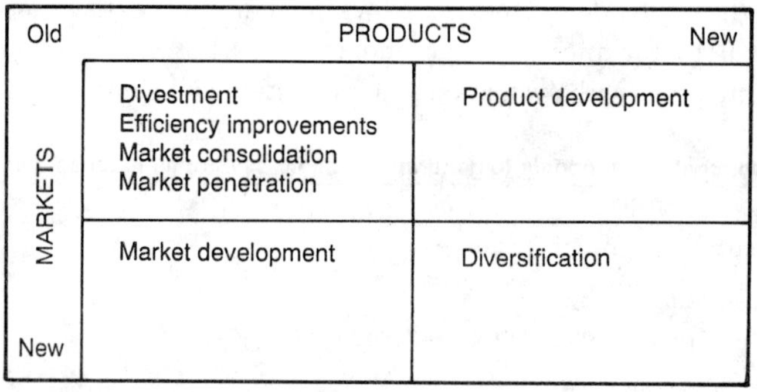

Old	PRODUCTS	New
MARKETS	Divestment Efficiency improvements Market consolidation Market penetration	Product development
	Market development	Diversification
New		

Figure 9.1　The product/market growth vector.

Divestment is a potential strategy for organizations that have identified a distinct section that is incompatible in some sense, such as management, cost basis or technology, with the remainder of the organization. This strategy furthers wealth-creating objectives by providing management with a greater opportunity to concentrate on the activities of the more compatible areas of the organization. It is also a method of raising capital, for example, for organization owners reaching retirement age or for strategists wishing to pursue new product/market developments. Market decline situations, once anticipated, can also signal divestment as an appropriate strategy.

Efficiency improvements have been particularly appropriate for much of British industry during the 1980s. In essence this strategy involves re-arranging organization processes to reduce resource inputs and/or improve prices charged, and thus margins earned, for existing products in existing markets.

Market consolidation requires actions to maintain sales value in a declining market or to maintain share in a growing market. The aim here is to ensure that either sales value or market share remains stable.

Market penetration is achieved when, in existing areas of operation, the organization increases its market share by taking customers away from the competition.

Market development strategies might be based on the findings of the segmentation exercises undertaken in strategic analysis. Such strategies locate and penetrate new segments where existing products can be sold profitably.

Product development encompasses two aspects of product change. Minor changes to the product might be made to achieve differentiation as a situation-specific 'one-off', development or as part of a dynamic development programme associated with ongoing, incremental changes. For example, because of a process of constant updating, today's cars are very different from those of the sixties.

Diversification can be related or unrelated to existing organization activities and outputs. To qualify for the description of diversification, however, the strategic development must take the organization into new markets and new products.

Development methods: internal development, joint development and acquisition

The product/market growth vector is designed to help strategists think about alternative development directions. In embarking on one of these development routes the organization has available three generic methods for negotiating the chosen routes. These are internal development, joint development and acquisition. This expression of what is merely a simple description of development methods is intended to encourage practitioners to broaden their thought horizons. Joint developments can be considered if the organization is short of resources such as cash, market knowledge or expertise. For example, franchise arrangements create wealth for both participants in situations where neither party is able to 'go it alone'. As another example, market developments into Europe might be best undertaken by small companies in collaboration with locally expert agents and distributors.

Acquisitions provide market penetration and market development vehicles for organizations that might find the market place too competitive to allow significant inroads to be made by self-development. Nevertheless, some markets are so new, or some organizations' research and development capabilities so advanced, that the best course of action could be self-development. The advantages and disadvantages of different development methods and advice on how to undertake particular methods are covered more fully in other texts.[3-5] At the very least, exposure to the strategic development methods model should stimulate strategists to consider the relevance and feasibility of steps other than 'going it alone'.

Wealth-producing strategic developments: concepts and models

The basic objective of strategic decision-making is to create wealth. A central objective of the theorists who serve this area of endeavour has been, not surprisingly, to describe and prescribe the nature of *generally* successful wealth-creating strategic developments. This search for universally applicable prescriptions has developed on two fronts. One thrust has been aimed at discovering and publicizing *organization structure* strategies. These advise managers on the most productive organization designs, given particular business situations. Chapter 4 discussed theory's contribution to this problem area. The other thrust is the concern of this section. It has aimed to describe the nature of 'winning' *product/market* strategic developments. In this section some recurring, consistent ideas about the nature of wealth-creating product/market strategies for modern organizations are discussed briefly. Some of the research activity and models associated with these ideas are then considered.

Wealth-producing product/market strategy concepts

Over time, the literature of strategic decision-making has built up a store of contributions that support the following wealth-producing product/market developments:

Develop into growing market areas. The attractive market segment model introduced in the situational analysis section of Chapter 8 described 'potential for growth' as a key criterion on which to judge the attractiveness for entry of any particular market segment. It is generally accepted that in markets of rapid growth even inefficient, inadequately competitive firms can grow and prosper. In mature or declining market segments, however, competition is usually intense, profits are harder to come by and growth is not endemic. The high street retail industry had many claimants to the title of 'success of the decade' in the consumer spending boom of the 1980s. As consumer demand falls, however, many of these successes are now struggling through the 1990s. The car industry, too, is beginning to experience the problems of mature or declining markets. Some organizations have successful records based on a clear policy of seeking out growing markets for strategic developments.[6]

Develop to achieve the biggest size of operation and leading market shares. Another theme to emerge from the literature is that 'size equals success'. The underlying notion, here, is that the biggest market operators command the most powerful marketplace positions, particularly because of the effect size tends to have in reducing unit costs of operation in mass markets.

Develop to achieve greater quality. This generic strategy for wealth creation is sometimes referred to as a strategy of differentiation. High quality offered to the customers of an organization is assumed to generate loyalty and commitment from existing customers and to attract new customers, who perceive the opportunity to obtain better value. The nineties, like the eighties, is an era of quality improvement campaigns as businesses large and small jump on to the quality strategic development bandwagon in attempts to produce more satisfying products and services and to reduce costs of operation.

Develop in ways that focus activities. Marketing theorists have advocated, for some time, the wealth-creating rationale of targeting, rather than scattershotting, marketing activity. The aim of a focused product/market strategy is to be especially successful through doing particular things with greater expertise and/or efficiency than the competition.

Develop to generate synergy. Synergy is the concept of '2 + 2 = 5'. This prescription recommends developments that create new, combined situations perhaps by acquisition in which aspects of each situation work together to create wealth of a greater total magnitude than would have been created by the systems operating independently.

We now explore more fully these wealth-creating product/market concepts by recourse to research findings and models that are associated with the concepts.

The experience curve

The experience curve shows that the cost of doing a repetitive task decreases by a fixed percentage each time the accumulated volume of production (in units) doubles. For example, the total cost might drop from 100 when the total production is 10 units, to 85 (=100 × 0.85) when it increases to 20 units, and to 72.25 (=85 × 0.85) when it reaches 40 units. This direct and consistent relationship between aggregate growth in volume and declining costs of production – the experience curve effect – has been measured empirically in a wide range of industries, including broiler chickens and integrated circuits.[7] Increased size, the theory proposes, generates cost savings through learning (the more we do a task the more efficient we become at it), through specialization (size enables division of labour, which intensifies learning and enables productivity-producing standardization), from product and process improvements (as volume increases the product mix can be rationalized, materials can be better utilized and improved technologies, layouts and storing processes can be introduced) and through economies of scale (increased buying 'muscle' and the sharing of central resources, for example). These findings have helped to fuel the market leadership battles that endure in many mass markets. The rationale for market leadership in price-competitive markets is to gain wealth and power from cost reductions. As economies of scale and learning effects combine, costs fall over time and lead to greater wealth production. Figure 9.2 demonstrates how, if the experience curve theory holds good, those with the highest market share (and hence the highest volume of production) make more profit per sale and more sales than the competition. It also demonstrates how the major source of wealth creation in these types of market situation is reducing costs. In order to put Figure 9.2 into a real industry context we might imagine that company X is Rover, company Y is Ford and company Z is General Motors.

Strategists thinking of adopting the experience curve prescription should be aware of some pitfalls associated with its use. First, reliance on an *average* slope of cost reduction will fail to take note of the effect of, say, recent technological advances. This type of reliance is also indicative of a general danger of over-emphasizing the experience curve model as a success generator and, as a consequence, becoming too focused on cost cutting and insufficiently active in monitoring the environment and in seeking diversification or differentiation opportunities. Market share is not the only wealth generator. The PIMS research, discussed below, emphasizes the importance of quality as a success generator. In some speciality markets a large market share might be a disadvantage if customers perceive largeness as lack of exclusivity. This was a problem faced by the

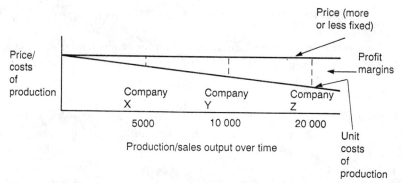

Figure 9.2 Wealth creation and competitive advantage through size, the experience curve and reduced operating costs.

Next organization as it pursued growth strategies in the 1980s. In all markets customers need to perceive value before they will buy. Furthermore, the experience curve is more significant in some industries than in others. A 5 per cent slope in retailing, for example, compares unfavourably with a 30 per cent slope in assembly.[8] The experience curve also suggests a uniform, common curve for every competitor in an industry. However, many industries have been changed completely by new entrants who arrive with a cost curve that behaves differently (often because of a different basic technology). New entrants can also learn from older competitors and so can come into an industry at a point well down the experience curve.

It is important to recognize that the theorists here are actually advocating size as a generic wealth creator – even though the literature tends to concentrate on market share. An organization with the largest market share of just one customer might, for example, be the smallest firm in the industry. Size, therefore, can lay claim to being a generic wealth-creating strategic development concept. However, the above caveats demonstrate again the fact that there are few simple answers to the complex problems of strategy-making and that the size concept needs to be operationalized with great managerial care.

The Boston Consulting Group's Growth/Share Matrix

Inevitably, the directions and methods chosen for strategic developments will have resource implications. The Boston Consulting Group (BCG) matrix, introduced in the strategic analysis section of Chapter 8, reminds us of the need to maintain a balanced product or sub-unit portfolio. In particular, this model combines the 'high market growth area' and 'high market share' prescriptions to advocate maintenance of a supply of 'star' products or strategic sub-units. 'Stars' occupy strong positions in attractive, growing market places. Use of the BCG matrix at the strategic development generating stage of the decision-making process can help to encourage thought about potential developments as investments. The BCG matrix prescribes that better investments are those that re-allocate, with successful consequences, 'cash cow' funds to 'question mark' and 'star' activities. On the other hand, disaster investment routes are those that expend funds on 'dying dogs' or 'falling question marks'.

While the underlying prescription of investing in high growth market situations seems inherently sensible the BCG matrix investment route model should not be used as a tightly prescriptive generatory and evaluatory tool. Michael Porter, for example, refers to the above average success achieved by Worthington Steel through its specialist activities in the USA 'dog' steel industry,[9] and Hanson Trust's renowned success has been forged through a policy of acquiring unglamorous 'cash cows'. (See also the BBA case study in Chapter 3.)

The PIMS research

Since the early 1970s researchers from Harvard Business School, inspired by earlier work at the General Electric Company, have been collecting data on the profit performances of an increasing number of corporations. Findings from this research support the theory that there is a profit impact of market share (the research undertaking has been labelled PIMS). Larger market share, according to the PIMS findings, produces a higher return on investment (the ratio of net, pre-tax operating income to average investment, where investment equals equity plus long-term debt). However, the PIMS research also supports the quality prescription. Higher product quality can compensate for a lack of significant market share. Small-share organizations often perform better than larger-share firms when they are perceived to offer better-quality products and services.

The PIMS research reveals that heavy marketing expenditure is no substitute for inferior product quality. In fact, heavy marketing spenders with inferior quality outputs perform worse in return on investment terms than do lower marketing expenditure, inferior quality offering organizations. While the best of all returns seem to accrue to the top market share, best-quality firms, Luchs[10] has suggested that if strategists are faced with a choice of *either* quality *or* market share then the surest wealth-producing strategy will be quality-orientated. Of course, quality and market share can be related. The biggest organizations are often those with most resources to spend on research and development and on improvements to products and services. Garvin[11] points out that quality has two dimensions – an internal, cost-saving one and an external customer-satisfying one – and that both can create wealth and increased market shares.

Interestingly, the PIMS research suggests that it is better to aim to be a top performer on at least one scale (market share or quality) rather than to seek to occupy the middle ground on both criteria. Some other contributions discussed later are also clear about the need to avoid 'getting stuck in the middle' when it comes to product/market choices.

Focused-effort strategies

As has already been stated, the theory of marketing advocates the breaking down of markets into smaller sub-segments. These then become the targets for focused, 'rifle-shot' marketing campaigns. The undifferentiated, scatter-shot mass market approach has been criticized for many years. 'It is rarely possible for a product or brand to be all things to all people'.[12] Undifferentiated marketing becomes increasingly less appropriate. Modern-day mass-market strategists seek success through focus. Sir Kit Macmahon,[13] formerly of the Midland Bank, spoke for the high street banking industry generally when he declared: 'A low-cost production and distribution system is one essential prong of competitive strategy – differentiation of product/service and intense focus on the customer is the other.' However, general concepts such as focus beg the question of how they might be operationalized in practice.

Michael Porter, again, assists strategists to think about the types of focus choices they might make.[14] For fragmented commodity type, highly competitive markets, for example, he recommends specializing by product type (as per Tie Rack), by customer type, by geographic location or by offering a 'bare bones–no frills' service.

Many productivity consultants suggest that big improvements in profitability can flow to organizations that, for the first time, concentrate marketing activity on their most profitable customers.[15] A rule of 80:20 often seems to apply whereby 80 per cent of the wealth generated by an organization comes from its interactions with just 20 per cent of its customers. Often, however, these clients and other potentially important clients receive minimal effort and attention. The converse of the 80:20 rule applies – 80 per cent of resource expenditure goes, wastefully, on contacting and servicing the less important clients.

Shapiro et al.[16] have noted that many organizations do not know or do not think about their ability to serve different classes of customers or the profit levels to be earned from them. They have provided a customer profitability matrix and advocate that strategists choose the matrix quadrant in which their organization will locate itself. *Bargain basement* customers are undemanding in terms of costs of service but expect the supplier to charge prices that incorporate a smaller profit margin. *Passive* customers pay a high price but are not costly to serve. This is the type of customer who perceives switching costs to be high or simply lacks a professional approach to buying. *Carriage trade* customers demand costly service inputs (special features in products, design, services, rapid order-to-delivery systems, for example) but they do expect to pay a premium price for the special service provided. *Aggressive* customers are often large, highly professional organizations that can offer large orders and substantial profits but expect, in return, total quality, extra responsiveness of service and low prices. Marks & Spencer has a reputation for being this kind of buyer. Shapiro et al. do not suggest that one particular quadrant is most attractive, generally, although they acknowledge the attractiveness of serving passive customers wherever and for as long as they can be found. However, they do advocate choosing, at the micro level, one quadrant in which to focus effort. 'Don't get stuck in the middle', they advise, in a similar vein to the prescription arising from the PIMS researchers' findings on middle quality, middle market share organizational performances. A firm operating mainly from one quadrant, they suggest, will begin to receive enquiries from buyers of the chosen quadrant type. Shapiro *et al.* also remind us of the need for continuous monitoring of customer profitability. They note a general movement by buyers towards becoming aggressive transactors.

This model provides another perspective for the process of thinking about potentially profitable focused strategic developments. It does, however, tend to push decision-makers towards present operation-related strategies, when strategies that take an organization out of present business areas might provide useful ways forward. Use of the customer profitability matrix might also provoke analysts to return to the strategic analysis stage of the decisional process. Shapiro *et al.* advise that many organizations suffer from the major weakness of not knowing the costs of serving different customers.

'Sticking to the knitting' and 'getting close to customers' are separate-focus strategies that are discussed here together, because they are prescriptions from the same theorists – Peters and Waterman. In their investigations into the best-run companies in the USA, Peters and Waterman[17] found that two common characteristics of the best performers (defined by reference to a number of wealth-creating performance indicators over a period of years) were an obsession with quality (again) and with making every aspect of the business customer-responsive, and product/market development policies that undertook new ventures only if they were associated with existing business areas and existing business strengths. Since the publication of Peters and Waterman's best-selling book, *In Search of Excellence*, some of their 'excellent' companies have under-performed. However, to the extent that we can rely on their principles of excellent performance two further lines of thought are recommended to analysts thinking about ways forward for their organization. Strategic developments, according to Peters and Waterman, should be closely related to existing 'excellences' and should seek to intensify organizational desire and ability to understand and satisfy customers.

Synergistic strategies

As stated previously, synergy can be described as '2 + 2 = 5'. When Dixons acquired Currys in the mid-1980s, Dixons' aggressive marketing style, its strong market position in 'brown' goods and its predominantly young clientele combined synergistically with the older-fashioned, older-clienteled and 'white' goods stronghold that was Currys. The combination produced profits generally agreed to be well in excess of those that would have been generated by the two organizations operating independently.[18] The concept of synergy is kindred to that of sticking to the knitting. It advises against use of the BCG growth/share matrix, for example, if such usage is aimed at bringing into the business portfolio business units or products that merely 'tack on' to the existing businesses in conglomerate fashion. Rather, strategic developments should be aimed at creating *additional* wealth through the fusion of the new with the old.

Michael Porter comes down firmly in favour of the search for synergy and against conglomerate, unrelated development.[19] He advocates a three-point test to guide successful acquisition choices. First, he advises that the acquisition should take the organization into an inherently attractive market (the *attractiveness* test). Next, the organization should be careful not to pay too much for the acquisition (the *cost of entry* test). Thirdly, the acquirer should look for synergistic potential (the *better off* test). Synergy is a vague concept but theorists and practitioners seem convinced of its very real existence and impact. Analysts therefore should channel their thoughts towards synergistic developments when undertaking the strategic development idea-generating process.

Generic competitive strategies

Choices of the development directions to be taken and the methods of achieving these developments are only first choices along the road to successful wealth creation. Once into a product/market area of operation the organization will have to earn its living through competing effectively. Michael Porter's immense popularity as a modern-day strategy guru has arisen because (a) he has perhaps most clearly articulated the concept that better wealth creation is to be earned through beating the competition; and (b) he has produced a generic competitive-strategy model that integrates the prevailing wisdoms of size, share and cost-reducing strategies; quality and differentiation strategies; and focus-orientated strategies. (In his separately enunciated better off and attractiveness tests Porter also embraces the principles of synergy and market growth area orientated developments.) His prescriptions for the basic methods of gaining competitive advantage (earning higher than average profitability) lead strategists to think about the strategies they might choose in order to be top competitors in their chosen market places. Porter claims[20] that higher than average industry profitability will be earned by competitors who align themselves most favourably against the five forces of industry competition. Central to the attainment of competitive advantage is the ability of management to choose and implement a winning generic competitive strategy. According to Porter, this choice is 'clear-cut'. Firms must choose to be one of the following:

1 A least-cost producer. This implies that the organization will compete on price and through attaining lower 'bottom line' costs than the competition. This prescription, of course, aligns with the underlying messages from the PIMS market share findings and the BCG growth/share model.
2 A differentiator. This generic strategy aims to produce extra value in the eyes of customers sufficient to attract a price premium. This strategy is not primarily focused on costs of operation. In fact it might involve the incurring of

additional costs if these produce extra customer value leading to a higher price premium.

The choice of which of these generic strategies to adopt needs to be made after the decision of where to compete. The choice here is again of a 'one from two' nature. Porter divides markets into broad segments and focused narrow segments. Ultimately, the generic competitive strategies available to any firm include:

- a broad-market, least-cost producer strategy;
- a broad-market, differentiator strategy;
- a focused-market, least-cost producer strategy;
- a focused-market, differentiator strategy;
- a focused-market, least-cost and differentiator strategy.

Weaknesses inherent in Porter's generic competitive strategy model include the regularly present problem associated with strategic decision models. The final choice of generic strategy is left to the strategist. Porter does not offer specific prescriptions. The choice of which organizational changes are necessary to achieve competitive advantage via the chosen generic strategy is once again left to the decision-makers concerned. Strategic decisions, ultimately, have to be taken by strategists. Further, the delineation of a broad from a narrow market – or indeed of any market – is not dealt with by Porter. His recognition of broad, undifferentiated, markets seems to fly in the face of the prescriptions identified earlier, which suggest that all markets should be segmented and 'rifle-shot' targeted. Critics claim that Porter's emphasis on the either/or nature of choices between a least-cost and a differentiated position misses the relevance of a dual route that can be taken to productive effect by an organization.[11] The PIMS research referred to earlier, for example, illustrates the attractiveness of being a large, low-cost, high-quality institution.

Despite these caveats Porter has stimulated much useful thought among strategic decision-makers about the ways in which they might develop to compete more successfully. Porter also stimulates thought through his very clear prescription, similar to that arising from other sources discussed earlier, that a strategic mistake is made by organizations that 'get stuck in the middle', not having made clear choices about where and how to compete.

This section has been concerned with the research findings and prescriptions that have been generated on the topic of generic wealth-producing strategies. It will be obvious from the discussion that the findings and the prescriptions serving this area have not been unequivocally accepted as being totally reliable or valid. Nevertheless, the repetitious manner in which the concepts of market growth areas, size for cost reduction, quality for differentiation, focus and synergy continue to appear suggests some inherent worthiness of the concepts in their roles as aids to the generation of strategic development ideas. An interaction between theory and practice promotes the adoption of these recipes. In such a situation organizations often need to practise the prescriptions simply to remain competitive.

Competitive tactics

Up to this point this chapter has concentrated on the broad generic competitive strategies that a firm might adopt. In larger organizations more tactical, shorter-term competitive strategies are sometimes best designed in detail, as part of the implementation stage of the strategic decision-making process. However, an overview of the range of tactical competitive strategies available to the organization can help top strategists in their general choices of competitive tactics. These can then be communicated to marketing departments or operating subsidiaries to act as a guide for their shorter-term plans. A consideration of potential competitive tactics should, of course, be undertaken with the results of previously conducted industry structure and inter-firm analyses in mind.[21] Competitive moves can be viewed as being located on a continuum ranging from offensive, through collaborative or non-threatening and on to defensive (see Table 9.3).

Table 9.3   The competitive tactics continuum

Offensive moves
   brute force
   unobtrusive moves
   difficult to follow moves
   moves that denote mixed motives
   commitment-communicating moves

Collaborative/non-threatening moves
   industry-improving moves (regardless of whether competitors follow suit)
   industry-improving moves (provided competitors follow suit)
   firm-improving moves that are considered to be non-threatening by rivals

Defensive moves
   raise structural barriers
   raise perceptions of retaliation
   lower the attractiveness of the market

'Offensive' moves seek to achieve sustainable competitive advantage by creating new, favourable alignments of the organization to the industry's forces of competition. So the organization needs to create the favourable situations implied by the checklist of questions relating to the five forces of competition and provided in Chapter 8. Unsophisticated competitors often see 'brute force' as the way to change industry structure. This can be an effective means of achieving a swift, sharp 'shake-out', in which a very strong competitor makes big price reductions suddenly, and thus quickly attracts larger market share and simultaneously makes the new price level unattractive to smaller, less efficient opera-tors. However, brute force is often met by retaliation – sometimes to the point of irrationality. The result is a marketplace where all competitors are worse off. Prices come down and marketing costs escalate. Only customers are better off. If offensive moves are to be undertaken it is usually better to employ a certain amount of finesse. Tactically, this finese should seek to achieve a 'no retaliation' or, at least, a 'delayed retaliation' response from competitors.

'Unobtrusive' moves are taken quietly, away from competitors' centres of attention. New product introductions in minor markets or with selected cus-tomers can be undertaken quietly to provide a strong base for a more general launch, before the competition realizes what is happening.

'Difficult to follow' moves take advantage of the competition's resource problems. For example, successful research and development activities can place an organization years ahead of the competition. Smaller organizations can some-times offer a flexibility and responsiveness that bigger firms find difficult to follow in the short term.

'Costly to follow' moves put the competition into a dilemma. For example, does the big competitor respond to a price cut made by a smaller operator in selected markets by reducing *all* its prices?

'Mixed motives' moves usually create indecision in the competitor and produce a time lag in its response to offensive moves. For example, the introduc-tion of polystyrene as a packaging material left many wood- and cardboard-based packagers in two minds over whether and how to respond to this substitute material threat. Adoption and promotion of polystyrene implies an acceptance of its attractiveness as a packaging material and means a demotion of the traditional 'cash cow' materials.

It is essential that, once agreed upon, the competitive move is clearly sup-ported. The organization needs to communicate its commitment to the move, unequivocally.[22] This commitment will be communicated effectively if the firm: (a) is perceived to have the resources, ready for deployment, to execute the move; (b) demonstrates a clear intention to carry out the commitment, and has a history of adherence to past commitments; (c) is perceived as being unable or unwilling to back down; (d) is perceived as having the required level of sophistication in its sensory systems to know when it is necessary to take market action to demon-strate commitment.

For example, in 1988 Thomson Holidays, the market leader in the UK air tours industry, publicly announced its preference as being to 'compete on quality, but combined with a determination not to be beaten on price'. This public announce-ment was well reported in the popular press and set out Thomson's powerful resource-supported intentions before the holiday season began. It thus clearly warned off early price-cutting moves from smaller competitors.

Collaborative and non-threatening moves seek to improve the firm's market place position without threatening the positions of inter-firm rivals. For example, work by one organization alone with a major industry supplier on the improvement of product quality can lead to a general improvement in market image, and so in consumer demand, for the benefit of all industry players. Price rises by a firm, which are followed by other players without adversely affecting total market demand, will increase the total profitability of the industry. Non-threatening moves can also include situations where the organization selects new areas of activity that do not interest its rivals.

Defensive moves are of three basic types. Threatened by a potential new entrant or by an existing rival seeking to encroach into its traditional market places, the organization can: (a) raise structural barriers; (b) increase anticipation in the hostile competitor of the defender's retaliation; (c) reduce the attractiveness of the segment under attack.

Raising structural barriers is a tactical move, which can be operationalized in many forms. Patent protection, for example, can make entry difficult. On the other hand, an extremely valuable customer interaction (as perceived by the customer) can make switching costs for that customer too high to be acceptable. This high level of value might be made up of the combined effect of many features of the organization's products, services and value chain linkages. In food and confectionery retail markets, manufacturers that have managed to 'lock in' prime positions on supermarket shelves find this control of the critical distribution outlet a major barrier to the successful entry of new competitors or the successful launch of new products by existing competitors. By increasing perceptions of a strong retaliation a firm attempts to warn off threatening competitive moves. The firm demonstrates its commitment to retaliation by exhibiting the characteristics already described in the discussion of 'communicating commitment'. The third type of defensive tactic involves reducing the attractiveness of the market being attacked rather than increasing the cost of entry into it. For example, reductions in the prices charged in the market can be made, to make the investment proposed by the potential entrant not worth while. Of course, this also incurs a cost for the organization concerned.

In defensive strategy-making, timing is particularly crucial. The aim should be to dissuade the competitor from further offensive thoughts and moves before it has built up a high level of commitment and investment. Ideally, competitors should be dissuaded at pre-entry stage – when market studies and initial deliberations are being undertaken. The next stage at which the competitor might be 'defensively attacked' is at entry, when the competitor is testing markets, organizing operations and developing product and process expertise. The sequencing stage sees the new entrant with a foothold in the market and concerned to develop a long-run strategy. Product lines might then be broadened, expansionary investment undertaken and an 'ever-present market occupant' image developed. The post-entry period sees the well-established competitor thinking as a defender.

Thinking about the tactical moves that might be undertaken, in a systematic and comprehensive way, enables analysts to improve the rationality of the strategic development generation process. In particular it avoids the dangers of neglecting this important aspect of strategy development and of simply competing in an unsophisticated or inappropriate brute force fashion. It also reminds the analyst that market places do not have to be arenas for zero-sum games. A proactive approach to strategy can improve the total market wealth available to everyone.

Key resource area changes

The choices eventually made with regard to development directions, development methods and wealth-producing strategies to be undertaken will involve commitments to action – resources will have to be deployed. At this stage of the strategy-generating process the analyst can usefully return to the key resource area models used initially in the strategic analysis exercise. On this occasion models such as the value chain can be used as a backcloth to stimulate thought about the types of organizational changes that will be necessary, or at least helpful, to the successful achievement of strategic developments. In particular, given competitive market situations, resources will need to be attracted and/or re-arranged to support market growth, least cost, differentiation and focused based, synergistic intentions. The specifics of how resources are to be deployed should be established when the implementation stage of the strategic decision-making process is being planned. Here, the aim is to generate potential wealth-creating, resource change strategies and to provide an early consideration of how resource capability can be made to match potential product/market strategies. A more detailed evaluation of potential wealth-creating strategies, including their resource implications, will build on this early generating/evaluating exercise when it is conducted in the next, evaluatory, stage of the linear sequential approach to decision-making.

Brainstorming

Use of the models contained in this part of Chapter 9 will have enabled the generation of a wide range of potential strategies. The aim of generating a long list is to offset the tendency displayed by 'most companies to choose their final set of strategies from a rather brief and unimaginative list'.[23] One way to facilitate an imaginative list is to use the technique of 'brainstorming'. This involves groups of between four and eight people, working together for periods of no more than one hour to generate lists of strategies. The basic rules of brainstorming should be explained to the group at the start of the session:

- the more ideas the better;
- no idea is too outlandish to be expressed;
- laugh *with*, not *at*, contributors;

- combinations and modifications of ideas are welcome;
- *evaluation* should not be allowed.

The list of strategies that evolves, finally, from the strategy generation process, including the brainstorming session, provides the basis for the next stage of decision-making: the evaluation and choice stage. Models are available to help in conducting this stage in a more rational way, and some of these are discussed in the next section.

Models to assist the evaluation and choice of strategic developments

Not all the potential developments generated from the systematic procedure outlined above will be suitable for implementation. The organization will, for example, be unable to afford to 'go ahead' across all potential fronts. Some strategies might be unlikely to produce wealth because of their incompatibility with the firm's resource base or likely environmental situation. Important stakeholders might simply not want the organization to develop in particular ways.

Other strategies might seem attractive in terms of wealth potential but might be judged to be too risky. This part of this chapter considers some of the evaluatory or choice-assisting models that are available in the theory of strategic decision-making. They seek to help strategists to work through their list of potential developments to reach conclusions on the developments the organization will pursue. The evaluation or choice models can be categorized as:

- financial and risk appraisal models;
- suitability and the TOWS matrix;
- a stakeholder support evaluatory model;
- fit with theory's wealth-producing prescriptions;
- a strategic fit ranking matrix.

The discussion of these models follows a process that might be undertaken after the brainstormed list of potential developments has been sieved to remove the obviously impractical strategies. Briefly, the process subjects potential strategies to a number of tests. The first-category models – financial and risk appraisal – are most concerned with tests of profitability and liquidity and with the generation of insights into the uncertainty or riskiness associated with particular strategies. Next, the process tests for the suitability of particular strategies by evaluating their 'fits' with findings from the previously undertaken strengths, weaknesses, opportunities and threats analysis. A stakeholder support model then helps in the assessment of the acceptability of strategies in terms of the aspirations and power positions of important stakeholders. Next is a test that makes reference to theory's wealth-creating prescriptions by asking the question: 'Does the strategy make sense in terms of being a theoretically recommended way of creating wealth?' Finally, in an effort to make the process as comprehensively rational as possible, and to find (or confirm the already obvious) clear-cut choices of strategies to be implemented, a matrix is introduced to draw together all the evaluatory findings and to facilitate final choices of 'best fit' strategies.

Financial and risk appraisal models

The basic task of the strategic decision-making process is to create wealth. Even survival strategies, which might lay claim to being *the* fundamental type of organization strategy, are undertaken as optimistic prerequisites to the survivor organization renewing its wealth creation and distribution capability. Rationality demands that decision-makers understand the nature of each potential strategy in terms of how much wealth it will create. However, precise estimates are rarely obtainable in the constrained circumstances (identified in Chapter 1) that apply to the strategic decision process.

Financial and risk appraisal models aim to help analysts make better estimates of the returns to be earned, the resources required and the risks associated with particular strategies. Return on investment and cash flow models inevitably require analysts to consider the resource and environmental contexts of developments and so to build a data bank that improves the assessment of risk. By subjecting potential strategies to systematic tests involving the models shown below, strategists can move towards a more comprehensive and detailed assessment of the alternative ways forward. This requires careful investigation into: (a) the sources and sizes of costs, revenues and cash flows of different developments; (b) the resources available for investment and the size of those that will be needed if following particular courses of action; (c) the opportunity costs to be incurred by adopting one strategy, or one set of strategies, rather than others; (d) the risks associated with particular strategies; and (e) the decision-makers' and other important stakeholders' propensities towards risk taking. Collectively, these financial and risk evaluation models invoke discussion and investigation centred on resource, environmental, wealth target and human values issues. The models considered here are:

- gap analysis;
- the return on investment concept;
- discounted cash flow investment appraisal techniques;
- break-even analysis;
- payback period analysis;
- cash flow forecasts and liquidity ratios;
- sensitivity analysis, simulation modelling and scenario planning.

Gap analysis

Gap analysis is a relatively simple technique for assessing the wealth shortfall that will have to be made good if important stakeholders' aspirations are to be satisfied by the organization. It is also helpful in quantifying stakeholder aspirations and setting organizational objectives. It thus provides another example of a strategic decision-making model that can be used in different stages of the decision-making process. At this evaluatory stage, it assists in the assessment of a strategy's contribution to the wealth-gathering aspirations of the enterprise. Imagine that the two owners of a small business, which has made only a small profit over the past year (say £1000 net profit), have agreed that next year they require the business to achieve at least £20 000 net profit. Further, they require annual salaries of £20 000 each instead of the £10 000 each they received this year. Figure 9.3, in gap analysis style, demonstrates the wealth-creating problem facing the owners and provides a framework against which to assess the significance of the wealth expected to be generated by any strategy under scrutiny.

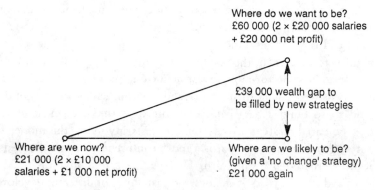

Where do we want to be?
£60 000 (2 × £20 000 salaries
+ £20 000 net profit)

£39 000 wealth gap to
be filled by new strategies

Where are we now?
£21 000 (2 × £10 000
salaries + £1 000 net profit)

Where are we likely to be?
(given a 'no change' strategy)
£21 000 again

Figure 9.3 Gap analysis: a hypothetical example.

The return on investment concept

The concept of return on investment (ROI) is fundamentally connected to the basic strategic problem of wealth creation. The measurement of ROI will vary according to the definitions used for the profit and capital inputs that go into the ROI performance ratio.

$$\text{ROI} = \frac{\text{profit}}{\text{investment}} \times 100 \text{ per cent}$$

The organization should be expected to produce a ROI that is better than a risk-free market rate of interest.

One problem arising from an over-emphasis on ROI as a measure of success is related to the residual nature of net profit. Small business people, for example, depend on their businesses for their day-to-day livelihoods. Their salaries and pension funds and other, less tangible, rewards are earned before a net profit figure is calculated. These benefits, of course, would be lost if the business was liquidated because of a weak ROI performance. Furthermore, the ROI concept neglects the emotional commitment many organizational personnel have to the maintenance of their enterprise or to the undertaking of a pet project, despite poor, or potentially poor, financial performances.

Nevertheless, the concept and its derivatives, such as return on sales (ROS), are important concepts for strategy evaluation in many businesses today and should be employed more generally as tests of the wealth-creating potential of strategies under review. Some organizations seem to prosper by adopting these measures as their most important evaluators of success. The highly successful organization BTR, for example, is reputed to work to a maxim of 'if it doesn't earn 10 per cent ROS either sell it or shut it'. Readers might wish to review the section on financial ratios in Chapter 4 at this time.

Discounted cash flow investment appraisal techniques

Developments that require resource inputs now in order to generate wealth in the medium to long term are amenable to the techniques of investment appraisal. Two principal techniques in use in business today are *net present value* and *internal rate of return*, which fall under the broad category of discounted cash flow (DCF) techniques. Perfect rationality would enable calculation of the wealth that would flow from potential strategies, in precise terms. However, decision-making is undertaken under constrained circumstances, as discussed in Chapter 1. Constraints are most significant when strategic decision-makers are considering longer-term implications in changing environments.

The DCF techniques aim to improve rationality by forcing decision-makers into a more comprehensive and detailed analysis of the cash flow outcomes – from cost and receipt perspectives – that are expected to accrue over the lifetime of the strategic investment under review. The processes involved in this formal assessment of investment opportunities should generate better decisions than those that underpin many 'gut feel' or 'rose tinted', blissfully ignorant, embarcations into new ventures. Attempts to put figures to the investment's lifetime cost and receipt categories should generate deeper understanding of the risks and uncertainties associated with particular developments. DCF techniques force strategists to assess the costs of capital currently accruing to their business and to test investments according to the significance of their real contributions to the 'wealth gap shortfall' – after they have repaid their own interest costs or some agreed minimum rate of return. They stimulate decision-makers to consider the opportunity costs of following one strategy, or one set of strategies, instead of others.

In total, therefore, DCF-type investment appraisal techniques help to widen and intensify the investigation into resource positions, environmental situations, riskiness and stakeholder aspirations. Problems are inherent in such models, however. These techniques, like many quantitative techniques, distil what are usually highly uncertain situations into 'hard and fast', one specific amount, answers. The sums that go into the many cost and revenue categories over the projected life of an investment, for example, are usually based on highly uncertain assumptions. Such techniques also fail to take account of emotional values (although the process of using them often brings these issues, beneficially, to the surface of the decision-making situation). Some very lucrative investments are unattractive for social reasons. In a similar vein, these models do not easily lend themselves to the inputting of social costs and benefits. These types of costs and benefits have to be quantified in some way in order for them to be fitted into the model. Productive (in ratio terms) investments need to be judged against less productive but larger total return generating investments. Nor do the DCF models automatically take account of whether the organization can afford a particular investment.

Fuller treatments of investment appraisal models are available in standard management accounting texts.[24]

Break-even analysis

Break-even analysis (sometimes described as cost–volume–profit analysis) helps the analyst to think about the impacts different levels of activity have on the profitability of a potential product/market venture. Costs are analysed into their fixed and variable elements, and the expected outcomes at different levels of activity can be calculated and expressed graphically.

In simple terms the break-even sales volume can be ascertained by dividing the value of total fixed costs by the contribution (sales value per unit less operating costs per unit) earned by each unit sold. Break-even analysis helps the evaluating decision-maker to consider: (a) how much volume (and market share) has to be achieved before the venture becomes a net wealth creator; (b) whether the break-even, or better, position is achievable; and (c) whether the decision-makers are prepared to accept the risks perceived to be involved in an attempt to make the strategy a wealth creator. The technique is also useful as a motivational and control aid for strategic implementation. Even at this evaluatory stage, strategists considering the implications of break-even modelling will focus their attention on the targets and budgets that seem appropriate to the realization of a successful strategy. Once again, the discipline involved in working through the likely costs of the development and in thinking about the way in which costs will actually behave enhances the rationality of the evaluatory process, as does the technique's implied demands for careful assessments of environmental situations and revenues.

The model's limitations lie in its rational economic assumptions – decision-makers do not always favour the best break-even proposition. Another important limitation lies in the underlying assumption of linearity, i.e. that costs and revenues may be represented by straight lines. In real life, in the short term at least, many variable costs are fixed, factory operators continue to receive minimum wages, for example, even when the production line is at a standstill. Often the market situation demands step-like increases in new capacity and sometimes, in order to facilitate increases in production, new, non-linear, injections of costs need to be made.[25]

Payback period analysis

'Payback' refers to the number of periods of net cash inflows required to recoup the original investment. Thus an initial investment of £10000 will have an expected payback of five years if net inflows of £2000 per year are anticipated. The payback model ignores profitability issues – it is more concerned with liquidity and the speed with which investment expenditure is to be recouped. Given that longer-term investments are generally considered to be the most uncertain and risky an investment that 'pays back' more quickly will tend to find favour over other, longer, investments offering similar expected returns. Research by Manchester University[26] found that for the respondents questioned the most favoured formal technique of investment appraisal was, in fact, the simple payback method. However, the research also found that the most favoured and used approach of all was that of reliance on the investment decision-makers' subjective judgements. Subjective judgement must provide a major input into the evaluation of potential strategies and the decision-maker's judgement reigns supreme at the moment of choice. However, it seems that, in practice, strategists tend not to avail themselves of the relatively easy-to-use models that are available to improve decision-making rationality and so to underpin and improve judgement.

Cash flow forecasts and liquidity ratios

The discussion presented here on financial and risk appraisal models has been structured to deal with models in a particular sequence – from models primarily concerned with wealth and productivity assessments, to models concerned primarily with impact on liquidity assessments and on to models primarily concerned with risk assessments. Each of the models presented builds on the knowledge gleaned from earlier assessments.

An assessment of the impact of a strategy on cash flows and organizational liquidity is particularly essential. It is not lack of profitability that forces a firm into liquidation but a lack of sufficient liquidity. Important tests of the risk inherent in a proposed venture should include cash flow forecasts, which calculate the extent of net cash inflows or outflows. The aim is to determine whether the company can afford, or can attract, finance to facilitate the projected outflows. Many strategists more easily and quickly perceive the risks involved in a strategy when they are crystallized in terms of the cash that needs to be found to finance it. Key ratios that help managers to assess the forecast liquidity performances (and to review actual performances during implementation) include the gearing ratio, the current ratio and the acid test ratio. These ratios are explained in Chapter 4.

Sensitivity analysis, simulation modelling and scenario planning

The sensitivity analysis technique has gained more widespread use with the availability of computer spreadsheet packages that are specifically designed to facilitate 'user friendly' sensitivity analysis exercises. The technique involves identification of the important assumptions behind the expected financial performance of a venture and the subsequent asking of 'what if these assumptions were changed?' questions. New assumptions about such issues as market demand, production cost levels and prices charged are fed into the computer to establish how sensitive profit and liquidity performances are to the underlying factors and their new values. In this way strategists obtain warnings about the financial effects that might apply if important strategic variables occur in a less optimistic manner than expected. Sensitivity analysis thus clarifies the important ingredients for the successful implementation of a strategy and also promotes discussion of and insight into the chances of these variables being different from those expected. It paves the way for contingency planning, which attempts to remove, reduce or insure against the risks associated with key variables.

Simulation modelling extends the sensitivity technique. Rather than simply selecting important variables, assigning them 'what if?' values and then modelling outcomes as the sensitivity approach does, the simulation method seeks to assign probability distributions to all the important factors and then to simulate the way each of these factors in each of its profitability values might interact. Simulation requires three steps to be performed:

1 Estimate the range of the values for each of the important factors (for example, range of selling prices and range of sales growth rates).
2 Select at random one value from the distribution of values for each factor. Then combine the values for each factor and compute the rate of return from the combination.
3 Do 2 over and over again to define and evaluate the odds of the occurrence of each possible rate of return.

This technique involves an intense analysis of every aspect of a potential strategy. It also involves the participation of knowledgeable personnel if realistic probability distributions for important success factors are to be calculated. The resultant model describes a range of outcomes with probabilities of occurrence values for each outcome. It also demonstrates variability from the expected (most likely) outcome and thus enables a choice of strategies that demonstrate low variability (and presumably less risk) to be made.

Computers can be used to carry out the trials in very little time and at very little expense. Hertz[27] describes one trial of 3600 discounted cash flow calculations based on nine input factors, which took just two minutes and cost just £15 for computer time. Despite these perceived advantages of the simulation method, difficulties in understanding the underlying theory, a lack of modelling and computing expertise, and the need to undertake detailed analysis, including precise probability assessments, tend to make the method too unwieldy for general adoption by business.

An important distinction between 'What if?' sensitivity analysis and scenario planning is the descriptive element of the scenario. Paul Samuelson[28] identifies a problem with forecasting: 'I think that the greatest error in forecasting is not realising how important are the probabilities of events other than those everyone is agreeing upon'. To combat the problems that can arise from an inappropriate choice of the strategy associated with what is regarded as the most probable future environment, many organizations now consider the possibility of several environments. Linneman and Kennell[29] provide a practical approach to multiple-scenario analysis, which they claim is within the capabilities of even the smallest companies. Their ten-step approach leads to the design of distinct scenarios. Two scenarios is too few, they claim – one automatically assumes the mantle of 'good', the other 'bad'. Four scenarios are usually sufficient to cover the markedly different situations that the organization might face. The scenarios should develop descriptive themes around different key variables and should be written in no more than two paragraphs. Each scenario should be different but all should be plausible. A most likely scenario should be included (but should not be described as such, to avoid leading analysts into concentrating on that scenario). 'Deadly enemy' and best scenarios should also be included. The scenarios should be written from the viewpoint of someone standing in the future and describing conditions at that time and how they developed. Thus scenario planning used at this stage of the evaluatory process is an attempt to get people to think about the possible future situations that the firm might face and then to consider the risks inherent in the strategies being evaluated, in the context of the different scenarios. Scenario planning might also have been used in the identification of opportunities and threats, earlier in the corporate planning process, during the strategic analysis exercise.

Financial and risk appraisal models are most concerned with testing potential developments in terms of their likely impacts on profitability and liquidity and the risks they bring to the organization and its people. Other types of models provide different 'test' perspectives and the discussion now moves on to consider some of these.

Suitability and the TOWS matrix

The test of 'suitability' refers to the 'extent to which a strategy addresses itself to the situation described in the strategic analysis'.[2] In Chapter 8 it was explained that a useful method of analysis of a business situation is to compile a list of internal strengths and weaknesses and external opportunities and threats. These SWOT analysis findings can be grouped into a TOWS (threats, opportunities, weaknesses and strengths) matrix, which helps in choices of suitable strategies. The TOWS matrix helps strategists who might not have made the connection that different combinations of SWOT factors 'may require distinct strategic choices'.[30]. Preparation of the TOWS matrix involves the drawing up of a matrix of the form illustrated in Figure 9.4.

	Strengths	Weaknesses
Opportunities	Strength–opportunity matching strategies	Weakness–opportunity matching strategies
Threats	Strength–threat matching strategies	Weakness–threat matching strategies

Figure 9.4 The TOWS matrix.

The matrix identifies strategies that are either suitable or unsuitable depending on whether and how they address TOWS combinations. Strength–opportunity matching strategies are 'maxi–maxi' strategies that capitalize on sound organizational characteristics and market opportunities. A strength–threat matching strategy is a 'maxi–mini' strategy that aims to maximize the former while minimizing the latter. For example, an organization with a good record of social responsibility might use this to take the sting out of a current pressure group attack. A weakness–opportunity matching strategy is a 'mini–maxi' strategy. Thus, a manufacturer with an attractive, in terms of market opportunity, new product but with little resource available to launch the product effectively might seek out a suitably resourced joint-venture partner. A weakness–threat matching strategy is a 'mini–mini' strategy. This is the worst situation in which a firm might find itself and the strategic decision-making process should endeavour to avoid it. Nevertheless, these types of situation do occur and strategies have to be found to deal with them. A firm that is very illiquid and facing intense competition, for example, might seek a coalition or merger with a willing competitor as a way forward. Thus, the TOWS matrix forces strategists to refer back to the strategic analysis outcomes and to think in very specific terms about strategies that fit the resource and environmental situations facing the firm. It also highlights any dangerously unsuitable 'pet' strategic developments that have been 'kept in the running' by their 'owners'. At this late stage, the TOWS matrix can also generate new strategic development ideas.

A stakeholder support evaluatory model

In the mid-1980s Barclays Bank sold off its profitable South African operations because of increasing pressure from its customers and shareholders (and its potential customers and shareholders). Many of Barclays' stakeholders found the continuance of this wealth-creating strategy unacceptable on social, political and moral grounds. The ultimate success level achieved by a strategy depends more upon the support it receives from important stakeholders than upon any inherent economic, wealth-maximizing rationality it might be perceived to possess. If key stakeholders find a particular strategic development unacceptable then either the strategy will be unimplementable or the consequence of 'forcing' implementation will be a reduction and perhaps even reversal of the hoped for level of wealth. Despite this importance of people, their power positions and propensities for or against particular strategies, there are few explicit models to help strategists think through the political viability of a strategy. The largely rational/economic basis for corporate planning tends to ignore these important aspects of strategy-making and so provides a less rational approach than is desirable. It is important that, in the context of a proposed venture, careful consideration is given to the positions which might be adopted by important present and future stakeholders.

Drawing from the political analysis of Chapter 2 it is suggested that the analysts need to: draw up a list of important stakeholders; assess each stakeholder's perceived ability to influence organizational activity against the wishes of the strategic decision-makers, for example by withdrawing critical resources necessary for implementation; assess the propensity of each stakeholder to support a decision or to take adverse action. Table 9.4 provides a crude evaluatory technique for this purpose. The value of this 'stakeholder support model' lies not so much in the numbers it generates but in the systematic analysis and the debate it forces upon its users. At the end of such an analysis the decision-makers should have a clear idea of the most important stakeholders for the success or failure of the strategy being evaluated, whether the strategy remains feasible with or without modification and whether political bargaining strategies are appropriate in order to ameliorate or take advantage of the perceived positions of stakeholders. This evaluation can lead not only to a decision on whether to proceed but also to one on how to proceed.

At one extreme, the conclusions reached from stakeholder support analysis might lead to a 'no go' choice and an associated divestment of resources, as in the Barclays example. Alternatively, a choice to go ahead might be made but with amendments to the strategy as originally conceived and with an implementation programme that paid particular attention to 'winning over' important but reticent stakeholders. Rosabeth Moss Kanter[31] recounts, for example, how an acquisition by Delta Airlines of Western Airways was implemented in a caring, communicative and participative fashion in order that commitment to organizational success was engendered in 'acquired personnel'. At the other end of the political bargain-

Table 9.4   A stakeholder support model, with example scores (strategy being evaluated: change of plant location)

Stakeholder/stakeholder group	Power to influence for or against (0–10)	Propensity to influence for (+) or against (−) (−10 to +10)	'For' or 'against' scores (power × propensity)
Workforce (unskilled, high unemployment)	3	−3	−9
Management (supportive of relocation)	6	6	36
Suppliers (monopoly situation but unmoved either way)	8	1	8
Unions (given labour situations not over-powerful but also not happy with move)	5	−5	−25
Shareholders (see this as a productive move)	10	7	70
Bankers (important source of funds but supportive of business plan underpinning move)	6	8	48
Competitor A (strong and likely to use relocation as a period for attack)	7	−7	−49
Totals	15	−15	−83
	30	22	162

ing strategy continuum is the approach that goes for the originally conceived strategy, undiluted and unamended, in the expectation that opposition will be ignored or crushed. Some Fleet Street re-organizations of the mid-1980s seemed to adopt this approach, as did the British Coal restructuring strategy of the same era.

Fit with theory's wealth-producing prescriptions

In a preceding section theoretical prescriptions of the generic means for creating wealth from product/market operations were discussed. In that context these prescriptions (quality, size, synergy, focus and growth market opportunities) were presented as aids to the generation of strategic development ideas. Once again, the corporate planning process backtracks. On this occasion the prescriptions are used as a backcloth to test whether potential developments actually appear to make sense in theoretically prescribed terms. Business consultants, who are well versed in these prescriptions, often find practising strategists blissfully and dogmatically pursuing their own, theory contradictory, developments. This test, even at this late stage in the 'evaluation leading to choice' process, provides a further occasion on which proposed strategies can be viewed dispassionately. This is not to suggest that generalized theory should take the place of individual judgement. Hofer and Schendel,[32] for example, advocate the testing of potential strategies against the emerging rules of the marketplace – rules derived from the practice, theory and research of management strategy. However, they also remind practitioners that 'When using such rules of the market place one must keep in mind both the limited evidence on which they are based and the fact that there will always be factors unique to each situation that may have an important bearing on the success of the strategy which is adopted.' Hofer and Schendel remind us that at the moment of choice judgement remains supreme. At this point in the decision-making process strategists can and should: make their own theories; create their own strategies; and make their own decisions.

A strategic fit ranking matrix

If he or she has followed the process of first generating and next evaluating potential strategies, as outlined in this chapter, the decision-maker should be ready to make more rationally based choices about the developments the enterprise will undertake. She or he should, at this stage, be in a position of having considered carefully the pertinence of a wide range of alternatives. The process should have sharpened understanding of the really important resource, environmental and aspirational variables. Given this enhanced state of rationality, 'best' in the context of strategic choice is a subjectively derived measurement based on the decision-maker's views of how each potential strategy fits with and contributes to the aspirations, resources and environmental factors perceived by the decision-maker.

A final aid to the choice stage of the strategic decision-making process is the strategic score-card.[23] Here, theory recommends that prime-candidate strategies that remain 'on the table' at this late stage of the evaluatory process should be scored in terms of their congruences with the major variables of aspirations, resources and environment. A ranking matrix is used to score and rank these strategies. The strategic score-card requires decision-makers to express quantitative scores on qualitative judgements and so is subject to difficulties associated with people being uncomfortable about this 'soft to hard' conversion exercise. A further difficulty is created because different people infer different mental weightings from the same numerical figures. Usually people also bring different weightings to bear on the categories against which strategies are being evaluated. Very rational (in economic terms) strategies that seem to fit resource and environmental situations very well can lose out to lower-scoring strategies because the decision-makers, despite all their previous deliberations and the message emanating from the score-card, want to pursue the lower-scoring strategy. In this case the aspirations category is being given greater weight than the other categories. Despite the introduction of 'hard and fast' numbers into this last evaluatory exercise, the final choices often remain difficult; there can remain little to choose between final-strategy candidates. However, the introduction of numerical assessments via the strategic score-card can provoke meaningful discussion that will improve, even further, the rationality of the process leading to strategic development choices.

Models to assist choices of whether to involve other organizational personnel in the strategic decision-making process

The picture painted so far in Chapters 7, 8 and 9 is of a top-management decision-making process. This is the mainstream view of corporate planning that probably represents the reality of much corporate planning in practice. However, there is a body of opinion within management theory suggesting that the involvement of personnel other than the top managers in the strategic decision-making process is beneficial. Benefits flow from the rationality to be achieved up to the choice stage (more perspectives and more information inputs create a situation closer to global rationality) and from commitment to implementation of the chosen way forward.[33]

Personnel issues need to be considered before the corporate planning round begins; they are not simply strategy implementation issues. David Hussey, who has spent a lifetime in corporate planning, advises that the corporate planning approach sometimes fails because of a lack of commitment to the plans by the people of the organizations. He insists that the chief executives must demonstrate commitment to the process, that it should involve management generally and that control mechanisms should ensure that managerial personnel are not allowed to opt out of the activity. However, 'planning by committee', arising from the desire to involve, should not become the norm. Further, specialist corporate planners should be involved as facilitators of participative managerial decision-making rather than as 'planners for the managers'.[34]

Despite these calls for personnel involvement in the decision-making process many managers seem oblivious to the benefits that might flow from a more participative process. Their natural style of decision-making continues to fit the mould of the classical theorists (such as Frederick Taylor and Henri Fayol),[35, 36] who tended to emphasize management's roles of planning, controlling and commanding. In the context of Tannenbaum and Schmidt's 'managerial decision-making style' model (see Figure 9.5), many top strategists are located almost exclusively at the left-hand, authoritarian side.

William Ouchi[37] informs us that the Japanese strategic planning culture encourages collective responsibility. Important decisions take longer, and all managers who would be affected are consulted about possible options. When

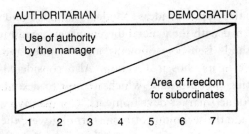

1 Manager makes decision and announces it

2 Manager 'sells' decision

3 Manager presents decision and invites questions

4 Manager presents tentative decision subject to changes

5 Manager presents problem, gets suggestions, makes decisions

6 Manager defines limits, asks for group to make decision

7 Manager permits subordinates to function within limits defined by superior

Figure 9.5 Managerial decision-making styles.
Source: A. S. Tannenbaum and H. Schmidt, *Harvard Business Review*, 1958; March–April: 96.

consensus is achieved in this fashion it generates a great deal of commitment. This is physically manifested in the fact that, for example, a document proposing a change in procedures may typically show the seal of approval of 20 or more managers before the director puts his or her final seal of approval on it. Of course, not all decisions lend themselves to this participative, time-consuming decision-making style – often major strategic decisions have to be made quickly and secretly, and the corporate planning process has been attacked for failing to provide solutions to the problem of how to handle urgent, important decisions. Nevertheless, theoretical and practical exhortations to involve people in strategic decision-making are strong and serve as thought-provoking, change-stimulating devices for strategists who are accustomed to making decisions by themselves in their own ways. By stimulating wider and deeper information contributions these exhortations also act as an aid to even greater rationality in the strategic decision-making process.

Conclusion

This chapter has concentrated on the generation, evaluation and choice stages of the strategic decision-making process. It has discussed, in a systematic, corporate planning stylized way, many of the models of strategic decision-making theory.

First, the discussion centred on models to assist the generation of a wide range of pertinent strategic development ideas. Models examined under this category included those concerned with the general directions an organization might take and the general methods (self-development, joint venture and acquisition) it might adopt to move in its chosen direction. Also considered were some of theory's wealth-creating prescriptions, which attempt to describe the nature of wealth-generating product/market developments. Competitive tactics, resource deployment changes and the technique of brainstorming were then examined.

Next, the chapter examined a variety of models to help decision-makers evaluate particular potential strategies and make final choices over the developments to be implemented. Here, the discussions centred on: financial and risk appraisal models that collectively help to improve understanding of return on investment, liquidity and risk issues; the assessment of stakeholder reactions to particular strategies; the fit of potential developments with the resource and environmental situations facing the organization; and the value of proposed strategies in terms of their apparent congruencies with theory's wealth producing prescriptions. The final choice of strategy was set in the context of a strategic score-card, which generates scores for particular potential developments, using the criteria of aspirations, resources and environment.

The final section of the chapter stood back from the linear, sequential process described and adopted by Chapters 7, 8 and 9 to consider the case for the involvement of other than top management in the strategic decision-making process. In this section, more recent exhortations of the benefits of wide involvement of personnel were compared with the classical approach to decision-making, which emphasizes the manager as a planner, commander and controller. It was suggested that, given an appropriate situation, involvement of personnel in the strategic decision-making process generates greater rationality – the *raison d'être* for each of the models introduced in Chapters 7, 8 and 9 – and commitment to the implementation stage of the decision-making process. Implementation is the subject matter of Chapter 10.

Case study 9

This case illustrates the generation of a scenario for planning purposes.

Advances in technology and design have made the automobile of the late 1990s safer, more reliable, and nearly service-free. From the viewpoint of the car fuel retailer, however, the most significant change in the automobile has been the tremendous increase in fuel efficiency over the past two decades. Better mileage has offset the effects of increases in the number of cars on the road. Overall market demand has grown at an average of only 1–1.5 per cent per year.

Because of a low rate of market growth and a high cost of capital, the ▷

number of retail petrol stations has increased only slightly since the late 1970s. Rapidly escalating labour costs and the 'service free' automobile have been responsible for the demise of the full-service filling station outlet. The high rate of inflation has made price-conscious consumers extremely receptive to the economies of self-service stations. The price competition between majors and independents is head on, so there is no pump-price spread.

Notes and references

1 H. I. Ansoff, *Corporate Strategy*. Penguin, Harmondsworth, 1968.
2 For example, G. Johnson and K. Scholes, *Exploring Corporate Strategy*, 2nd edn. Prentice-Hall, Englewood Cliffs, NJ, 1988.
3 J. Patterson and W. Richardson. 'How to acquire success', *Sundridge Park Management Journal*, 1988; Spring: 32–8.
4 A. Van de Vliet and D. Isaac, 'The mayhem in mergers', *Management Today*, 1986; February: 39–41.
5 R. Lygo, 'Strength in numbers', *Management Today*, 1989; November: 1.
6 See E. Newbeginning, 'Oxford Instrument PLC', a case study available from the Case Study Clearing House of Great Britain and Northern Ireland, for information on an organization that declares its primary objective as seeking new opportunities in high growth market areas.
7 See, for example, B. Hedley, 'Strategy and the business portfolio', *Long Range Planning*, 1977; **10**(2): 21–7.
8 A. C. Hax and N. S. Mjluf, 'Competitive cost dynamics: the experience curve', *Interfaces*, 1982; **12**(5): 50–61.
9 M. E. Porter, *The Business of Excellence*, video, Episodes 1–3, Thames Television, 1986.
10 R. Luchs, 'Successful businesses compete on quality – not costs', *Long Range Planning*, 1980; **19**(1): 12–17.
11 D. A. Garvin, 'What does product quality really mean?', *Sloan Management Review*, 1984; Fall: 25–43.
12 B. Gardner and S. Levy, 'The products and the brand', quoted in P. Kotler, *Principles of Marketing*. Prentice-Hall, Englewood Cliffs, NJ, 1980; 312.
13 K. Macmahon, *Midland Bank Chairman's Report*, 1989.
14 M. E. Porter, *Competitive Strategy*, Free Press, New York, 1980.
15 R. Hirsch, 'Getting the ratios right', *Management Today*, 1990; April: 107–10.
16 B. P. Shapiro, Y. K. Rangan, R. T. Moriarty and E. B. Ross, 'Manage customers for profits (not just sales)', *Harvard Business Review*, 1987; Sept–Oct: 101–8.
17 T. J. Peters and R. H. Waterman Jr, *In Search of Excellence*. Harper & Row, New York, 1982.
18 D. Isaac, 'Dixons doubles up', *Management Today*, 1985; November: 58–65 and 124–5.
19 C. Lorenz, 'The trouble with takeovers', *Financial Times*, December 1986: 14.
20 M. E. Porter, *Competitive Advantage*. Free Press, New York, 1985.
21 For a useful discussion on sustainable competitive advantage, see K. P. Coyne, 'Sustainable competitive advantage: what it is, what it isn't', *Business Horizons*, 1986; Jan–Feb: 54–61.

22 M. E. Porter (14) describes commitment as 'the single most important concept in planning and executing offensive or defensive moves'.

23 J. Argenti, *Practical Corporate Planning*. George Allen and Unwin, London, 1980.

24 See, for example, T. Lucey, *Management Accounting*. DP Publications, Eastleigh, Hants., 1983.

25 D. Edwards and H. Mellett, 'Break-even analysis – problems posed by the real world', *Banking World*, 1989; October.

26 These findings are discussed in *The Gamble of Investment*, video, Business Economics, Open University, 1983.

27 D. B. Hertz, 'Risk analysis in capital investment', *Harvard Business Review*, 1979; Sept–Oct: 169–81.

28 P. Samuelson, 'Two poor years for the forecasters', *Business Week*, 1974; 21 December: 51.

29 R. E. Linneman and J. D. Kennell, 'Shirt sleeve approach to long range plans', *Harvard Business Review*, 1977; Mar–Apr: 141–50.

30 H. Weihrich, 'The TOWS matrix – a tool for situational analysis,' *Long Range Planning*, 1982; **15**(2): 54–66.

31 R. M. Kanter, *When Giants Learn to Dance*. Unwin, London, 1990.

32 C. W. Hofer and D. Schendel, *Strategy Formulation: Analytical Concepts*, West Publishing, St Paul, MN, 1978.

33 Involvement for commitment is a major prescription of Frederick Herzberg's work. See *Work and the Nature of Man*, World Publishing Co., 1966.

34 D. E. Hussey, *Corporate Planning: Theory and Practice*, 2nd edn. Pergamon, Oxford, 1984.

35 F. W. Taylor, *Scientific Management*. Harper, New York, 1947.

36 H. Fayol, *General and Industrial Management* (trans.). Pitman, London, 1949.

37 D. S. Pugh and D. J. Hickson discuss the work of William Ouchi in *Writers on Organisations*. Penguin, Harmondsworth, 1989; 109.

10 Rational Decision-Making – Implementation Issues

The approach taken in this book has been to adapt prescriptive models of the decision-making process within a framework of constrained rationality. An objection to this approach is that in many working situations the constraints are so great that they become the dominant variable. If this is the case it may be that implementation and behavioural problems have been underestimated. Relegating these factors to the role of mere constraints rather than keeping them as the basis of the analysis is convenient for the purposes of constructing a model. However, this approach needs to be examined critically to establish where it actually meets the overall purpose given at the beginning of the book – of improving strategic decision-making.

In this chapter we critically review the decision process approach examined in the book and identify the likely problem areas that may arise in the process of its implementation. To do this we look at each stage in the decision process and then at the process as a whole, to see the interrelationships between the stages and the dynamism of the process. The objectives of this chapter are to:

- outline the debate about the relationship between rational and incremental models;
- examine the problems of implementing a new mission statement;
- analyse why identification of the need for a decision must be a separate stage in the decision-making process;
- suggest ways in which the problem definition stage can be improved;
- identify areas of bias during the search stage;
- recognize the issues involved in using models of strategic choice;
- understand the importance of monitoring decisions.

Planned versus incremental change

Johnson[1] has suggested that there are three theoretical approaches to the process of strategic management: the rationalistic, the incremental and the interpretative.

Chapter 1 examined these issues in detail but it is useful from an implementation point of view to recap. The first is usually associated with corporate planning and is essentially rational and analytical, but as it bears little resemblance to 'what strategic management is in actuality' (p. 17) it is of limited usefulness. The incremental perspective arises primarily from Mintzberg's empirical observations of how strategic decisions were actually taken (see also Lyles[2] and Hickson *et al.*[3]). These studies are 'academic' in that, while reporting on what happens, they do not help in the making of future decisions. Quinn[4] described this approach as 'logical'. It is important that lessons can be drawn from any findings, so the incremental approach is also of limited usefulness. The interpretative perspective 'sees strategy as the product of the sense-making of managers',[1] who form relatively simple 'recipes' that can be applied to cope with environmental complexity. There is no suggestion that these are ideal – the contrary is suggested by Grinyer and Spender[5] and Pettigrew.[6] Again, in terms of practical advice for creating and implementing a strategy, little emerges.

Johnson's work was partially aimed at seeing the relevance of these perspectives in practice. He concluded that as well as incremental changes there were also fundamental shifts in strategy, and that managers had a relatively commonly held set of core beliefs and assumptions. Johnson called these paradigms and said that they dominate strategic thinking. They are essentially a cultural phenomenon, so they are obvious to outsiders but not to insiders. In many organizations they will radically affect the implementation of strategy, as the attitudes and beliefs behind the paradigms must be changed before strategic changes can be implemented. The implications Johnson draws are that managers need to be better planners, by being more objective and analytical, and to be better managers of social, political and cultural processes of change. Thus any rational model must take cognizance of behavioural matters in much the way that the McKinsey 7-S framework does (see Chapter 3).

It is useful to continue to use the decision process framework to discuss the extent to which each stage experiences constrained rationality or is dominated to such an extent by constraints that when this approach is considered it is no longer possible to talk in terms of rationality. At each stage possible methods of overcoming the constraints will be discussed.

Mission statements and objectives

The rational model requires that objectives form the beginning of the decision cycle and are the end to which it is working. Thus they are crucial. Chapter 2 looked in detail at the problems of implementing objectives. Although Case study 10 shows a series of clear objectives, the mission is not always easy or simple to identify. For example, if a confectionery manufacturer believes it is in the business of 'sugar confectionery', it will automatically exclude certain options that a wider mission statement, including the business as being in 'impulse snack foods', would not. Similarly it is easy to misconceive the mission by relating business to certain inappropriate geographical areas or inappropriate stakeholders as well as market areas. Only the experience of the participants in the process will guide top management to the 'correct' mission. Techniques to ensure the mission is appropriate include the use of outside consultants to check that management has taken as wide a perspective as is necessary and has recognized changes in the environment that might affect the fundamentals of the business. Alternatively, internal brainstorming sessions or assignment of critical evaluation to a group will help to test the validity of the new mission statement being devised.

Once an acceptable mission exists, the problem of generating strategic objectives from it is relatively simple. It is more difficult to ensure that lower management do not misinterpret the objectives or deliberately alter them to suit their own personal goals. The misinterpretation can be overcome by the use of special communication networks (as described in Case study 3). The extent of the dissemination of information that is necessary is much greater than the rational model would suggest. If changes are to be understood they must be communicated using several methods, such as literature, meetings, briefing sessions and slogans. They also need to be understood both intellectually and emotionally.[7] The gradual moulding of objectives to suit personal goals can be reduced by the use of appropriate reward systems and techniques, such as management by objectives; this will, of course, also assist in reducing misinterpretation of objectives (see Chapter 2).

Howe[8] suggests that leadership is vital at this stage, and so 'adequate incentives to motivate senior management to achieve the chosen strategic goals' (p. 95) are desirable. From the findings of Khandwalla,[9] it would seem that the most appropriate strategy for implementing a new set of objectives is to recruit a new management team, because certain management styles are more or less appropriate to particular strategic environments. However, this is not generally feasible, so management development work and communication systems must be provided to assist in the change process.

The fit between new objectives and the prevailing culture is very important. Frequently a change in objectives, or a new mission, implies or requires a change in corporate culture. So implementing the former requires that the latter be considered. Chapter 3 points out some of the problems, but a holistic approach, which coordinates training, recruitment and reward systems, is more likely to be effective than a piecemeal approach. The cascading group membership model used by the company in Case study 3 is also likely to be successful. An organization that is resistant to change is probably going to require both and the process could be extremely costly.

The need for a decision

This stage is frequently treated as part of the problem definition stage but it can be argued (see Chapter 1) that it needs separate treatment because of special problems that can arise. The rational model takes it as given that the need for a decision is known. This is because it is essentially reactive, not proactive. Empirical research shows that this is not so, except possibly in a crisis situation. The environmental monitoring systems in Chapter 8 suggested how external expected eventualities could be anticipated, but it is the truly unexpected that it is so difficult to provide for. Unexpected events can only really be handled at the level of individuals, rather than organization systems.

At its simplest, on an internal basis, a staff suggestion box is an attempt to recognize that management is not omnipotent and cannot anticipate everything. Milliken Industrial, for example, has introduced 'opportunity for improvement' forms, which represent a systematic attempt to harness employees' ideas and knowledge so that any perceived problem can be dealt with quickly. All suggestions are investigated and many result in the establishment of central action teams. Quality teams, as described by Richardson and Richardson[10] for example, are another attempt to involve personnel in spotting internal problems not readily identified by normal reporting systems. Spotting external changes that suggest a need for a decision is more difficult if systems have not picked them up. However, all personnel have some external role and may identify situations where there is a need for a decision. Accepting this is important. Peters[11] stresses that 'we all guess wrong about the future' (p. 199), so methods of recognizing the need for change, other than planning systems, must be found.

Problem definition

The rational model assumes that it is relatively simple to define the problem or the decision that is needed. However, people's perception of problems varies enormously because of their past experiences, within the organization as well as outside it. Additionally, in Johnson's[1] terms, management paradigms, which help in the interpretation of problems, vary widely. The findings from Chapter 3 on culture are relevant here, for some organizations react to opportunities while others only respond to crises. The work in Chapter 4 on structures is also relevant, for the type of structure can affect both the level in the hierarchy at which a problem is handled and the likely response made to it.

Some of these shortcomings can be overcome by the use of culture as a strategic tool, team-building methods and training. Chapter 3 suggested that culture can have a considerable impact on the interpretation of perceived events and therefore will affect the way a problem is defined. All the methods outlined in that chapter are relevant to the establishment of an appropriate culture. It is unlikely that any two organizations will arrive at exactly the same way of handling this issue, for the existing culture and the prevailing environment must be taken into account when devising an appropriate culture. Team-building is an excellent method of generating creative ways of handling problems, encouraging involvement by everyone and communicating ideas. If there is overlapping membership of teams, a cascade effect will greatly facilitate the development of an overall approach so that similar decisions are handled in similar ways. Training schemes can increase awareness of the difficulties of problem definition so that some of them can be avoided. However, if these are carried out in isolation from other policies, they are unlikely to be successful. What is needed is a holistic approach.

Search

The basic rational model assumes that all relevant information is available. This is clearly not the case in practice. Information is expensive so judgements are continually being made about what to search for and how far to extend the search. Research shows that the process is sequential and frequently certain areas are ruled out as a result of previous findings. This is a logical or rational way of handling uncertainty, but if the decision about what to exclude is mistaken then the whole decision process must be recycled once the mistake is discovered. If the mistake is not discovered until after the whole decision has been taken it is likely that the specified objectives will not be realized.

This problem can never be completely overcome. Calling for more and more information is frequently a behavioural response to a desire to defer taking a decision. Training of staff to increase their awareness of filtering mechanisms, and systems that require the explicit consideration or explanation of why certain avenues of thought were excluded, are both helpful. Case study 10 illustrates the importance of perception and the filtering of information, as certain potentially problematic areas were not considered until they were presented as actual problems. Time and budget pressures and the international nature of the project were contributory factors but it is likely that relatively simple production problems were ignored because other problems were perceived as more important.

Judgement plays an important part here. Hogarth[12] claims that decision tools are insufficient for the tasks at hand, so judgements, both evaluative and predictive, become important. Judgement is frequently intuitive or instinctive. The sources of bias that may affect the search stage include: using only easily available information, interpreting events using one's own experience, anticipating results, disregarding conflicting evidence, assuming spurious correlations, being inconsistent, failing to revise opinions, and underestimating joint probabilities.[13]

Numerous training programmes and games are available to help overcome these problems,[12, 14] but it would be unrealistic to assume they could be eliminated. But being aware of the problems will help to improve judgement. As well as individual bias during the search phase, the role of political behaviour in organizations should not be forgotten. Pfeffer[15] suggests various ways of understanding political behaviour and methods of mitigating its detrimental effects on decision-making.

Evaluation of alternatives and choice

The rational model requires that clear alternatives are identified and compared to agreed criteria, derived from the objectives, so that the best alternative can be selected. Chapter 9 looked in detail at models to help in strategic choice but Case study 5 showed the problems of interpretation of a situation and implied that making the 'correct' strategic choice was a difficult matter. There is unlikely to be general agreement on the correct choice of action, even with the benefit of hindsight. The popularity of different strategic choice models varies over time and there is a tendency for fashions to develop: for example, many firms adopted the experience curve and portfolio models approach, replaced it with ideas derived from the profit impact of market strategy work and then adopted Porter's model or the corporate cultures approach. If many businesses move in the same direction at the same time, this will inevitably increase competition. An interesting alternative approach adopted by BBA (Case study 2) was to move against the prevailing trend: taking a sunset industries approach rather than a sunrise industries approach has been a very successful strategy for that particular firm.

Implementation

Within an overall strategic approach there will be many possible strands of activity that, when linked together, form the overall strategy. Although criteria will be established at divisional and departmental levels to contribute to these strands, there is frequently considerable opportunity for discretionary behaviour. This may take the form of pursuit of personal career interests or stakeholder needs rather than departmental objectives or organizational needs. Various schemes for overcoming such behaviour and for ensuring the survival of new ideas through the organizational hierarchy, aside from reward systems and management by objectives, have been suggested. Product championing (mentioned in Case study 10) helps to ensure that a project is seen through to successful completion.[16] However, in Case study 10 the responsibility was not assigned to one individual. Mr XYZ had an overall 'sponsorship' role, which was successful, but having several 'champions' in several different international subsidiaries was not successful.

Monitoring and feedback

This final stage is essential to the rational model, for it is at this point that the success or failure of the decision can be established. It is considered good practice to review the outcome of decisions and monitor the achievement of objectives. However, the practicalities of this are often very difficult in complex, long-run decision-making. Furthermore, unless a decision is a spectacular success or failure, it can be difficult to decide if an average outcome is satisfactory or not. The performance measures may not be accurate, may be inappropriate, may not distinguish short-term from long-term benefit, or may capture a specific return and not the overall return accruing to the organization. These can be overcome by improved measurement and control systems but this area is not the exact science some accounts would like it to be.[17] The role of structure (see Chapter 4) in this area is crucial.

A particular difficulty is to distinguish long-term trends from short-term fluctuations. The extent to which an unsatisfactory outcome requires action or can be seen as an aberration is, in practice, very difficult to establish. This is amplified by the reluctance of many to recognize failure and to accept and use it to provide a learning situation for the future. Small firms, as Chapter 6 showed, do not always have this opportunity, for one failure can be the end of the firm itself. The portfolio models of Chapter 8 assumed that large-scale organizations have a number of distinct strategic business units and do not face the same risk as small firms, which have 'all their eggs in one basket'. However, even large firms that are diversified within an industry will face problems if they have failed to recognize a long-term structural decline. Use of the techniques discussed in Chapter 8 should help to mitigate this, as should an adaptive corporate culture.

The whole process

Although looking at each stage individually helps to pinpoint areas of concern and to suggest methods for overcoming identified weaknesses, it is still important to view the process as a whole. The dynamism of the whole process is very important. If it operates quickly with relatively few episodes of recycling it will be more successful than a slow, laborious process with many periods of back-tracking to previous stages. Similarly, it is important to take a holistic view of any decision, but particularly of a strategic decision. For it is easy to forget the original purpose of all the activity – as happened, for example, in the nuclear power decisions in the electricity industry. The desire to provide cheap electricity was originally associated with the use of nuclear power, and this central belief was never questioned internally despite evidence to the contrary. Those standing back from the industry were the only ones able to take a holistic view, but because many of them had other objectives, to ban all nuclear activity, their views were ignored. The use of non-executive directors is an excellent mechanism for ensuring that a holistic view is taken.

Conclusion

The whole of this book has used the rational decision processes model as a basis for its structure. At each stage weaknesses in the model have been identified and a number of methods and techniques offered to help overcome them. Thus the central thrust has been to demonstrate how rationality in decision-making can be improved. It is unlikely that many would propose the opposite view and advocate increased irrationality. However, many would take issue with the prescriptive nature of the approach adopted. The justification for it is that this is not only a piece of academic work but that it is also aimed at improving decision-making abilities. While it is both interesting and acceptable to undertake academic studies pointing out the absence of rationality in real business decision-making, it is not very useful to prospective practitioners. Practitioners typically want to draw conclusions from findings, so that their effectiveness can be improved and good practices can be established. If this is possible, not only should academic findings be analysed but also lessons for the future must be highlighted. However, it is essential that these two quite separate dimensions are made explicit. This book has attempted to do so to ensure that the theoretical perspectives are used to model reality more effectively. The aim of this approach is to enable readers to assess recommendations themselves and select and apply the models most useful to the situation in hand. They should also be able to 'fit' new theories and findings into the basic framework. Additionally a critical evaluation of prescriptive advice, both current and prospective, can be made. Readers should, therefore, not be left in a position of discovering that a method no longer works and that they need to search for another 'recipe' – they should be able to adapt the existing models or evaluate new ones critically.

Case study 10
New product management

This case illustrates the problems associated with launching a new product. It shows that no matter how well the process for implementation is ▷

designed, if the strategic decision to undertake the project is misconceived because of poor research then failure will result.

Background

This case describes the process of developing and launching a new product used by a large multinational involved in pharmaceuticals and cosmetics.

At group level in Australia an analysis of products, distribution of sources of income and profits indicated that there was a strategic need for a new product. The new product was to fill perceived gaps and had to satisfy the following criteria:

1 Be capable of being mass-produced.
2 Have a worldwide appeal.
3 Be lightweight for ease of distribution.
4 Be novel.
5 Be as free as possible from controls by any government agency.
6 Use skills already existing in the group, particularly those associated with production and marketing.

The solution suggested at group level was a Tic-Tac type pellet, that is, a sweet in various flavours in a novelty box. An international name was selected and the box was to be a Lego-type cube that could be collected and used as a child's building brick. The production of the sweet used the confectionery know-how of an Australian subsidiary. As the box would require expensive tooling, the market had to be worldwide. This product met all the conditions outlined by the strategy team. The UK and French subsidiaries expressed interest in the idea and they, with Australian support, became the 'product champions'.

Preparation for the launch

At group level outside consultants were employed to advise on the optimum location. After consideration of four sites in the world, Ireland was recommended because of the tax advantages and grants offered.

Mr XYZ was selected to organize the process of launching the product. He was given a May to March time scale (ten months) to establish a factory, manufacture the product and launch it in three countries.

He established that the following activities needed to be carried out:

1 Find a site and factory.
2 Negotiate with government agencies to achieve 1.
3 Manufacture the sweets.
4 Find or design machines to fill boxes to contain sweets.
5 Find or design machines to make boxes.

To achieve 1 to 5 he decided which people to involve and when and how ▷

they should be involved. He decided that in order to establish commitment he would involve everyone very early in the process.

For each of the activities outlined above, he established what was required, what primary functions were involved and who the managers of those functions were. He then called a series of meetings involving those concerned with each area of activity.

He set up communication links with, and working parties of, the various interested groups concerned with the project. These included those internal to his subsidiary, contractors, outside advisers, government agencies and international group interests. The internal working party consisted of finance, legal, manufacturing, quality control, engineering, packaging, design, purchasing, research and development, marketing and personnel representatives. The outside advisers were French bankers, Irish lawyers, Irish accountants, tax specialists (Irish and British) and American location advisers. Government agencies were the Irish Development Agency, the Ministry of Labour and local authorities in Ireland. The international group's interests included marketing, finance, engineering and personnel functions.

Working details

Mr XYZ set criteria for the working parties based on time (because of the tight deadline) and money, designating the limit in money terms of each group's authority. He also attempted to ascertain the commitment of participants to the different working parties and their sub-groups. Finally, communication networks were formally established in an attempt to speed up decision processes and ensure that information was disseminated to those who needed to know.

The tools of analysis were selected by Mr XYZ. First, critical path analysis, summarized by simple flow charts, was carried out to ensure that the complex process could be completed in time. Secondly, financial plans and cash flow charts were drawn up to ensure that budgets set internationally were met. Finally, project leaders were appointed to take responsibility for 'trouble-shooting' problems as they cropped up or referring them quickly if that was felt to be necessary.

Mr XYZ called a meeting of all the managers involved who had previously done some preliminary work, and agreed a timetable of activities, responsibility procedures, including who could take what type of decision, and their financial limits. A schedule of future meetings was drawn up and included draft agendas and proposed report forms. Mr XYZ also established an emergency procedure.

Problems encountered

Factory location　The location in Ireland, which was selected by the consultants, was in a rural area although the Dublin area had been preferred by the ▷

internal working party. The reason for the choice was the Development Agency (DA) offer of higher grants on a country site. Towards the end of the decision period the EC objected to the taxation holiday offered by the Irish government and the financial projections had to be redone. Additionally, the Irish DA realized that it had been too generous in its grant offer, which was 40 per cent of the assets of the manufacturing company. Some of the assets were not held in Ireland, because they were tooling for the moulding of boxes subcontracted to a Birmingham firm, and so were technically not eligible as part of the basis for grant calculations. Eventually the Irish DA, after threats of withdrawal, allowed 60 per cent of assets in Ireland, on condition that the agreement was secret. The loan associated with the training of employees encountered problems, which were resolved. The manufacturing process involved the use of a great deal of water, which was pumped untreated back into the river from whence it came. Local authority officials pointed out that it was polluted and needed treatment. This would have required an expensive piece of equipment and pushed the factory outside the budget. Mr XYZ threatened to pull out unless the condition was waived – it was.

Manufacturing process The tableting machinery, based on in-house technology, worked well with the sweets but the shelf life of the sugar coating was not sufficient as discoloration occurred with certain colours. The problem was referred back to the research and development department. The box moulding equipment caused far more problems. It was a new area for the company, the moulds were more expensive than anticipated and the loose waste pieces of plastic caused problems with the filling machinery. The manufacture of these boxes had been subcontracted and the subcontractor was having problems in meeting the deadlines at the required quality.

Marketing problems The French company objected to the colour of the plastic boxes and wanted packaging display changes. It also raised problems it thought might arise from the EC, which required that each item (sweets and box/building brick) be priced separately (compare this to Kinder chocolate eggs, which contain a toy). The Australian company would not approve the advertising material prepared in the UK. Lego threatened court action unless the container was changed. This involved altering the whole design of the box, which had originally been compatible with Lego. A change to make the box just a container was rejected, as the re-usable nature of the box was intended to distinguish it from Tic-Tac sweets, which were the market leaders. The Australian company's marketing function began to revise its assumptions for projected sales and as a consequence financial pressure increased.

Achievements and failures

The project was completed on time, both the factory and the production of ▷

the product. The capital costs were to budget and the project cash flows were met, which meant the grants expected were received.

The quality of the sweets remained a problem, with two colours mottling within a short period (below the anticipated shelf life of several months). The quality of the boxes was a problem and for certain periods the boxes had to be hand-filled, which involved considerable overtime payments. The contractors were sued but teething troubles continued for six months. The running costs of the factory were above budget, for even when the filling machines could be used they were slower than anticipated. The commitment to the product by the French company waned and, with the replacement of its managing director, went completely.

Mr XYZ believed that his management of the process of the product development and launch was correct and that the detailed planning, establishment of criteria and communication networks were essential. Despite this the product was not a success and he believes that managers and teams associated with such projects must accept that some fail. They must not alter the psychological commitment and energy needed for such a project to be implemented, but must be prepared to cope with the let-down at the end if it fails.

References

1 G. Johnson, *Strategic Change and the Management Process*. Basil Blackwell, Oxford, 1987.

2 M. A. Lyles, 'Formulating strategic problems – empirical analysis and model development', *Strategic Management Journal*, 1981; **2**: 61–75.

3 D. J. Hickson, R. J. Batter, D. Cray, G. R. Mallory and D. C. Wilson, *Top Decisions: Strategic Decision Making in Organisations*. Basil Blackwell, Oxford, 1986.

4 J. B. Quinn, *Strategies for Change*. Richard D. Irwin, Homewood, IL, 1980.

5 P. H. Grinyer and J. C. Spender, 'Recipes, crises and adaptation in mature businesses', *International Studies of Management and Organisation*, 1979; **9**: 113–23.

6 A. M. Pettigrew, *The Awakening Giant*. Basil Blackwell, Oxford, 1985.

7 See, for example, H. Woodward and S. Buchholz, *After Shock – Helping People through Corporate Change*. John Wiley, New York, 1987.

8 W. S. Howe, *Corporate Strategy*. Macmillan, London, 1986.

9 P. N. Khandwalla, 'Some top management styles, their context and performance', *Organisation and Administrative Sciences*, 1976–7; Winter: 21–51.

10 B. Richardson and R. Richardson, *Business Planning: An Approach to Strategic Management*. Pitman, London, 1989.

11 T. Peters, *Thriving on Chaos*. Guild Publishing, London, 1987.

12 R. Hogarth, *Judgement and Choice*. John Wiley, Chichester, 1987.

13 R. Hogarth and S. Makridakis, 'Forecasting and planning: an evaluation', *Management Science*, 1981; **27**(2): 115–38.

14 P. Moore, *The Business of Risk*. Cambridge University Press, Cambridge, 1983.

15 J. Pfeffer, *Power in Organizations*. Pitman, Marshfield, MA, 1981.

16 See, for example, P. Drucker, *Innovation and Entrepreneurship*. Heinemann, New York, 1985; C. Gore and K. Murray, 'Changing to an enterprising corporate culture', *Sundridge Management Park Review* (in the press).

17 See, for example, R. Kaplan, *Advanced Management Accounting*. Prentice-Hall, Englewood Cliffs, NJ, 1988.

Index